Y0-EIA-924

SHARING THE COURSE

A Guide to Group Study and
Individual Application of
Spiritual Principles

Nancy H. Glende

Noelani Publishing Company, Inc.
P.O. Box 24029
Cleveland, Ohio
44124-0029

Kind acknowledgment is given for the following permissions:

Portions from *A Course in Miracles* © 1975, reprinted by permission of the Foundation for Inner Peace, Inc., P.O. Box 1104, Glen Ellen, California, 95442

Pamela Levin for Think Structure as shown in *Becoming The Way We Are* used on p. 232, "Think Structure"

Oman Ken for words taken from "Give Me Your Blessing" on audio tape, *Holy Messengers,* by Oman and Shanti used on p. 241, "Mirror Talk"

John Diamond for ideas on forgiving mother used on p. 311,"Mother Love"

Photography by Eric A. Glende, Jr.
Author Photo Copyright © 1993 by Eric A. Glende, Jr.

Cover Design by Nancy A. Burgard
Cover Illustration Copyright © 1993 by Nancy A. Burgard

Printed in the United States of America

Copyright © 1993 by Nancy H. Glende
All Rights Reserved
ISBN 0-9636216-9-6

Library of Congress
Catalog Card Number: 93-83759

Published by
Noelani Publishing Company, Inc.
P.O. Box 24029
Cleveland, OH
44124-0029

The Soul Is.
For the Soul there is only Life.
That Life is Now.

(see page 360, *Sharing the Course*)

DEDICATION

To the One who invites me to See

In Seeing, I choose to Serve

WITH HEARTFELT GRATITUDE

To the multitude of authors who gave freely to me
and guided my awakening

In return, I extend a hand to you

NOTE

This book is meant to inspire, include, and unite people. We believe that *Sharing the Course* is compatible with, augments, and enhances current understanding of major religious teachings.

The ideas represented herein are the personal interpretation and understanding of the author and have not been endorsed by The Foundation for Inner Peace, copyright holder of *A Course in Miracles*.

Integration of principles from *A Course in Miracles* with other techniques has not been endorsed by the Foundation for Inner Peace, copyright holder of *A Course in Miracles*.

Throughout this book, in places where the information helps to clarify points, the author tells about her healing. Nowhere does she intend blame in stories she tells. Each is to make a point about the healing process.

The author has used all methods, processes, and exercises in this book for her own growth as well as for facilitating individuals and groups. She has given information simply and clearly to assure proper application. Used as intended, these tools and guidelines are completely safe. The author will not assume responsibility for any problems that arise due to lack of understanding of the healing process.

Noelani Publishing Company, Inc.

ACKNOWLEDGMENTS

I am grateful to:

The One who taught me that Mother's Love is available to me through any person who is committed to being truly helpful.

All students who have received me. Through you I know that I gave, and that my giving was worthwhile and meaningful.

All students who wrote Loving reviews for this book when it was only an idea. You served as beacons of Love.

All students who committed yourselves to grow into the unknown with me. You have been faithful.

Michael Root, for your gifts of music.

Nancy Burgard for your gifts in the cover art.

Eric Glende for your gifts in the photo art.

Michael Root, Bill Greenberg, and Eric Glende, your Love sustained me at my hardest times.

Those of you who gave generously of your abilities as readers and editors: Paulie Alma, Paula Amicarelli, Nancy Burgard, Pat Durjava, Eric Glende, Bill Greenberg, Roz Kapczuk, Karen Klyn, Michael Root, Ksenia Roshchakovsky, Bruce Sherman, Denise Simunic, Kathy Stanitz, Marianne Tompa, Beverly Wehr, and Nancy Wendling.

Eric Glende, my partner for Inner Peace and Love. I thank you for reflecting Loving-Kindness and True Goodness that I might know these qualities in myself. I celebrate you on your own journey and am grateful that your path joins and complements mine. Noelani thanks you and applauds your courage.

FOREWORD

Sharing the Course is a guide to spiritual growth. It calls each of us to expand in safe and Loving ways. It is for anyone willing to be their magnificent self. We, Nancy's students, use her excellent internalizing processes. We attest to the power of the included information and processes to transform lives. We tapped into the Universal power that unites us all by expressing our most tender selves in a safe environment. We share because we experience joy from changing our lives.

Nancy lives the message she shares. She models a reverence for life that inspires all who know her. Results of her vigilant, disciplined search for Truth are in these pages. She writes with convincing simplicity, certainty, and clarity. Her book demonstrates the choice to fearlessly and generously give her gifts. Examples of her own healing read like pages from her personal journal. Both she and *Sharing the Course* demonstrate the simple truthfulness which comes from integrating principles of *A Course in Miracles*. *Sharing the Course* is a guide to reap rewards of spiritual growth. It first assists by presenting concepts to the intellect. Then it provides a missing link, ways to apply the spiritual message. Tools given throughout this book take concepts into action where the truth of them is experienced, felt, and known.

Through *Sharing the Course*, the spirit of *A Course in Miracles* is easily understood, experienced, and integrated into daily life. *Sharing the Course* lends itself to individual or group study. In both cases, emphasis is on doing spiritual homework which calls for a change in ourselves. Miracles are our rewards when we realize we have been refusing to receive Love by waiting, blaming, and hating.

Sharing the Course is destined to uplift the world's energies. It supports the growth of anyone ready and willing to learn. Exercises are appropriate to beginners and the most advanced students as well. We are privileged to be part of this journey. We invite you to live the message with us and support the spiritual shift taking place at the Universal level. May your life be as blessed as ours have been.

Nancy, we honor you for your willingness to accurately name things. Once named, they will be healed. We applaud you for *Sharing the Course*.

With great Love, affection, and gratitude,
Your students

PREFACE

I AM READY AND WILLING TO SHARE MY GIFTS WITH YOU.

In 1987, my first husband died of multiple sclerosis. I was not welcome at his funeral. We had separated 10 years earlier and I had since remarried. I invited my friend Sally to talk with me about having a small funeral service that I could attend. My goal was to recognize his death as an event in my life. I imagined a group of six women with whom I would talk and cry, believing I would then feel complete. Sally asked me what it meant for me to be recognized. I had no answer for that.

As a young newlywed I learned that my husband had MS. During the next eighteen years I did everything I could to keep him functioning at his best, to maintain our marriage, and to keep our family of four together. My best wasn't enough. At my point of despair I was rejected and blamed by family members for all sorts of things. Certainly there was no rejoicing for all I had courageously given in search of my goals.

Sally recognized the need to celebrate me for who I had become through my experiences over the years. Sally had Vision. She planned a day to celebrate me. On September 3, 1987, six "mothers" and my current husband, Eric, tended me for a day of unconditional Love.

I prepared for three months, as one would for any rite of passage. When the day came, I was wrapped in a burgundy blanket to represent the womb. For two hours I listened to drumming heartbeats and Loving voices anticipating and welcoming my birth as a Soul. My new birth celebrated the end of *trying to get* Love in all the ways that don't work. The rest of the morning was devoted to welcoming, nurturing, bathing, and feeding.

In the afternoon a crowd of invited guests came to expand the circle of Love. This segment of the day was devoted to reliving my childhood. The purpose was for me to experience in the presence of Love, that which was once painful. We celebrated with music, dance, and snacks appropriate for childhood. During this segment of the day I declared both my new identity and my new direction as a Soul born to Love.

> I resolve to live by Higher Principle - which is Universal Law - to honor God as my Source. I accept Grace. I acknowledge that happiness is harmony with God, and accept Harmony. I choose to live ON PURPOSE, serving Love to all who seek to Love and be Loved by me.

That evening we had a holy ceremony with music, dance, and food appropriate to the occasion.

Two months later, without a physical symptom, I knew I was dying. That was before I truly understood how Love heals. It was before I realized that resolving to live in higher energy is a prayer. I didn't yet understand that what I was experiencing was my prayer being answered. My ego was dying that I might be fully alive. My energy was reversing from *trying to get* Love, to being a receiver of Love. I only knew I was dying and could only think of one person who might know how to save me.

Louise Hay had been my mentor and model for some years, though I only knew her as an author and a voice on audio tapes. I wrote to her. Louise invited me to a week-long intensive training program for professionals. I went. On the fourth day we were doing an exercise in accepting (forgiving) based on the premise that our bodies hold pain until we tell our truth. I lay on the floor with a partner leaning knuckles into knots in my back and shoulder muscles.

For what seemed like a very long time I stated a litany of "I accept" statements as instructed. "I accept that that hurts." "I accept that I hurt." Then the "knuckler" said, "You have gifts to give that you aren't giving, don't you?" I began to sob. I sobbed through the whole next segment of the workshop, right there on the floor in front of the stage.

I was not free to give my gifts until I knew the experience of being received with Love. Once I was celebrated on the day Sally and I planned, the pain from not being celebrated released.

It was four months after this event that I was invited to teach *A Course in Miracles* to a small group. During the time since then I have learned how Love heals. It is our magnificence and glory that we hold as our deepest secret, not our unworthiness. It is truly our magnificence and glory that we need to accept. I released unworthiness to accept these gifts, and I give them to you.

v

THIS BOOK IS FOR YOU IF YOU

- ◆ are seeking to understand spiritual principles.

- ◆ are seeking to understand spiritual development.

- ◆ want practical information on how to grow spiritually and live miraculously.

- ◆ want to know how to integrate the thought system of *A Course in Miracles* into your own life.

- ◆ have been reading *A Course in Miracles* and want to share with others.

- ◆ are considering leading any group for the purpose of personal growth or spiritual development.

- ◆ currently lead a group for personal growth of spiritual development and want to expand and deepen your leadership skills.

- ◆ currently lead a group for personal growth or spiritual development and seek ideas or inspiration to broaden your group's experience.

- ◆ participate in any personal growth or spiritual development group and want to expand and deepen your experience.

- ◆ are a teacher, minister, health professional, counselor, coach or leader of any group and want to increase caring and sharing within your group.

- ◆ aspire to be one who supports changes taking place at the planetary level to bring Peace on Earth.

HOW TO USE THIS BOOK

A Course in Miracles focuses on changing our thought system. *Sharing the Course* takes information from *A Course in Miracles* along with spiritual principles found elsewhere, and integrates these at the feeling and behavioral levels. Thoughts, feelings, and behaviors become integrated by practicing techniques from many traditions. Integrity is completion, and completion is Joy.

Read the entire book for meaningful information and inspiration.

Reread the entire book with deeper understanding after seeing how concepts are applied.

Review the book by reading sentences in bold print.

Read any section or chapter that appeals to you.

Use the book as a resource for understanding *A Course in Miracles* or spiritual truths found in other resources.

Use the index to research a spiritual term or concept and see its application in everyday life.

See Section II for information on joining with spiritual language and reading with others.

Invite someone to read this book with you so you have someone with whom to share your experience.

Do Healing Methods, Chapter 5, because you want to live their results.

Use the book to guide, comfort, and assure you as you experience the effects of healing. See Chapter 6.

Do Practice Exercises and Spiritual Homework, Chapter 25, as an individual, couple, family, as friends, or support group, to join and know happiness.

Make a regular practice of using basic skills for spiritual growth found in Section Two of Chapter 25.

Some Practice Exercises are appropriate for a social event. See Section Ten of Chapter 25, Inspiring Creativity.

Tape the visualizations in Chapter 26 and heal yourself using your own voice.

When facing a problem, select a Practice Exercise that feels appropriate, or let the book fall open in the Practice Exercise section and do the exercise before you.

Use the book as a guide for selecting, starting, or participating in a group whose purpose is to seek deeper meaning in life.

Use the book as a resource for lesson planning and teaching.

Teachers around the world, share information in this book with our youth.

Clergy, share information in this book through your sermons.

Health professionals and counselors of all kinds, share this book with those who hurt for whatever reason.

Review this book in different stages of your growing. You will find Loving support on your journey.

Information in this book is pure and powerful. If you feel overwhelmed, rest for a while and let what you have read assimilate. Then return to your reading. Know that you will begin again at the perfect moment. You do not read this book alone. Spirit is always present, guiding you.

TABLE OF CONTENTS

INTRODUCTION

We are meant to be happy.
We are meant to live miraculously.

In the first phase of our life we seek to connect with others to *survive physically.* When we are comfortable in the care of others we are content. When we experience no one as there for us, we respond with emotion that calls for care. There are times when we fail to get the care we need. Nature provides us the ability to defend under these circumstances. This puts us on hold until our next phase of life.

In the second phase of life we seek to *heal emotionally.* Wherever we did not find comfort as a child, we use our own grown-up Thinking Nature (inner parent) to reverse energy that we diverted to defenses. This healing brings us to the third phase of life in which we *enjoy connecting* with God.

Survival is achieved by restricting.
Happiness is achieved by undoing those restrictions.

Our Soul's intent is to be happy. *A Course in Miracles* contains information precious to us for our soul's growth and development. It excites and awakens spirit once restricted and now dormant within us.

I am often told by people who have read *A Course In Miracles* or more recently, *Return to Love* by Marianne Williamson, that they do not know how to apply the information to their own lives. *Sharing the Course* is meant to be a companion book to *A Course Miracles.* It is my intent that *Sharing the Course* bridge the gap between information you have read, and living a life that fulfills the message.

I have been leading groups of one kind or another all of my adult life. I began sharing *A Course in Miracles* in 1988. This quickly became the joy of my life and I resigned all other teaching jobs to devote full time to this work. *Sharing the Course* grew from my experience of healing myself and sharing my methods with others. I have used all the methods and exercises in this book to undo my survival restrictions. I share about my healing throughout the book where examples from my life are meant to help you see possibilities for yourself.

I teach in groups no larger than ten people. Currently, I have four groups that meet weekly. Members of my groups were eager to participate in sharing their lives with you. Their contributions are throughout the book. Where their name is signed, it came directly from them. Examples of dialogs are not actual personal work.

In *Sharing the Course* I speak conversationally, sharing deep understandings I gained through transforming my life and assisting others. I see this book as unique in that it serves as a bridge in several ways.

First, it is a bridge between the symbolic and abstract language of *A Course in Miracles*, and the simple language and common experience of our lives. Upon beginning to read this book we intuitively respond with, "This speaks to me!"

The second bridge is between the meaningful wisdom of *A Course in Miracles* and the actual practice of the principles which brings results in our everyday lives. This aspect of the book leads us to inwardly respond with, "I can do this!"

The third bridge is between being an individual studying *A Course in Miracles* alone, and that of applying its principles within a group setting. In a group setting we may experience Love for the first time, and sense that we finally belong somewhere. Both of these bring a refreshing sigh of relief.

Healing is something we do for ourselves.
***Sharing the Course* explains spiritual healing and gives simple methods for doing this.**

Part I, Surviving Physically and Healing Spiritually, offers simple explanations of Universal Laws we must understand to receive Love. When restricted in survival (fear) we see the world as hostile, punitive, depriving, and demanding our sacrifice. We heal this to see the world as friendly, comforting, gifting, and asking our service which has built-in rewards. This section includes healing methods to be applied immediately for undoing survival restrictions. In working with these methods we see a world that is *for* us rather than *against* us.

Part II, Joining with *A Course in Miracles*, is about the book itself and benefits of studying it. *A Course in Miracles* is written both in masculine and Christian language. It also uses terms

2

differently from what we are accustomed. So to receive the message, we must first join with the language and understand the terms.

Do not be concerned if you do not understand a term or concept the first time it is presented. Concepts are introduced throughout *Sharing the Course* where you see their application. Terms are made understandable within their application. For example, to pray is to ask. There are twenty Practice Exercises titled "Asking" which demonstrate asking as a process of prayer. There is also an index to help connect concepts with their application.

It is only in our thoughts that we believe we are separated from God.
We are not sinful, only mistaken, and we are to correct our mistaken thoughts.

Thoughts directed to defense deny the presence of God or Love. Every thought that does not include God, or the presence of a Loving Greater Being, is an incomplete thought. Every incomplete thought seeks to be redirected to be completed. We change our minds to heal this separation.

Part III, Changing Our Minds, addresses transforming our thinking from survival thinking to creative thinking. This change includes going from perception to Vision. Perception is the distorted way we see things during survival adaptation, and Vision is the clear way we see things with enlightenment.

Part IV, Meeting in Groups, assists in finding, leading, or participating in a group study of *A Course in Miracles*. This section emphasizes the need for creating a safe space and tells how to do it. Group rules and structure serve to provide safety to express. Therefore, they increase spiritual freedom rather than impose restrictions. Many of the students in my groups wrote letters to you about their experiences in group. These reflect the freedom to express tenderly that comes from sharing in a safe environment.

Part V, Sharing the Course, includes listings of ways to open and close meetings and offers suggestions for teaching content. This section offers an extensive listing and description of practical exercises for living the principles of *A Course in Miracles*. Each exercise has an accompanying spiritual homework assignment. Needs for stability and variety are met in using a consistent structure and varying the content of each step as proposed in *Sharing the Course*.

Weekly exercises gently bring us to awareness. They set up anticipation as we awaken to experience life as Joyful. We learn that by first applying principles in a safe group setting, we then carry the message into the world and make a difference there.

We know miracles when we consistently choose to follow processes which transform our thinking.
We learn to be people expressing what we want to see in the world.

Part VI, Bringing Things to Completion, includes ten sample lessons from my own teaching. They demonstrate both how I use structure and give content. In closing I share with you what it is like for me as a teacher. There is no separation between learning and teaching. The more I learn, the more I teach; and the more I teach, the more I learn.

Our language does not lend itself to describe that which is non-physical, or spiritual. Traditionally capital letters are used for terms relating to the spiritual, or to Being. Capitalizing calls our attention to the spiritual level of experience.

When we read a capitalized word our mind is drawn to the higher vibration of Love.
Capitalizing letters is meant to convey an experience of the spiritual which we can know, and not describe.

Sharing the Course has a companion set of audio tapes by Michael Root. Michael has participated in my groups from the beginning and has sensitively provided musical backgrounds for practicing principles of *A Course in Miracles*.

My husband, Eric Glende, took all the photos in this book. They were set up to help you see how we do things in group. In some photos, only one or a few are doing what we would all be doing in our actual group setting.

A Course in Miracles was first published in 1976 with a second edition in 1992. I quote from the corrected second edition and use the following notations in this book:

A Course in Miracles	ACIM or the Course
Text	T
Workbook for Students	WB or Workbook
Manual for Teachers	MT or Manual
References are to both editions	First/Second

4

PART I

Surviving Physically
and
Healing Spiritually

1

UNIVERSAL LAWS

In this chapter I share about Universal Laws. We must understand these Laws to receive Love. The Law of Being that governs our Soul has two parts. First, it requires that we view a Being greater than ourselves as capable of Loving, protecting, guiding, and nurturing us. Secondly, it requires that we view ourselves as worthy of receiving this Love. Note the relationship here. We are the receiver from a giver. We must be willing to receive.

Universal Laws are those laws that govern our Being. They are those laws that are true for all people, have always been, and will always be. These laws are absolute and impersonal. For example, at the physical level, the law of gravity is absolute and impersonal. The law is absolute in that any person who steps off a roof will be pulled to the ground. The law is impersonal in that it does not matter who that person is who steps off the roof.

Now, consider an airplane. I still marvel that anything that heavy can take flight. Do you? How is flight accomplished? An airplane can function by the law of gravity or the law of aerodynamics. To take flight, an airplane switches to a law which supersedes that of gravity. The law of aerodynamics is a higher law than the law of gravity and allows for release of the physical level law.

It is the same for us. **There are laws that govern our physical survival and laws that govern our Souls.** Laws that govern our Souls give us all the freedom and expansiveness of flight. They supersede laws of physical survival. The law of gravity and law of survival still exist when we choose to follow higher laws. In choosing to follow higher laws we experience marvelous results like airplanes in flight. We call them miracles. They are our natural way of Being.

A *Course in Miracles* is about higher laws which govern our Souls and bring us miraculous release. These laws are just as appropriately called Laws of Being, Spiritual Laws, Principles, Universal Principles, or Lord. Lord means Law. Check this out by reading a Bible verse such as Psalm 37 substituting the word "Law" for "Lord."

Universal Laws all have in common that they cannot be broken. We do not break Universal Laws when we fail to live by them, we break ourselves. At the physical level, we may break a leg falling off a roof. At the spiritual level we recognize failure to follow the law by feeling unhappy. Learning Laws of the Soul and aligning ourselves with them is a choice we are all called to make. Happiness is our natural state and comes from fulfilling the law.

To fulfill laws that govern our Being, we must first understand them. As energy Beings, we are subject to laws of electromagnetic systems. **One characteristic of Being is that energy moves from a positive pole to a negative pole. The positive pole is giver and the negative pole is receiver.** Traditionally these have been named masculine and feminine. Masculine is not the same as male gender, nor is feminine the same as female gender. On an electrical outlet, the wall socket is the feminine receiver of the pronged plug which penetrates it.

As Souls, we are all feminine receivers of masculine penetration by Spirit. We are literally inspired. Each in-breath is called an inspiration. Each out-breath is called an expiration. Death of the body is also called expiration, and is the moment of our last out-breath. Use your breath right now to experience the Force that inspires you. Allow yourself to relax your chest, letting your breath go all the way out. Then feel the power of Life itself as it breathes you. Did you feel the force of Life deep within the center of your Being?

Another characteristic of Being is that there are two major phases to life. The first phase of our life deals with physical development and the second phase deals with spiritual development. Like baby teeth and permanent teeth, our beliefs and behaviors related to physical survival. along with their effects, are meant to give rise to something more solid and permanent. In letting go of our baby teeth we may get scared, angry, cry, need the help of a string, a parent, or a dentist. Sometimes we bleed, and sometimes the tooth fairy comforts us with a reward for our ultimate courage to give up a tooth. The transition from baby teeth to permanent teeth is a long-term process. So is our transition from functioning on laws that govern physical survival to functioning on laws that allow our Souls to mature. **We call the process of switching from laws of physical survival to Laws of the Soul spiritual growth or spiritual healing.**

The Law of Being that governs our Soul has two parts. First, it requires that we view a Being greater than ourselves as capable of Loving, protecting, guiding, and nurturing us. Secondly, it requires that we view ourselves as worthy of receiving this Love. Note the relationship here. We are the receiver from a giver. We must be willing to receive.

This Law does not say we need to view the giver as a man, nor does it say we need to call the giving Force any particular name. I knew a woman who effectively grew spiritually by conversing in her mind with what she identified as her grandmother who had died before she was born. Note that she grew because she followed the law for her Soul's growth. In her mind, she both viewed her grandmother as capable of Loving, protecting, guiding, and nurturing her, and she knew she was worthy of receiving this care.

Laws of physical survival allow us to use our energy to restrict ourselves when needed to assure our safety. In my physical survival phase, I learned to keep my mouth shut. I believed that it was the best way to keep myself safe. I survived by restricting my natural ability to speak for myself. This was only one of many abilities I restricted to survive physically. Spirit never stops calling me to free the abilities I once restricted. I am not unlike you in this. What did you restrict? Do you hear the call to express these abilities? The call may feel like an unhappiness with the way something is going in your life. You may feel an inner restlessness. You may be ill.

I heard the call. And, at some point I began speaking even though I was terrified. Remember, I believed that I needed to be silent to survive physically, so I also believed I was going to die if I opened my mouth and said what I had to say. When I did have courage to risk that I wouldn't die, I felt angry when at first I was not able to make myself heard or understood. A voice coach endured years of struggle with me as I made the switch from being voiceless to speaking truth with authority.

Writing this book is part of my Soul's journey which reverses restrictions I imposed on myself in survival decisions. I make the choice every moment either to have writer's block and be voiceless, or to know I am safe to speak now. Since you are reading this book, you know that I am disciplining myself to follow the Law of Being. This requires both holding to the belief that I am loved by a Greater Being, and that I am worthy of receiving this Love. You, too, make this choice every moment to restrict, or expand under the Law of Being.

Both surviving physically and healing spiritually are natural processes. **Healing releases the restrictions we place on ourselves to assure only our physical safety, and includes care to our Soul as well.** In *Sharing The Course* I share with you how to make the transition from surviving to healing. To understand what we release in the switch, I first describe the adapting and separating process we all go through to survive physically.

2

ADAPTING

In this chapter I share the process we were given first to survive, and then to be radiantly alive. Growing up physically is automatic. We age. We grow old. **Growing up spiritually is not automatic. Life provides a process for us that allows us to reverse our early life restrictions. It is voluntary.** When we give consent, we mature spiritually. When we open to receive Love to our Souls, we become youthful. We become young in Spirit. We become radiantly alive.

A Course in Miracles **is a course in undoing our restrictions.** The Introduction to *A Course in Miracles* says we are free to choose when we do this and not free to choose the process. This is another one of those things that is absolute and impersonal. The process is the same for all of us. It doesn't matter who we are when we make decisions to restrict our abilities as part of surviving, we always experience their effects. When we choose to release those restrictions we experience freedom from their effects. *A Course in Miracles* is a gift to us that both invites us to freedom, and tells us how to get there.

For years I have shared my understanding of this process with others. I have been inspired by their growth. I want to share with you, too. In order to understand the process of spiritual growth, which is the undoing of restrictions and receiving of Love/Light, we must first understand our process of adapting. *A Course in Miracles* says, T p. 203/218, "Miracles are merely the translations of denial into truth." We are meant to live miraculously. Sounds good, doesn't it?

Early in life, we function on our Feeling Nature which is feminine receptive. Our own Thinking Nature, which connects with Higher Thought, or the Mind of God, is not yet developed. **When our Thinking Nature develops, it provides the link between God and our Feeling Nature making us one with the giver from whom we receive. When we bring these two poles**

(Thinking and Feeling) together, it is like connecting two poles on a battery. Juice begins to flow in us, and this juice is Love.

These two natures are often referred to as our inner parent and inner child. Connecting these natures begins our spiritual journey. It also begins our healing. In Chapter 5, Healing Methods, I share with you simple ways to make this connection. **In healing we save ourselves from our own restrictive survival decisions that separate us from Love.**

Until we make this connection within ourselves, we depend on grown-ups to be aware of our needs. They read signals of our physical needs as hunger, sleepiness, and danger. Ideally they take appropriate action to solve our problems. They read signals of our emotional needs as fear, anger, and sadness. Ideally they take appropriate action to solve these problems, too. Parents are like our baby teeth. They are supposed to serve us this way. It is our inner parent that is permanent and fulfills our spiritual needs, making us happy.

Truth is, most parents are still functioning entirely in their own survival mode at the time that they have children of their own. They, too, have not as yet reversed their own restrictions and freed their Souls. So, they are raising children who are *trying to get* Love while they themselves are *trying to get* Love from outside of themselves. Or, in others words, they have not as yet acknowledged the Law of Being. They have not accepted that a Being greater than themselves is giving them Love, and that they are worthy of receiving that Love. They are not yet happy.

This does not mean that either parents or children are bad. All of humankind is growing in its ability to create and extend Love. Each generation is intended to be able to extend Love from a higher level of awareness. This is spiritual evolution. We are where we are in evolution.

Meanwhile, life IS safe. **Nature provides all of us an absolutely marvelous way to survive those times when our parents and society fail to protect us.** We all adapt. Adapting is like squeezing a balloon. The more we squeeze one part of it, the larger another part will become. The whole volume is still the same. We are like that...whole.

The more we restrict ourselves to survive, the more we build within us a part which is capable of taking care of someone restricted just like we are. We call the restricted part our wounded child. We call the expanded part our Higher Self, or inner parent.

A *Course in Miracles* calls this expanded self the Holy Spirit which is God's answer to the separating we do in the process of adapting to survive. The Holy Spirit is the part that remembers what we deny. It is the Voice we hear within, the One that speaks to us as a Loving Mother or Father. When we identify as the wounded one, it is joining with this expanded self that completes us, heals us, and makes us happy. We long for this Loving union with Spirit. We loosen the restriction on our balloon to know Love again.

The process of joining with the Holy Spirit is simple, yet we experience it as difficult because it is contrary to all we think is true. It is contrary to what we have been taught by society, within the institutions of society, by parents, and within our extended family. That's about everybody, isn't it!

We naturally experience fear of dying as we let go of a survival pattern. We make physical level survival decisions to assure care of a parent while we are dependent on them for our well-being. We believe we will die if we do not follow our self-imposed restriction. So when we begin to do or be what we once prohibited, we face our belief that we will die. Secondly, we face threat of rejection and non-support from all the people and systems that support our restricting.

Rejection or non-support may come from religious, educational, governmental, financial, or medical institutions. It may come from public media. It may come from those closest to us. Growing spiritually can feel like standing alone for ourselves with everyone against us. While it takes courage to face our fear of dying, blaming our parents when we are not happy as adults is like walking around with a string tied to a baby tooth, too afraid to pull it.

Because of fears of rejection and dying we often begin our spiritual growth only after some *seeming* tragedy in our lives. We need to be more afraid of spiritually dying from the results of our restricting, than of physically dying from rejection. And then, when we finally have the courage to do what we must to live, we may experience lack of support from others as a vote for our dying.

Note that I said a *seeming* tragedy may be our turning point. Most of these events are just that, places for us to turn from surviving to healing, from restricting to expanding. This reminds me of an event in my own life. In my thirties I put concerted effort into getting certified as a Transactional Analyst. I set up a counseling practice in my home which flourished by word of mouth. I was offered an opportunity to get a Masters degree in

Mental Health Nursing with federal funds made available during the presidency of John Kennedy. I accepted. This degree allowed me the credibility to teach at a local university as well as counsel.

Meanwhile, the psychologists in my state passed a law stating that they were the only ones qualified to do psychological counseling. I joined with other counselors and social workers in our state to pass legislation that would include us in the practice. It took a lot of years to achieve this. I then applied for licensure under the newly passed bill. Five years later I was declined. The reason given was that I lacked sufficient college classes on theory of personality. It *seemed* like a real tragedy for someone to tell me I was not qualified to continue counseling in a practice that I had spent so many years preparing and developing. It was ME and I loved what I was doing.

Other forces had been at work here, though. During the time that the licensing board was poring over piles of applications, Spirit had led me to *A Course in Miracles*. I understood it because of what I had learned in Transactional Analysis training. I had begun teaching the Course. So many students came to learn that I had quit teaching at the university and used the money in my retirement fund to build a classroom in my home. I assume that if someone passes a law against teaching *A Course in Miracles*, Spirit will invite me through another door. Maybe I'm supposed to be a full-time author!

My freedom to do what I most love is due to more than just listening to Spirit's guidance. It requires my acting on the Law of Being. I acknowledge that a Greater Being is giving Loving guidance to me. I also forgave psychologists who feared, and who chose to restrict. I forgave a legislature that feared, and that chose to deny me license to practice.

We have to forgive in order to fulfill the second part of the Law of Being which is to believe that we are worthy of Love. If we do not forgive those who support our restricting, we continue to believe our unworthiness to receive, and stay restricted, bitter, and blaming toward them. Every *seeming* tragedy is an invitation to grow spiritually. When we choose to release a restriction and any blame that goes with it, we release the tragic nature of the troublesome event.

As for the licensing board's belief that I lack understanding in theory of personality, I leave that up to you to decide. Now we will look at how we survive by restricting, and then see the marvelous built-in plan for release.

14

3

SEPARATING

In this chapter I share the process of separating. Life provides us the ability to use our energy to survive the absence of Love from human care givers until we are mature enough to create Love within ourselves. In understanding our separating, we see what we must do to heal our separation.

DEFENSE

Squeezing the balloon is known as defending. (See Chapter 2 for balloon analogy.) It has also been appropriately called building an ego, putting up walls, closing our doors, numbing ourselves, putting on masks, adapting, building our personality, becoming addicted, taking on roles, becoming compulsive, falling asleep, and going into darkness. *A Course in Miracles* calls this embodied defense our ego. **No matter what we call this process, the end result of defending is separating from God and setting up the condition of guilt.**

Guilt is what we experience in the absence of Love when we are separated from the flow of Life (Light/God). It is our identity when we live in darkness. This temporary identity is meant to give way to knowing our true and permanent identity. As we accept the breath, or Spirit of the balloon back into the part that we squeezed, Light enters the darkness. With it comes knowing ourselves as an innocent, Beloved child, or as more frequently called in *A Course in Miracles*, a Son of God. **It is our decision to defend that separates us from God, and it is this decision that we change to heal and to release guilt.**

DISSOCIATION/DENIAL

This is how we defend, which is also known as dissociation and denial: Suppose as a child we are frightened. Our parent may not be around, or may be the one who is frightening us, or may simply be frightened, too. There is no one to comfort us in our fright. As a child we see our parent as the Greater Being who Loves and protects us. So, we experience a threat to our life while abandoned by the one who protects us. We believe there is no Love available to us, and we fear dying.

The law of survival automatically takes over and sets up the instinctual process of defending. This process takes place thousands of times during our growing up years with a cumulative effect. The following steps take place rather instantaneously, and not necessarily in a progression as I list them here.

Feelings that accompany this abandonment are too intense for us to bear as a child, so we deny (repress) the visual memory. Blocking the visual memory dissociates our awareness from our feelings. This sets the scene of threat outside of our awareness where it waits for us to be mature enough to look at it anew. Holding this memory in our past sets up "time" as defined by *A Course in Miracles*. We know Love in the present and defending takes us out of the present.

When we defend we reverse the natural flow of Life through us. Our energy is demagnetized, now anti-God. This move sets up the *seeming* separation from God. I say *seeming*, because Life itself gives us this ability to survive by defending, and Life continues to feed us energy.

This reversal is like what we do at the physical level when we stop modeling our parents and start resisting them as teenagers. We believe that in doing the opposite of our parents, we are free and independent. Meanwhile, our decisions are entirely based on what our parents do in order for us to do the opposite. And, in believing we are independent, we ignore the full range of support we are receiving from our parents.

When we defend we use Life energy to build our walls, mask our faces, and hold our breath. Grief accumulates from this separation from Love. Floods of tears get stored behind our wall. Healing, which reverses our defense, is accompanied by sobs and sighs which release our tears and also our restricted breathing. I remember at one point believing that if I ever started to cry I would never stop. It wasn't true, of course. I still cry when I reverse an early scene and remember the presence of Love.

16

Since it is the flow of Life through us that nourishes and heals us, when we defend we set in motion circumstances that lead us to sickness and death. We do not realize this, of course, for it is the nature of the whole process of defending that we deny that we have dissociated. Sickness is a sign that we are using physical survival means when we have reached an age when spiritual maturity is appropriate. *A Course in Miracles* is quite clear on the point that all sickness comes from separation and that death is not real. In other words, God does not create death. For the Soul there is only Life.

Ego denial is literally a deadening process. When we numb ourselves, we numb our ability to see abuse and violence for what they are. When functioning in our ego we always mis-name and justify our behaviors. We both participate in, and are subject to both abuse and violence. Without seeing them for what they are, we fail to change ourselves and to give appropriate responses. Instead of using power to heal, we use power to destroy. Numbness at the collective level is behind the massive abuse and violence of Mother Earth. As we wake up from denial, we refuse to abuse ourselves or tolerate abuse from others. The same awakening corrects our abuse and violence of others and Mother Earth.

Once we defend, or squeeze the balloon, we do not see the whole of who we are. All participation in abuse or violence indicates we are refusing Love rather than refusing darkness. Just as light is still beyond the window when we pull down a shade, Love of a Greater Being is there for us, too. In order to reconnect with this Being, we need to lift the shade. This means that we need to bring back to awareness those scenes and feelings from which we have dissociated. They wait in our unconscious, outside our awareness. You will find scenes to clarify this point in Chapter 5, Healing Methods.

PROJECTION

A feeling is energy in motion. **When we dissociate from a feeling, it doesn't simply disappear.** It continues to move. Blocking energy by defending builds tension which functions as a propellant. The feeling energy is sent to the solar plexus of a parent or care giver. The sending out of energy in this manner is called projecting. We are all created to pick up such signals at our solar plexus (pit of our stomach).

Projecting a feeling is our innate way of calling for someone else to help us before we are mature enough to think for ourselves. We project like a movie projector. The feeling does not leave us like the film does not leave the projector. In deciding to defend, however, we deny awareness of the feeling, so we think it is gone.

One characteristic of a projected feeling is the quality of blame that accompanies it. Since we dissociate from awareness of our part in the process, we believe someone else is at fault for our not feeling Loved and happy. Workbook Lesson No. 5 in *A Course in Miracles* says, "I am never upset for the reason I think." We are truly always upset because we defended and separated from God. Since, as a child we can only see our parent as a Greater Being, we do not realize there is a Being greater than the one who was unable to Love us at the moment.

Another characteristic of projection is a result of the switch in magnetism. When we defend, we are no longer feminine receptive in our Feeling Nature. We have reversed polarity and have become a masculine giver. Projecting from our defensive stance is one of exerting control, or manipulating. This is commonly called "laying a guilt trip" on someone. We *try* to make someone give us care by making them wrong.

> When we project from the Feeling Nature (which is intended to be a receiver), we are closed to receiving Love from God. When we remain a receiver from God we are free to extend Love, and receive Love extended to us by others. When demagnetized, *trying to get*, we repel our Good and keep it from coming to us.

Energy projected to the solar plexus of another carries a charge that is reversed and therefore in disharmony with the natural flow of Life. These are masks for the true feelings which we deny in the reversal. We think they are real. Since substitute feelings are not genuine they do not resolve. They continue to build and we continue to use them to *try to get* Love which we cannot receive while our energy is reversed. When we use feelings by our ego, we use the same substitute over and over, harder and harder, or longer and longer. We do not acknowledge that what we are doing defensively has not, is not, and never will bring us the Love we desire.

Have you known someone who was sad two years ago, they are sad now, and you are quite sure that if you see them two years from now they will still be sad? The same pattern could be true for anger or anxiety. These are non-genuine feeling displays masking genuine feelings. A substitute display of sadness, like whining, irritates others and we want to say, "Knock it off already!"

Genuinely expressed sadness calls for others to move in tenderly and give care. We express genuinely as we heal and become Joyful. Projection is intended to be used for infants and young ones to survive. For example, the scream of a child alarms us and motivates us to solve their problem. We want to solve the problem to bring an end to the feeling of alarm in our gut.

When defensive behavior is used beyond these young years, we experience such projections to our gut as attacks. When we receive them we often move to defend, too, and respond to the attack with a counterattack. We project a feeling back which also carries with it the intent to blame the other for our separating from Love and going to fear.

Though we are sending intimidating attacks, we still and always identify as a child receiver. We do not realize we are sending the attacks and only see the responses coming back to us. (This is why all parties in a troubling situation "feel" like victims.) We start to replace our image of a Loving parent with that of a cruel, abandoning, or rejecting one. We carry this attitude into other relationships expecting others to be cruel, abandoning, or rejecting also. We do not realize we are being cruel, abandoning, or rejecting, first of all to ourselves, and secondly to others.

Then, as we grow up, we tend to transfer the images we have formed of a parent, onto God. We determine that God is cruel, abandoning, or rejecting. So, once defended, we identify as a wounded child without a Loving Greater Being. Until we heal our separation, we listen to a voice in our mind that sounds cruel, abandoning, and rejecting. We feel worthy of no more in our darkness, in our state of guilt. Only when we heal this separation do we know ourselves as a Beloved Child of a Loving God. And only then do we see that every other human being has defended, also, and each has the task of healing to once again know Love.

PERCEPTION

There is one other thing I would like to share now on the topic of defending. Remember that defending starts with a decision to block visual memory so as to not see what we don't want to feel. This sets up what *A Course in Miracles* calls perception. Perception is always a distorted way of seeing because we don't see the whole picture. Believing God doesn't exist because a parent is not able to Love is perception, not the whole picture. Seeing the whole picture is Vision.

Several years ago, after wearing glasses for thirty-five years, I was able to take them off. In allowing myself to See what I had denied, my eyesight began correcting itself. I was accepting Vision, willing to See the whole picture again. Our ability to deny is meant to be our baby teeth. We are then to wake up to See that which is permanent, the ever present Love of God.

Defending is an ability given to us for physical survival only. We reverse our decisions to defend as we heal spiritually. To remain in a defensive stance beyond its time is to suffer. To blame anyone including God for our suffering is to refuse to See. Willingness to See is willingness to know God as our Source of Love.

SUMMARY: ASPECTS OF SEPARATING

We experience a threat to our life.
We deny visual memory.
>This sets the picture in mind.
>This holds our mind in the past.
>This sets up "time."
We dissociate from feelings.
>This reverses our polarity.
>We become demagnetized.
>We repel our Goodness.
>We set up conditions of sickness.
We embody our ego.
>We hold our breath.
>We build our walls.
>We store our grief.
We project feelings - attack and invite attacks.
We receive counterattacks and justify more attacks.
>Pain and unhappiness build.
We suffer and blame others.
We see others and God as cruel.
We remain unaware that we denied.

4

HEALING OUR SEPARATION

In this chapter I share the process for healing our separation from the Love of God. True communication is a joining. Joining is the coming together of a masculine giving pole and feminine receiving pole. This is the basic Law of Creation. **Our Soul's growth is the healing of our separation which we set up during our period of dependency.**

Healing is correcting the energy reversal of our ego used for survival. During our period of physical dependency, we each set up patterns for *getting* others to be the thinker for us. We have been calling for others to tend our feelings by sending out alarms, without realizing that they have experienced these as attacks. Now we are mature enough to Think for our own Feeling Nature. All of the Healing Methods in Chapter 5 are designed to join these poles. We are undoing the patterns we made to *get*, and are Giving awareness to our own feelings. I call this doing Spiritual Homework. It is something no one can do for us. **The means are simple and the rewards are great.**

Our spiritual journey begins with an inner connection, the joining of our inner parent and inner child. Ultimately, the joining is between ourselves as Souls, and God. I have found, both in my personal growth and in guiding others, that the gap between pure energy of Love offered by God and our closed states of fear is too great to join directly. We first need to develop a kind voice within us and gain trust of our inner child. As we open to our own kind voice, we also open to the Love of God.

This process in our growth is like a five year old asking where a baby comes from. We as adults have much information to offer. If we truly think about it, spiritually, we may need to admit that we really don't know. It is one of the miracles of Life itself. However, all the five year old really wants to know is that the baby comes out of a mother's tummy. That is wonder enough at that age. The function of Jesus Christ and other

Teachers has been to help bridge this same gap for us, making mysteries of Universal Law easier for us to grasp.

What we realize as we grow is how firmly we have entrenched the habit of blaming. We even blame God and do not see that WE made all the moves to separate from Love in the first place. **The way to God's Love is simply to be willing to stop waiting and blaming, and do what WE need to do to correct ourselves.** The energy direction of blame is demagnetizing. In blaming we repel what we most need and want. The inner connection made in healing remagnetizes us. We become magnets of Love.

Put most simply, we join our inner parent and inner child. **Only then do we know happiness.** Happiness comes naturally when we release our demand and blame of others for not fulfilling our desire to be happy. As we open ourselves to Love, we connect with Inner Guidance. That which we've learned in our period of adaptation is general information for survival. During our stage of spiritual development we listen inwardly for who we are as unique individuals, and extend our Being as gifts to the planet.

No matter where we are in our survival and growth, we are *always* listening to a parent voice. When we identify as our ego, we listen to a voice that controls, criticizes, hurts, restricts, abandons, etc. This is **the voice of the ego** that **demands.** When we identify as a Beloved Child we listen to a voice that encourages, praises, helps, gives us permission to go ahead, and supports our process of individuation. This is **the voice of the Holy Spirit** that **invites.** To come to completion is to accept the invitation of the Holy Spirit. **Accepting back into awareness all that we denied, or squeezed into another part of the balloon, fulfills our individual purpose. This, and this alone, brings us to Joy.**

In applying the following methods, it is necessary to learn to discern these two voices. It is rather easy in that one hurts, and the other feels good. We are so used to feeling hurt, however, we hardly know what it would feel like to receive a Loving response to help us grow.

There is always a part of us that does know, and does remember the state of happiness. That is why we so persistently seek to be happy. The Loving parent voice comes from conscious thought, from imagining how a most Loving parent would respond to us. This is not the voice impressed on our subconscious in the solar plexus exchanges in which others were attacking to *try to get* Love from us at the same time we were attacking to *try to get* Love from them. These were the attacks that separated.

It is wonderful if we have known Loving people, perhaps a parent, a grandmother, or a teacher whose words serve as a model for us. **I believe whether we have known a Loving person or not, we all know deep within our Beings the words we long to hear. We can also speak them. They are the words that heal our separation.**

At first we may feel like we are pretending as we hold these healing conversations. This is natural. What we are doing is preparing ourselves to receive higher energy. It is like switching from a radio station that plays hard rock to one that plays soft favorites.

Our task is to learn to join, which begins inside. The energy of joining is a higher energy pattern than that of resisting which sets up the separation. We grow in our ability to extend higher energy through practice. Joining allows Life Energy to flow. This means we are willing to once again be aware (Thinking Nature) of feelings (Feeling Nature) we denied. This means we extend Love from our heart rather than depend on solar plexus attacks. This means we See God as Loving rather than cruel, and extend Gratitude for Love we receive in joining.

Our ultimate goal is to be of one energy with God, that of Pure Love, Pure Joy, Pure Peace. This energy is completely free of all attack, all harmful intent, all intent to *get* from another. We are fulfilled in our Giving and extending of the Love that flows through us.

I have observed some recent happenings with interest. For quite a few years it seemed that people who would ordinarily have found mates or married in their early twenties, were totally frustrated in their desires. I would put this in the category of *seeming* tragedies. Many of them are now mating, or marrying in their thirties or forties. They are raising children after beginning their Soul's journey. I believe there is an important step taking place here. Do you see the hope this offers?

In the next chapter I give you methods for joining. For each method, I give you instructions, an example, call your attention to key points, share with you problems I've observed as people have used the method, and suggest what to do about those problems. As with any Universal Law, we only realize the miraculous results by fulfilling the Law, which means to put it into practice. Now, for the methods that heal separation. I bless you on your journey.

SUMMARY: ASPECTS OF HEALING

Willing to connect with God.
    Believe Love is available to us.
    Risk that we won't die if we open.
Willing to stop blaming.
Willing to See.
    Remember what was dissociated.
Willing to tend our own feelings.
    Listen to our inner child.
    Speak kindly to ourselves.
Release embodied ego.
    Breathe, cry, dissolve our walls.
Listen for Inner Guidance.
    Accept Light into darkness.
Identify as Innocent/Beloved.
Acknowledge that Life is safe.
Express Gratitude to God.

Some of our "young ones."

5

HEALING METHODS

In this chapter I share Healing Methods which are all processes to be continued over a period of years, if necessary. These methods work to release your intent to blame and demand of others, which is left over from your survival stage of development. Their healing power can only be known by doing them. Spiritual healing is returning your focus to God as your source of Life/Love.

I hope you will discover more ways to achieve your joining. You will first join the Thinking and Feeling Natures within you and then join the Father, knowing you are Loved, limitless, pure, and innocent. **If you seek to go directly to God without releasing your ego intent first, you simply blame and demand of God rather than open your heart to receive.**

"You are still My holy Son (child), forever innocent, forever loving and forever loved, as limitless as your Creator, and completely changeless and forever pure. Therefore awaken and return to Me. I am your Father and you are My Son (child)." (WB p. 445/455)

METHOD ONE: *USING IMAGINATION TO REPARENT YOURSELF*

INSTRUCTIONS

Imagine the most wonderful possible parent. Imagine the words you've longed to hear and the comfort you've longed to feel. Speak these words to yourself and feel yourself being comforted. Set up polarity by being the Greater Being capable of extending Love, and also the child worthy of receiving Love. I'm sure you are aware of the critical voice that makes you wrong and unlovable. **You cannot listen to the critical voice and**

25

your Loving voice at the same time. At every moment you are choosing which you will speak and which you will hear. The choice FOR one is a choice AGAINST the other.

Call yourself by name either using your actual first name, an endearing name you were called as a child, or some term of endearment, like "Honey." When I am talking to myself Lovingly, I think of my head as my Thinking Nature (Grown-up, or Nurturing Parent) and my stomach or solar plexus area as my Feeling Nature (Little Girl, Inner Child, or Natural Child). In the example that follows, I use "NP" to represent my Nurturing Parent voice and "LN" to represent Little Nancy. This is the actual conversation I wrote in my journal this morning.

EXAMPLE ONE

> LN- I don't mind writing this book "but" I don't like to be criticized and I know that people will criticize me.
>
> NP- Nancy, I appreciate how much you have been cooperating with writing this book. It has been a high mission. I hear that you don't like to be criticized. Of course you don't. No one does.
>
> LN- Sometimes it is easier to be invisible.
>
> NP- Yes. I can understand that a little girl sometimes feels safer when she thinks no one sees her. I see you.
>
> LN- Well, do you like what you see?
>
> NP- Yes, indeed. I see a courageous young one willing to follow the guidance of Spirit even if people criticize you. Anyone who criticizes you doesn't see the importance of your message to the public.
>
> LN- Every time I hear the word "public" I get scared. What if I have to go on the Oprah Winfrey Show?
>
> NP- Well, first of all, you don't have to go on her show.
>
> LN- Good. All those unknown people out there scare me.
>
> NP- To be on her show may be part of Spirit's plan for you. Spirit is seeking to reach all those ready for this message.

LN- Sometimes it is hard to follow Spirit.

NP- It seems that way, doesn't it. Are you remembering that I will be with you no matter where you go?

LN- What will you do for me?

NP- Suppose you are invited to be on Oprah's show. I will remind you constantly that she is one of the most visible people living the principles of *A Course in Miracles*. She loves *A Course in Miracles*. Anyone who lives by these Laws will only be kind and helpful to you. She wants people to hear your message and will help you deliver it.

LN- It won't be like the time when I was asked to do a radio interview and the woman challenged everything I said?

NP- No, Nancy. If Oprah has you on her show it will be because she wants to help you get your message out to the public.

LN- Do you think she will buy a thousand copies of my book like she did *A Return to Love*?

NP- She may. I can tell you are beginning to feel excited rather than scared. You can focus on exciting aspects of being on her show rather than all the scary things about it.

LN- "What if" I have to go to Chicago and I get lost?

NP- I'll be with you. I'll see to it that we get all the information and help we need to minimize the chance of that happening. And, if it does, we'll get ourselves found again just like we always do! Take my hand and we'll walk through this experience together.

LN- You won't ever leave me?

NP- I am part of you and I will be with you everywhere you go, always.

LN- Thank you for being here for me.

NP- I love you, Nancy, I really love you. You are precious to me. 1 will always look over you and keep you safe.

KEY POINTS FOR EXAMPLE ONE

a. **Your inner child has many questions. All of them ask one basic question, "Will I be safe?" Safety to a child depends on seeing a protective parent as present for them. In your dialog, you are that parent.**

b. Note at the beginning of this dialog that "but" is my child's transitional word to fear. My Nurturing Parent says "Yes" (with no "but") to what my child says and then ADDS some thought that will comfort. This is a "Yes, and" rather than a "Yes, but." While "Yes, but" has a diminishing effect, "Yes, and" leads your child out of fear to the limitless nature of Love.

c. Your Nurturing Parent hears what you fear, dislike, and what hurts you, and says "Of course" frequently.

d. **Answer every "What if" from your child with the highest level of information you have. Always assume your child is telling you where it doesn't feel protected and where it needs information in order to feel safe.**

e. The Nurturing Parent sees and praises Goodness.

f. Continue your dialog until your child feels safe with new information received. Information to your child relieves fear. The most important information here is that your Nurturing Parent is and will be present and aware of your feeling child. From conversations like this your Feeling Nature begins to trust your Thinking Nature to be there as a Greater Being. This trust is the reversal of willfulness, of survival/defensive resistance. The release of resistance opens you to flow with the Will of God. **Releasing fear ASKS for God's presence.** Asking comes from a child stance, "I am pure and innocent, deserving only Love." As you treat yourself this way, your Feeling Nature accepts this as true for you and receives Love from God. Anything you believe about yourself other than that you are innocent and deserve only Love came from the way you were treated by others. And, in resisting their treatment, you closed to God (became anti-God). Living closed to God brought experiences you used to prove to yourself you didn't deserve Love.

PROBLEMS WITH THIS METHOD AND WHAT TO DO ABOUT THEM

a. You continue to listen to the ego voice hassling and do not think to use this method to respond to your child who feels separated. Set up a regular habit of listening and responding. There is no problem too small or too great for this method.

b. You allow the critical voice to respond. It sounds like this: "Don't be scared, people won't criticize you." And, of course, you've just been criticized by the critical voice in your own mind. This voice made you wrong for feeling scared. Accept all feelings so the child trusts that you are there. Then, give information on how the two of you together will handle the feared situation should it arise.

c. You confuse your inner child with children you now parent. Your "inner child" is the accumulation of all stored memories which include images from what you saw, heard, smelled, tasted, felt, sensed in movement, and experienced as feelings such as mad, sad, and scared. Your inner child is ageless. Images come to awareness from all past ages for you to give care to them now. As a parent, your children will seek similar attending from you. One kind of attending is an inner process for healing yourself. The other is an external process for responding with care to another. Our Soul's growth requires many kinds of discerning. This is one.

METHOD TWO: *USING AN OBJECT (DOLL) TO REPRESENT YOUR FEELING NATURE*

INSTRUCTIONS

Open yourself to Love by using a doll, teddy, pillow, etc. to represent your Feeling Nature. As you rock, cuddle, and caress this object, imagine that you are loving your inner child. Speak and listen to it. You will find that your voice and manner will switch back and forth from being the parent to being the child. Expect your child self to want to be held securely. Expect lots of tears as you unite with your hurting child. They are tears of relief. They are tears that accumulated behind your wall of defense while you were separated from Love. You will find a teaching of Jesus related to this in the Beatitudes, Matthew 5:4 (Holy Bible, Revised Standard Version). "Blessed are those that mourn: for they shall be comforted." Releasing your tears to your own Thinking Nature is fulfilling this Law. Your result will be to receive the comfort for which you have longed.

EXAMPLE TWO

A close friend has an "ET" doll. It is the object that felt most like his little boy to him. Before using this method he often experienced intense anxiety. He found that by just picking up "ET" a conversation would start in his mind. He would soon know what his child's fears were and could give needed information. Note that the act of remembering and picking up the doll allows for the joining. His inner child feels the presence of a Greater Being. His Loving response to the child allows his Feeling Nature to know his worthiness to receive Love.

KEY POINTS FOR EXAMPLE TWO

a. You will know what doll or stuffed toy is right for you. You will feel emotionally drawn to it. Do not use anything to which you don't feel Loving. I found that when I was dealing with birth issues, I wanted to use a small infant size pillow. Usually I used a doll which wears size two clothing. I put this in past tense for me because I discovered after years of healing my inner separation (reversing resistance) that I began to relate as one whole Being to God.

b. Your object is not to be any living thing that has a personality of its own, as a child or a pet. It needs to be something onto which you project your inner child.

c. Privacy is important in doing emotional work. Others may not understand your healing process and could deeply affect you by laughing or ridiculing. Be alone for this.

d. You may get angry in doing this dialog, or any of these methods, as you realize how simple it could have been for someone to comfort you in your past. Recognize this anger as a pull to blame. Say "Yes" to your child self that is speaking to you. You will either continue to blame, or you will be determined to continue this process until you open to receive. **Choose to continue to Love yourself, giving yourself fully what you need.**

e. If you are in a group that is like-minded and appreciates the healing work you are doing, do take your "little one" for them to Love, also. We cannot receive too much Loving attention.

f. This method helps break down stereotypes that only girls play with dolls and only women take care of children. I love seeing a man in one of my groups attending to his "Buddy."

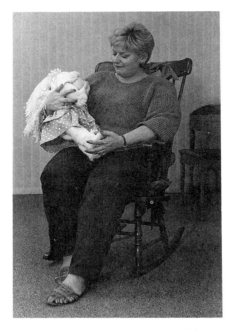

Nurturing your inner child.

PROBLEMS WITH THIS METHOD AND WHAT TO DO ABOUT THEM

a. There is a difference between keeping secrets and keeping things sacred. This method is not part of mainstream thinking and can be subject to misinterpretation. Recognize that it is a powerful healing tool you are using and your choosing to heal yourself is honorable. You need not tell people who would not understand what you are doing. This is what keeping it sacred means.

b. When we feel bonded with our doll or toy, we would like to take it everywhere. Do take it everywhere as an image in your mind and a feeling in your body. Hold your conversations in your mind, and you will feel results in your body and see results in your life. When out in the public, be the grown-up and stay aware of your child self.

31

c. People confuse their own self with their children or pets. See this point under METHOD ONE.

METHOD THREE: *USING A MIRROR TO JOIN THINKING AND FEELING NATURES*

INSTRUCTIONS

Preferably, sit in front of a full length mirror with your knees nearly touching it. You might also stand, sit on the floor, or use a hand-held mirror. Allow enough time to get beyond the initial tendency to adjust your hair and look for wrinkles, pimples, and bags under your eyes. This method invites you to look deeply into your own eyes to truly see yourself. While you can do this in whatever way feels right for you, I instruct people to think of the one sitting in front of the mirror as being their Thinking Nature - parent self, and the one in the mirror being their Feeling Nature - child self. Hold a conversation speaking with your two voices just as you would if you were writing the parts out in a journal.

Doing mirror work.

EXAMPLE THREE

Suzanne's dialog:
NP- (Nurturing Parent Voice) Hi Suzanne!
LS- (Little Suzanne) Hi!
NP- You are beautiful and I love you.
LS- I don't believe you.
NP- That is OK. I will still be here loving you.
LS- How can you love me? I'm so inadequate. I'm so stupid sometimes.
NP- Suzanne, there are times when you don't know things. That doesn't mean that you are inadequate or stupid.
LS- I feel stupid.
NP- Well, stupid isn't really a feeling. You believe you are stupid because people have called you that. What do you feel when you believe you are stupid?
LS- Scared. I feel scared that no one will love me. (crying)
NP- Yes, Suzanne, when we believe we are stupid we will also believe that no one could love us. Suzanne, look at me. See me. I am your very own loving parent. I am part of you. I am sitting here at the mirror with you to help you see that I am here for you. I see you as beautiful, and I love you.
LS- I don't think I can trust you. No one else has ever said that to me.
NP- Suzanne, I will be here for you whether you trust me "yet" or not. I love you, I really love you. (After continuing for some time, she sighs and smiles through tears.)
LS- Thank you for being here for me and not giving up on me.

KEY POINTS FOR EXAMPLE THREE

a. The mirror allows you to see facial changes and posture stances as you change back and forth from those of a parent to those of a child. You can actually see that the other is there and that both of these identities are within you.

b. Plan to sit long enough to break through any resistance from your child self. This is important in all of these methods.

Repeat the Loving message you want the child to hear rather than make any child response wrong. (Use "Yes, and.") Also, notice the word, "yet" near the end of this dialog. The word "yet" sets up a sense of hope, anticipation, and excitement that something desirable is coming. Generally speaking, the words "I can't" associate with hopelessness while "I haven't yet" associate with hope.

c. Mirror talk is a powerful healing tool. It is difficult to maintain a defensive wall while looking yourself in the eye. You can cry into a pillow for years and not heal. Do you know why? Healing means joining. **If you cry, seeing yourself only as the abandoned, wounded one, and do not bring in the nurturing voice to tend your child, you are not following the Law of Being, which is the Law of Healing.**

d. See to privacy for this method. If you have a friend whom you truly trust to be with you at very tender moments, it would be OK to have them in the room. They would sit quietly mostly to give you a big hug at the end of your dialog to celebrate your healing.

e. The person in the mirror may take on a different "face" from your own. You may realize at some point that you are speaking to a parent, mate, or friend. It may be someone who has died. Say what you need to say to them and then return to your parent/child dialog.

f. As with any of these methods, see the conversation through to completion. **A sign of completion is a sigh. This indicates the joining has taken place.** Notice how a sigh also opens your breathing and you take in more Spirit. This means you open to Love. You open to Life. You open to God. You no longer hold resistance, or an anti-God stance on this issue. Since you have separated off so many aspects of yourself, you will need to continue to use these various methods to reclaim these also. **When you sigh, say "The crisis is over."** I find it helpful to reinforce the joining by doing this several times with large, purposeful sighs repeating, "The crisis is over" after each sigh.

PROBLEMS WITH THIS METHOD AND WHAT TO DO ABOUT THEM

a. When you have spent your life surrounded by people who withhold feelings and you suddenly begin to feel, you may not realize the rightness of what is happening. Any time you have learned something that is wrong, as being right, then when you do something right, it will feel wrong to you. I have had people ask me if they are going crazy. I assure you that joining in this way is coming out of craziness. *A Course in Miracles* tells us our ego thinking is insane and we awaken to Truth which is sanity. We save ourselves by risking to reverse our thinking and behaving. Remember, the way you have been handling feelings hasn't brought you to happiness. Sometimes you need to do just the opposite of what you have been doing. There will likely come a time in your life when you learn to recognize Truth by the fact that it is the opposite of what is usually done in society. Social structures are built on fear and adaptation. **Truth is always simple, brings growth, and harms no one. Everyone gains from any action that you take based on Truth.**

b. Avoiding eye contact is one of the most frequent problems. This is a sure sign that you are avoiding feeling. I recommend you use your Nurturing Parent voice to gently and persistently call your child to see that you are there. "Look at me. I am here for you. I Love you even though you cry. Your tears are beautiful to me. I will be tender with you. I Love you, I really Love you." **It is in recognizing that you avoid seeing the presence of your own self as a grown-up that you truly see how much you hold a position of blame toward your parents and refuse to see that you are now a grown-up yourself.** Most of us doing this work are older than our parents were when they were raising us.

c. Most do not trust their Nurturing Parent Voice. Build it by speaking from it. Build it by acting "as if" you are a trustworthy and capable nurturer. We become skilled athletes by actually throwing, hitting, or kicking a ball. **We become skilled nurturers by actually saying Loving words and acting in Loving ways.**

METHOD FOUR: *USING IMAGINATION TO WALK INTO THE SCENE*

INSTRUCTIONS

Close your eyes and remember any scene from your childhood in which you felt pain of any kind which was not healed by comforting. Allow the scene to emerge in your mind. Notice that you know exactly what your child self needs. Imagine yourself, as the grown-up you are now, walking into the scene. Speak for your child to others in the scene, if needed. Give your child self the protection, Love, and comfort that was needed then and not received. Did you sigh automatically? This indicates your child received from you and fear was released. Notice that in healing a scene like this, you haven't changed what happened back then. You have changed the way you look on it, and therefore your feeling response to it changes. In the original early scene you experienced yourself as having no Greater Being to take care of you. By being there for yourself now, you have fulfilled the Law of Being that frees you. You gave Love to yourself and you received Love from yourself. In this joining, fear was released along with blame of the one(s) you perceived as failing to Love you. This is the process of forgiving.

An alternative to this method, as I have described it, would be to run the scene back as if it were a film, and start before the scene took place. For example, you see that harm is about to take place, so you take your child by the hand and get your little one out of the scene. This, too, doesn't change what happened in your past. It does free you to give a new response in your life now knowing you are joined with the one who took your hand.

EXAMPLE FOUR

Bryan's Scene: I am in my bed with the covers over my head. My parents are fighting downstairs. I'm terrified that someone is going to get hurt. They have done this before. Once I told them to stop and they yelled, "Get out."

Second Part of Scene: I, as the grown-up Bryan I am now, walk in and see that little Bryan is frightened. I greet him and gently pull the covers from his head. I tell him I am his loving parent. I see what is going on. I can do several things at this point. I have the power of imagination. Just as I am holding an image that I created in my mind at that time, I can create any new ending for the scene that I need in order to resolve my fear to Love now.

See KEY POINTS and PROBLEMS WITH THIS METHOD for suggestions.

KEY POINTS FOR EXAMPLE FOUR

    a. Any unhealed scene from your past has a pattern to it. **The disturbing pattern will repeat in your life until you give a different response to it.** For example, if you felt helpless when your parents fought, now at any time that someone starts to fight in your presence, whether fighting with you or not, you may become very anxious, feel helpless, freeze, etc., instead of acting effectively. Using this method in which you walk into the scene yourself, works especially well at seeing yourself give that new response. Then, amazingly, you give a new response next time a situation comes up in your life that follows the same pattern. This is when you experience a miracle. You don't make miracles happen. You stop preventing them from happening. You prevent them whenever you hold images that call out fear and separate you from a Loving Greater Being.

    b. When you see yourself in an early scene that remains unresolved to Love, (stuck in fear), you are at the point of decision. You either continue to wait helplessly, blaming another, or you detach and surrender. **To detach is to mentally let go of holding the scene in your mind that reminds you to be fearful.** Instead, you see yourself as capable of being the nurturer now. **To surrender is to emotionally let go and let your feelings flow to be tended by your own grown-up self.** You no longer have NEED for the person you were blaming to behave in some expected way. You may PREFER that they would. You are safe whether they do or not, however. You are also free to take unlimited options to fulfill your unmet need as soon as you detach and surrender.

    c. Since you are doing this healing within your imagination, you can bring in all the support you need. This includes anything like people, cocoons, tools, armies, or Guardian Angels. You could imagine yourself safely inside a Plexiglas bubble if you want. **Your goal is to change the way you see the scene so it is no longer fearful to you.**

    d. You have changed your perception of having no Loving person for you by being that person yourself in the scene. You also need to change your view about receiving that Love. You need to see yourself as innocent, and completely worthy of Love and protection. This is true even if the scene started with your making a mistake because you didn't know something. Not knowing something does not make you unworthy of Love. You are not unworthy of Love the day before you learn how to ride a bicycle and worthy of Love after you learn. Making any mistake

37

is a sure sign that you need a Loving, protective, and guiding parent to help you. I am still doing spiritual work to release my belief that if I need help I will be hurt by the other rather than helped. Each scene is a place where I am still in darkness, have not yet joined with Love, and experience guilt instead of innocence. It is no longer true that people only hurt me when I need help. I once experienced life that way.

e. All Healing Methods include tears. Tears come at the point of joining. They represent the healing of your separation. These tears need to be distinguished from depression. Depression is the dullness that comes from repressing your feelings, denying them, and keeping them hidden. Healing is the opposite. It is expression. When you express what needs to be expressed, you are not depressed. Depression is not something that happens to you. It may seem that way since you repress feelings as part of your defensive or denial system. You may have been told you have a chemical imbalance which is responsible for your depression. Every thought causes a chemical reaction in your body. Learn to be there for your inner child rather than medicate feelings away. Handle your thoughts responsibly and your depression will lift.

f. Note the change of direction for energy in this and all methods. Here, the parent within you reaches out to give Love to you, the child. This follows proper polarity of Greater Being giving to you. You, as the child, rightfully receive from the Greater Being. Until you heal this scene, or any like it, you will use defensive means to survive. This means you send out, or project unresolved feelings to be picked up by your parents (or others) at the level of their solar plexus. This is a reversal of proper polarity. You gave and they received. It was not Love that you sent out. Be aware, here, that I am referring to energy exchanges. I am not saying that parents are to do everything for their children. I am sharing with you the Law that governs our Soul's growth.

PROBLEMS WITH THIS METHOD AND WHAT TO DO ABOUT THEM

a. You experience a violation as unforgivable. I find using the word "accept" to be more useful here. To accept is to see what is truly there. This heals child perception. I recommend this exercise of speaking, or writing out as many accept statements as you can.

Example from Bryan's scene:
>   I accept that my parents could be solving problems in other ways.
>   I accept that I am not the one fighting.
>   I accept that I feel scared when they fight.
>   I accept that I don't have to fix them to feel safe.
>   I accept that I have my own inner parent now to take care of me.
>   I accept that I am no longer the helpless little boy in that bed.
>   I accept that I can use other ways to solve problems even if my parents didn't know any better way.
>   I accept that I prefer that they be kind to each other.
>   I accept that I can be kind to myself now.

This list could continue for some time bringing more and more into awareness. What I really like about this exercise in accepting is that I can make the statement that something is not acceptable to me. "I accept that it is no longer acceptable for me to see myself as helpless when other people fight." Do you feel the difference between the following two statements? "I forgive you for frightening me with your fighting," and "I accept that I was frightened by your fighting and know there is a better way for me to solve problems." **You need only accept a better way for yourself in order to be free, which is what it means to forgive.** You don't have to change your parents or wait for anyone to be different. You need only stop waiting and blaming, and accept a Loving way for yourself.

b. There are some scenes that were so traumatic for us that we need help from others to heal them. See Practice Exercise No. 70 in Chapter 25 for information on how to do this. I regularly hold "healing days" in addition to *A Course in Miracles* classes. At these events we each take responsibility for setting up scenes from our lives that need healing. Other group members take the parts of people involved in these early scenes. We also choose to bring Loving people into our scenes which is what we needed and didn't have when we were young. Experiencing this protection from outside ourselves builds our inner protector. Holy Bath, pictured in Practice Exercise No. 108, Chapter 25, and explained in Sample Lesson No. 5, Chapter 27, grew out of one of our "healing days." One student, who wanted to gift me, wrote a list of affirmations and set up the scene to surround me with Love at a point when I was taking a step in my growth.

c. Your child self is doing something harmful to itself or others and sees it as the only way to survive. Reinforce your protective presence by being firm in your actions. Tell your child self that you are here to solve this problem in a better way. Say what you will do. Be firm like a protective parent who gives a forceful "Stop" to a child about to run in the street. This is not an angry tone, it is one that feels good when you are about to be injured.

d. This is not a problem with this method. It is a problem that can be solved using this method. Your child self still identifies as being back in the scene of abandonment. In this case, tell your child who you are and that you have come to get him or her to come live with you. Take your child's hand, and speak to your parents or caregivers one at a time. Speak from your Nurturing Self explaining to them that it is time for your child to be with you now. They will either:

1. bless your taking the child, in which case you simply thank them, and feel any tears related to the parting;

2. act as if they don't care, in which case you accept that you are free to take your child with you, which is where your child now belongs anyway; (You DO care!) or,

3. resist one way or another. In this case, I recommend you picture a Guardian Angel present to take care of your parents' feelings so you no longer need to do that. (See how parents sometimes support the reverse direction, insisting that children take care of their Feeling Nature. In this case parents are using their children as idols, believing their children save them.) As you imagine your parents with an Angel to protect them you see them as having someone as their Giver other than you. Now, hand in hand, imagine yourself going to the home where you currently live. Tour your home so your child knows where you will eat, sleep, etc. Be aware of sighs. Say, "The crisis is over." Your separation is healed in this joining.

METHOD FIVE: *USING CHAIRS TO REPRESENT ASPECTS OF YOURSELF*

INSTRUCTIONS

When chairs are used to represent aspects of yourself or other people, you are dealing with images you hold in your mind. Therefore, the other people are aspects of yourself. There are several variations of this method. You could have one chair to represent your parent voice, and one your child voice. You could also have one chair to represent you, and one to represent someone else as Mom or Dad. This is a safe way to give your feeling child a way to have a voice in scenes where it didn't feel safe to speak. You can also set up three chairs, one being your feeling child, one the other person, and a third for the parent voice in you that will protect your child while you say what you need to say. Remember the importance of responses here. The goal needs to be that the feeling child experience the presence of a Loving Greater Being. If your Mom or Dad responds Lovingly to any hurt or accusations you make, that is fine. If not, then it is your job to give the Loving response in your own parent voice. Set up chairs in any way that is right for your situation. **Simply setting up chairs gives permission to your child to speak for hurts that have been held for a long time.** What a gift you offer yourself!

EXAMPLE FIVE

I give two examples here. First, I share with you the most vivid chair talk I remember from using this method to heal myself. Shortly after marrying, in my early twenties, I found out that my husband had multiple sclerosis. I took a defensive move to handle my terror. Of course, by definition of what a defensive move is, I did not realize what I had done. At the time I belonged to a church in which we went to the altar to take communion. One day, shortly after receiving this news about my husband, I knelt at the altar and bargained with God. "I'll 'Be Good' if only you will see to it that he does not become paralyzed." Over the years my husband did become paralyzed and I felt increasingly betrayed by God. I was sure that I kept my end of the bargain. In truth, what I had kept was my commitment to the ego defense pattern of being a "Good Girl" as a way of *trying* to save myself.

41

Then one day I had the following conversation picturing God on the other chair.

> Me- God, why have you betrayed me? (I sobbed for a long time.)
>
> Me- God, I only asked one thing of you. (I sobbed for a long time.)
>
> Me- God, why did you let him become paralyzed? (After sobbing some more I moved to "God's chair.")
>
> God- Nancy, you asked. He did not. (This response came so unexpectedly. It solved my biggest problem which was feeling punished by God.)

The second example is a piece of chair work between a man and his father (imagined on a chair). I will call the man Bill. Bill is a fine craftsman who has a habit of discounting his work and selling himself short when it comes to charging fees.

> Bill- I feel angry when I even look at you.
>
> Dad- You look angry. What are you angry about?
>
> Bill- You're never there when I need you. It has always been that way.
>
> Dad- I feel bad when you say that. I was always working to support the family.
>
> Bill- Yes, you were always working. But I wanted you to show me how to do things.
>
> Dad- Like what?
>
> Bill- Like, build a tree house.
>
> Dad- I never was very handy at things like that. I think you were always better at doing things like that than I was.
>
> Bill- You do! I didn't realize that. You mean the reason you didn't help me wasn't because you didn't love me?
>
> Dad- No, it was because I didn't want to feel like a fool.
>
> Bill- Then the reason you didn't praise me was because you felt bad when I did something well?
>
> Dad- Yes.
>
> Bill- I never thought of that.
>
> Dad- Please forgive me, Bill.

KEY POINTS FOR EXAMPLE FIVE

a. **It is OK to make blame statements to a chair in order to hear where your child feels abandoned or hurt.** Your parent self will be listening carefully here to give the needed response.

b. It only takes one new piece of information to get out of a stuck place. I was shocked when I had this conversation with God and received the response that my husband had not asked. That was a new thought for me. When I thought about this I realized I had been asking for my husband to be different so I wouldn't feel my fear. (See Sections No. 4 and 5 of Chapter 25 for things I might have asked for, and ways I could have asked had I known how at the time.) Ultimately, we betray ourselves by defending. The statement, "You betrayed me" is an ego statement of blame even when said to God. In the next chapter I will give you information about my adapting and healing process which will shed more light on this example. Bill was also surprised to hear himself give new information from the "Dad" chair. **One new piece of information allows you release from ego restriction and freedom to entertain options.**

c. It is safe to express anger to a person you imagine as being on a chair. When you truly understand how feelings work, you know that all feelings that you think you are holding inside are being projected to the gut of the other all the time; and you are denying this. So, expressing anger properly, as to a chair, lets you heal yourself. This ends projecting because as you listen for your child need you can meet it yourself. This heals the separation inside yourself as well as with the other. This is forgiving. If you feel very frightened of a parent (on the chair) use their first name instead of addressing them as Mom or Dad. They will seem less fearful this way.

d. In my scene, a load of heaviness lifted and my heart was lightened. **Our healed state is one of gratitude. This comes after the sigh.** It is as if the dam built of anger and tears breaks, and a flood of Love comes pouring through. All gratitude that flows through us, heals us. You might also want to share this Love with the other. (If they have died, imagine their presence and send Love from your Soul to theirs.) Realize that you have been holding a stance of attack toward them, perhaps for years. If you approach someone to share your healing and they do not welcome you, know that I welcome you as a person of courage who joins me in willingness to put Loving vibrations out to the planet.

e. Setting up the chairs gives permission to your child to speak for hurts that have been held a long time.

PROBLEMS WITH THIS METHOD AND WHAT TO DO ABOUT THEM

a. Those of us who adapted to "Be Good" may believe it is wrong to say anything unkind even to a person we imagine as being on a chair. (See point "c." under KEY POINTS FOR EXAMPLE FIVE.) You may have learned not to use vulgarities and profanities. I believe in clean speech myself. In doing any of these healing methods, I allow myself to use any language I need in order to express my intense feelings. I have written letters (in my journal - not mailed) in which I was so angry that pages rolled up from the pressure of my pen. I suggest you burn, or at least shred and discard a letter like this after writing it. **Your goal is to free your tender feeling child. Keep this goal in mind at all times.**

b. You may start in a position of hopelessness with the other and say to yourself, "What's the use of talking to them?" As you start moving back and forth between chairs, speaking from the different voices, your energy will shift and you will have the opportunity to take a stalemated conversation in a new direction.

c. People often ask me if they are to respond as they believe the other would, or as they would like them to respond. You may do this either way. If the person (whose voice you speak from the other chair) is not able to give you a Loving response, then you can either bring in another chair, or stand up beside their chair and give the needed Loving response to yourself.

d. If you believe this is all in your imagination, it is! And, so is the memory you have held that has kept you feeling abandoned and unloved. **Choose to use your imagination FOR yourself.**

My intent has been to give you enough information, clearly enough, that you can see the basic pattern for healing. **The principle is the same in all Healing Methods. Bring in a Loving Greater Being for your feeling child in a way that allows you to surrender blame and receive Love now.**

OTHER METHODS TO SPARK YOUR CREATIVITY

1. Notice that you have a sense of color that relates to your wounded child, or state of abandonment and blame. This may feel like "black hate" or a gray cloud. You also have a color that relates to your joined self, when you nurture yourself and feel safe. Perhaps this is "blue peace" or "white delight." Experiment with changing these colors in your mind. Notice changes in your body. I instantly release my breathing when I change my thought from "black hate" to "blue peace." I find my face releases to a smile when I think "white delight." To switch a color in our mind is to ASK for Love's presence. It is a prayer that is instantly answered. We go from ego to God, problem to solution. We ASK for the solution rather than the problem and the results are miraculous!

2. Write a letter to a Holy Figure (God, Mary, Jesus Christ, Guardian Angel, etc.). Write your own Loving response, also. You might be amazed how words start flowing onto your page that seem to be coming from somewhere other than your own mind. This is exciting.

3. Do a dialogue wherein you write with both hands. You will most likely want your dominant (writing) hand to speak as the parent voice, and let your non-dominant hand be your child voice.

4. If you enjoy drawing, use art as your medium. Your child would relish drawing, splashing out color to express feelings. One way or another, include the element of a Loving response. For example, if your child draws an angry scene with lots of red and black, respond by bringing in some soothing green and blue. You could draw a Loving Greater Being or holy figure in the scene. You could respond with written or spoken words to offer help and Love needed. One way or another, draw a scene of peaceful resolution.

5. If you enjoy music, sing a song as a dialogue using "Ah" as the parent voice and "Eh" as the child voice. For example, use "Tender and Innocent" on the audio tape *Musical Companion to Sharing the Course*, or use a song like J.S. Bach's "Bist Du Bei Mir" (also titled "Thou Art My Joy" and "Draw Near to Me"). Start with "Ah" on the first phrase and let "Eh" respond as your troubled child singing out feelings without needing to put them into words. Alternate phrases to make it a dialogue. The child needs to hear the reassuring parent voice.

6. You could hold your doll or a pillow while doing mirror talk. It feels comforting to physically hold something.

7. One day the phrase, "I wanted you to love me" was singing through my mind on a melody. I began to cry. I sat at the piano with my journal and a mirror. Each time I thought of a person from my past, I wrote their name and the phrase, "I wanted you to love me." I watched myself in the mirror as I then sang it. I sigh, even now, thinking about what a release I experienced that day. "The crisis is over!" What crisis was this? The crisis of "special relationships." These were all the people whose Love I thought would save me. In integrating my own thoughts and feelings here, I healed myself.

I have shared with you simple methods for inner healing which is what *A Course in Miracles* is all about. I know this work is not easy. That is why I have written a book about sharing the course of our healing. Read on.

6

HEALING PROCESS

In this chapter I share what you can expect in your healing process. "Love heals." No two simpler words have ever been spoken. "Prayers are always answered." No truer words have ever been spoken. To pray is to shift from fear to Love. **Prayer is reaching out with Love, to Love. It is communicating with God on the God channel, not from the fear channel. Prayer is a shift we must make to correct our errors.** When we answer God's call to return to Love, our prayers are always answered miraculously. Accepting the answers to our prayers often means changing the way we expect prayers to be answered. Healing requires accepting ideas that are contrary to everything we ordinarily believe. Healing is a most natural process. We just haven't understood it very well.

Love is an energy, a vibration in harmony with the Universe. It is a higher octave than the energy and vibration of fear. Fear is disharmony. The harmony of Love extends from our heart space rather than projecting from our solar plexus as disharmony does. The disharmony of fear begins to transform when we are touched by Love. Transformation is the breakdown or undoing of what *A Course In Miracles* calls the "body." This is the embodiment of our ego.

Our ego is a whole system of "holdings." We hold images of fear; we hold memories of words spoken; we hold memories of feelings and body experiences; we hold blame; we hold our breath; we hold muscle tension; we hold onto people, jobs, and possessions that no longer serve our well-being; and we hold to our defensive anti-God stance. These holding patterns have an electromagnetic and chemical component which affect every aspect of our Being. Opening to Love means releasing these holdings. The movement of Love within us is Spirit healing us at every level of our Being. As we heal, we experience symptoms physically, emotionally, and mentally.

Consider for a moment the idea that **symptoms appear at the point that a healing has begun.** That is very different from what we ordinarily believe. When energy starts to move in us and we feel mental unrest, emotional turmoil, or physical pain, we so often respond by medicating it away. **If we think of symptoms as our inner child waking up, we realize that drugs (all idols/addictions) say, "Stay asleep."**

When we get an inflammation, experience an injury, or even get cancer we call it "getting sick," not getting well. In fact, it sounds crazy to think of getting cancer as part of the process of Love healing us and making us well. The truth is that sickness exists only in fear. **Sickness is a lesson for us.**

I learned about sickness and healing from my own life experience which I share with you to illustrate this point. I intend no blame to anyone involved in telling this story. All of us did the best we knew how at the time.

When I was two years old I had pneumonia. The story goes that I had a temperature of 107° for four days, convulsed, and went into a coma. The doctor told my parents I would die. My father worked long hours to support the family, so I assume he was mostly not available to me or my mother. My mother paced in the hallway, terrified, I am sure. Her other two children were also ill. One was down the hall in another hospital room, and the other was being tended by a neighbor. I was in isolation, and I assume no one wanted to risk catching what I had. They all kept their distance at a time when I most needed comfort.

This was before the days of penicillin, when sulfa was the medicine of choice. I was fed food laced with sulfa, convinced that all those nurses were trying to poison me. (I didn't drink milk or eat eggs for years afterward.) The girl in the next bed also had pneumonia. I listened to her screams as they did a "cut down" (cut through her skin to place intravenous feeding more securely into a vein). They threatened to do the same to me if I didn't eat what they were feeding me.

I was so hot I told my mother my bed was on fire. She said it wasn't. This was perhaps the most frightening of all events. The comforter on which I depended didn't "see," or let me know she saw the alarming danger I was experiencing. She didn't realize this was the only way I was able to report my experience. I assume it was after this that I convulsed and slipped into a coma. My father attributed my survival to the night nurse who bathed me with ice water on the fourth night. After I recovered, he took me to see her about once a year to show her how healthy I was.

As a physical body, I had recovered. Meanwhile, what went unnoticed were events of my Soul. I returned home to parents who had been so terrified that their energies were in fear, not Love toward me. They had grieved my dying and detached from me. And, I had decided I could not trust any grown-up to be a safe comforter to me. I had "defended."

I chose a means to survive on fear energy. I chose an idol, a way to save myself. I set up a pattern of addiction. It is called being a "Good Girl." This role has recently become known as co-dependency. I was so intent on pleasing everyone, I completely sacrificed even knowing what I wanted. By the time I was a teen-ager I was called "so mature." This is a misnaming that is quite common. A mature person makes decisions based on inner wis-dom and I was functioning only on what I saw outside of myself. I was making sure at every moment that I didn't do anything that would lead anyone to reject or harm me. Without realizing it, of course, all the tension of my genuine needs going unmet built up inside of me and I was projecting out resentment all the while. I also whined to let off steam. Both of these made me very un-pleasing to be around, I am sure. Such is the nature of our de-fense system. (T p. 334/359, "Defenses do what they would de-fend.") **Defenses create just what we are *trying* to keep from happening.** Because I didn't want to be rejected, I tried to please everyone. In being untrue to myself, I rejected myself. The re-sulting disharmony made me unpleasing to others.

After years of being a "Good Girl," I became a "Good Nurse," carrying out my survival decisions into the next phase of my life. Just before graduating from nursing school, I married and be-came a "Good Wife." I was conscientious, efficient, fiercely loyal to doing everything "right." Soon after I was married, I found out that my husband had early symptoms of multiple sclerosis while in college. I went even more deeply into being a "Good Wife," burying more fear, anger, and sadness. I saw him as my savior, so I intended to do everything I could to save him. I had two children and was a "Good Mother." We looked like the All-Ameri-can family. Just for a while, however.

Meanwhile, I suffered. I suffered an inner hell that was mine alone, shared with no one. I trusted no one. I was always in the caretaker role. I believed all along that I was giving Love to eve-ryone and if only I would give enough, someday I would *get* the Love I so deserved. I didn't realize that I was functioning on fear energy, defended, living an act, projecting resentment, and ex-tending no Love. I had no Love to give. I was drained, empty, separated, and desperate, and unaware of all of this. I continued to work, and *tried hard* to make everything perfect.

By the time I was in my mid-thirties, my husband was paralyzed, my daughter was ill, and my son had planned his escape which he later took. I went for a routine checkup and my doctor said she was quite certain that she was feeling a tumor in the area of my ovary. She was right. I had cancer. This felt like the final blow at the end of years of *trying* to do everything to "Be Good." And, it was. I woke up. Yes, I woke up to my Soul.

I had already learned the lesson of secrecy so inherent in all addictive processes. My husband had insisted that his disease be kept secret. My desire to please him added to my private hell. Everything in our lives became deception. I was the social secretary that turned down invitations to events that would require any physical activity he could not handle. I became known as a "spoil-sport," while I was deeply longing to participate in the very events I turned down. His mother would call long distance and invite us for holidays. My husband would respond, "Sure, Mom." Then he would tell me he did not want to go. As social secretary, I would tell her we were not coming. She experienced me as placing a wedge between her and her son, and was hateful to me.

Through all this my Thinking Nature was growing. When faced with the possibility of cancer, I decided to <u>not</u> keep my diagnosis a secret. I told everyone I was going to have surgery. This new response allowed for care to my feelings. This was prayer. This was a shift from fear to Love. And, a most miraculous thing happened. I started receiving long distance calls before I was out of anesthesia. My room was filled with gifts. People came to tend me in all kinds of ways and I accepted whatever they gave to me. This included a tree planted for me in Israel, a membership in our local public television channel, and laying on of hands. I allowed people to comfort me. I opened to receive. I saw that I could trust again. Notice that this is another hospital scene, a chance to undo early life decisions.

I experienced the Loving presence of my own Greater Being in deciding to be truthful. I also experienced the Loving presence of all who attended me and blessed my life. I saw that I was Loved. I reversed my decision from when I was two years old that there was no Greater Being I could trust to tend me Lovingly. I saw that this was no longer true for me.

It is important to notice here that God did not punish me. Remember how I felt betrayed and punished by God when I had bargained with God at the altar in an earlier story. The truth is that I made the decision to defend and punished myself in not following the Law of Being. I went fear's way and separated from God. I had turned my energy to resist Life as a survival move.

Here is a most intriguing thing about life, the balloon of which I spoke in Chapter 2. My physical needs were met as a child. This means I was tended as a body. The Holy Spirit is God's answer to our defending. The Holy Spirit is the part of us that remembers every need that goes unfulfilled. We grow the ability within us to tend the inner child' who had the unfulfilling experiences. So, the Holy Spirit within me grew the ability to give attention to my mental, emotional, and spiritual needs. However, I made the same mistake that most people make. I used those abilities to further my addiction to "Be Good." I stayed fearful and continued to focus on the needs of others, *trying* to meet their needs with my abilities. At the same time I ignored the very inner child for which the abilities had developed. I did not understand God's marvelous plan for healing.

Then one day later in my thirties, the image of myself at age two lying in a coma in a hospital bed came to my mind. I, the grown-up me, walked into the scene and sat beside her bed. Every day I imagined visiting her. Over a period of six weeks she woke up, talked to me, sat on my lap to be rocked, and began to trust me. In my mind I then took her to play on a grassy hill under a tree. I asked her to stay there and never go back to the hospital scene. Soon, she was ready to join me and has been one with me ever since. I used my mind for joining rather than separating within myself.

In tending my feelings I began the long process of reversing my addiction. I was transforming being a "Good Girl," a machine-like "human doing," to knowing my true Goodness as a growing human Being. As I began to use Healing Methods described in Chapter 5, the higher Loving voice within me bonded with the isolated, suffering child in me. While I had had surgery for my body, this did not heal my separation from God. I healed this by tending my Feeling Nature which reversed my anti-God stance, and my Soul grew in Love. The more Love I received from the inner bond, the more Love I was able to extend to other people and receive from them. I was beginning to function on the Love channel instead of the fear channel. I was beginning to Give instead of *trying to get.* I was meeting my spiritual needs.

I have done all the exercises in this book. Most of them I have done many times over a period of twenty years. Each time, I release more survival behaviors and choose Loving ways instead. I've learned to trust Life, know Joy, and live as one with God.

This is Atonement. **Atonement is undoing our ego and healing our belief in separation. Our wounds are our separations. Accepting Love heals every wound.**

In the healing process we undo our survival mode. Two things happen that can feel alienating. First, feelings emerge that we denied in defending. These feelings include anger, sadness, and fear. We often misdirect them and attack people in our lives now. This is taking place at the same time that we are disconnecting from the other in a dependent "special relationship." Achieving our inner joining often feels like abandonment, separation, divorce, and war with others. We need to understand the healing process to accept that seeming separations are our spiritual journey. We heal "specialness."

SEEMING SEPARATIONS: *RELEASING SPECIALNESS*

A "special relationship" is based on the ego's goal of separation. Each person is functioning with their Thinking and Feeling Natures separated. Each is *trying to get* the other to complete them. (For example, "I can't think, you think for me!" or "You feel what I don't want to feel.") Since Love is created by connecting these Natures within, Love is never achieved in a "special relationship." Both people are separated from God for they have not yet begun to create Love. Both are separated from each other for only the energy of Love brings union, "communion" and "communication." Most of us have only known relationships based on ego manipulation or "specialness." We don't realize we are really living with the illusion that we are connected with someone. There is no Love in the relationship, only hope (which is really hopelessness in disguise) that Love will be there sometime in the future "if only." Blame of self and the other lies within the "if only." I'd be Loved "if only" the other would change, or "if only" I could do enough or Be Good enough to *get* them to change.

Growing spiritually is the undoing of these separations. We unite the Thinking and Feeling aspects of our own self. This opens us to receive from Spirit and extend Love. We release our demand on the other to fulfill us. We release our blame of the other. We release our "need" for the other.

We are mistaken to believe that it is good to be needed. As long as we "need" someone, we justify manipulating them to use (abuse) them for our own selfish purposes. **When we take our first courageous steps to freedom from a "special rela-**

tionship" we will most likely be called selfish by the one who has a selfish need to control us. Truth is, it is only when we no longer need the other that we can freely choose to be with them because we truly enjoy being with them. Only then are we free to be with them Lovingly.

When the other person in a relationship is not growing spiritually, they fear our growing and increase blame. It hurts to be made wrong when we are making decisions to go Life's way. We experience their blaming as not supporting our life, as not wanting us to Be. They, too, feel abandoned because they aren't building their inner bond, and we are no longer giving into their manipulations. Both people hurt in seeming separations.

Transforming a relationship based on fear to one based on Love is one of those life situations in which we feel wrong as we begin to do what is spiritually correct. This is because even though we've never been happy in our relationship, it is the only way we've ever known a relationship to be, so we assume it is the right way to be in relationship. There are few models for us from which we can learn to be Loving.

In the story of my life I said I was not aware of my harmfulness in what I thought was giving Love while being a Good Wife. I wailed for a long time the day I forgave myself. On that day I saw, truly saw, that I had a vested interest in my husband's paralysis. Every function he lost was another opportunity for me to do for him, and another way to *try to get* his Love in our special relationship. Before that day I believed in "chronic grief." **When I forgave all the people involved in special relationships, including myself, I opened to Joy.**

In truth, we are separated from God and that is the separation we heal. Once joined with God we are free to extend Love. We'd like to believe that this means our relationships would then be wonderful and happy. Instead, those of us who accept healing may be physically separated from those who do not grow with us. Avoiding these seeming separations is what keeps us separated from God (Love, Health, Abundance, and Happiness). This is a choice we make. **We live unhappily with a separation inside our Being, or we risk feeling separated from others who do not heal with us and accept our healing. When we seemingly separate from others through healing, we send Love to their Souls. Heartfelt Love is freely given, and invites others to heal without making any demand on them.**

We do not *get* Love from another while we are in fear. When in fear, we are separated from God. As we heal our separation from God, we experience the gift of Love which is the miracle for which we pray. This is the healing of the "special relationship."

UNCOMFORTABLE FEELINGS: *RELEASING TIME*

Feelings that accompany Love include Joy, Peace, Glory, and Gratitude. They live in eternity. Uncomfortable feelings live in time. They have a temporal component. FEAR deals with re-membering an unsafe situation in our past where we didn't see a safe comforter. We project our image to the **future** and anticipate harm coming to us. ANGER is blame and the desire to take re-venge in the **present**. SADNESS is related to having had some-thing in the **past** and feeling the loss of it now. The three go to-gether: fear, anger, and sadness.

In any situation that remains unhealed, or unforgiven, there is at least one of these feelings denied. If a person is angry now, was angry two years ago, and you anticipate that they will be an-gry if you run into them two years from now, they are denying either fear or sadness, or both. Likewise, if one is anxious now, was anxious last time you saw them, and you anticipate they will be anxious next time you run into them, they are denying anger or sadness, or both. The same is true of unresolved sadness, or chronic grief. When you have any problem situations, make an exercise of asking yourself the following questions in whatever order feels comfortable to you:

"What am I scared about?"
"What am I angry about?"
"What am I sad about?"

Remember that symptoms appear when a healing has begun. A problem is a "symptom." Here is an example from my life in which I solved a problem by asking these questions (not at first, as you will notice). A son from my second marriage owned a BMX bike. Our family of six had had several bikes stolen in the past so I felt justified in hounding him to get him to lock it. He was just as insistent that he was not going to lock it. Because he had not followed my rule of using a lock, I grounded his bike. Then, on the day that I returned it, I saw him take off on it again with no lock. I felt rage inside.

At last (it usually takes a long time to decide to look at our-selves!) I decided to sit myself down and deal with me instead of him. Note how I was not upset for the reason I thought. In allowing myself to feel my pain I got in touch with what was really going on with me. As a child I was subjected to sneaky violence by the trickster nature of my father. Theft is like that. Each time someone had stolen from us I felt that same helpless feeling of being harmed and unable to protect myself or take revenge called out in me. I let myself feel the untended pain from my childhood and tended it myself. Then I no longer needed to control my son to make sure I didn't feel the pain I was avoiding feeling. Note that this is the typical rescuing pattern. In the guise of saving him from losing his bike, I erroneously justified lots of attacks on him. With my early life pain tended, I was able to simply let the bike be his property. If it were stolen that would be his lesson to learn. This is what I realized in asking myself these three questions:

1. *What was I really scared about?* I was identifying as the wounded child of my father. The father, whose job it was to protect me, was harming me, and I had no protector. I felt helpless.

2. *What was I really mad about?* I was blaming my son for not obeying my rules. I presented my rules as saving him from losing his bike. I was really using anger to manipulate him so I wouldn't feel helpless. In my defended state I was waiting for my father to change and protect me (he had died many years earlier). I was now *trying* to change my son so I wouldn't feel helpless. I was making my safety depend on how he was behaving. This left me feeling helpless unless I could control him. Note here how defenses do what they defend. I was defending against feeling helpless, and ended up feeling helpless. I was still identifying as a child with no Greater Being to protect me.

3. *What was I really sad about?* In defending, I separated my Thinking Nature from my Feeling Nature and therefore from God. Sadness and helplessness come from separating from God. **Anger is an ego substitute for true power which comes through awareness and guidance from God.**

ANGER : *RELEASING BLAME*

Anger is the energy of blame. It is always part of our survival mechanism. It is always found in "special relationships." It is an attack on another to *try to get* them to change to be our Greater Being for us. As a Loving Being I, (yes, I said "I,") listen to the anger of my inner child to de-

termine what it is she is needing from a Greater Being, and I provide that for her.

It is true that people do things that are hurtful to us. Blaming them keeps us in a state of helplessness. This is the worst place to be when someone is being hurtful. Our anger indicates a need for us to change our response to someone who treats us hurtfully. **We need to learn to not cooperate with, give consent to, go along with, tolerate, overlook, disregard, condone, misname, give in, or "be nice" in response to harmfulness.**

Love is firm and does not put up with nonsense. Responses which are truly Loving may not seem Loving, for we have erroneously misnamed things as Loving that are not. Complying is not Love. We call it not "making waves" and not "rocking the boat." We call it "peace at any price." The price is not Love, for Love has no price to pay. It gifts us with miracles.

There is no anger in Love. Since most of us are not living Love's way, anger will come up in personal work, and in group work, and is subject to being misdirected. It is improperly directed as blame of another. It is properly directed as an internal dialog. Our inner child wants us to listen.

I allow NO anger to be expressed at another person in group meetings. Sometimes we have such a charge of stored anger that we must express it as anger to hear the message of it. Anger tells us we have an unmet need. **Our goal in expressing anger is to get beyond it to our tender feelings.** It is only our ego that wants to use anger to change or harm others.

Anger always calls for us to change ourselves to correct something in our lives. As children, anger and the expression of anger seem to be the same. In healing anger we distinguish the feeling from actions we choose to express it. As you use any of the means listed below, prepare a private space for yourself. Show care to anyone who might see or hear you by telling them what you are going to do and what your goal is. **Never justify harm to yourself, others, or property when you are angry. This only creates another problem that will need to be corrected.**

Here are some safe ways to express anger:

1. Write it out.

Write it out with as many profanities as you need to use to release it. Then shred what you wrote or burn it. Do not send or give it to anyone. When you have identified your tender hurts or needs, share those tenderly with a nurturing person. Most people can respond to tenderness and are repelled by anger. One day my current husband came home from work to find me writing a letter of forgiveness. It was soggy from tears, of course. It was also curled up from all the pressure of anger with my pen. It is something we still laugh about today.

2. Scream it out.

If you are alone, scream or growl. If a cooperative person is present, tell them you are about to scream. Maybe they would like to scream with you! Otherwise, go to your (parked) car or to the woods and let out your anger with your voice. If need be, scream into a pillow.

3. Pound it out.

You may do this alone, or with a Loving person beside you. **The rules are this**: You may say anything you need to say and strike as hard as you need to strike. You may not hurt yourself, anyone else, or any property with your anger. Either be alone in the house, or at least tell others what you are about to do so they are not frightened. Now, take off any jewelry and watch, loosen any tight clothing, and remove anything else that might be in the way when you swing your arms. Kneel on a pillow beside your bed. Fold your hands palm to palm so you do not injure your fingers. Put your clasped hands over your head and bring them down onto the bed with all your strength. Meanwhile, put words with each swing. Most often I hear things like:

> "I hate you"
> "Stop hurting me"
> "Get out of my life"
> "Leave me alone"
> "This is my body"

You'll know what to say. When your rage is spent you will collapse in a comfortable fatigue onto the bed and cry tender tears. It is comforting at this point to have a friend beside you, so you can fall into their arms. In *deciding* to express anger this way, you use your own

Thinking Nature, so you will not *feel* alone even if no one is present with you.

I have both imagined myself pounding on a bed, and have also imagined my little child throwing a royal temper tantrum. I had freeing results with no one knowing what I was seeing in my mind's eye. You, too, can **imagine yourself doing this technique if your body is such that you would harm yourself (have arthritis, diabetes, cardiovasular disease, etc., or you are a smoker).** Use your imagination to do this when you are somewhere that you are not free to pound.

Releasing anger.

4. Sing and cry it out.

Your voice is a powerful healing tool. All feelings naturally heal through vocal expression. Let your body sing what it wants to sing. Make the sounds you want to make.

5. Stomp around.

Inform anyone in your space what you are about to do. Then, CHOOSE to stomp around the room. This is different from stomping around the room or slamming a door to get someone else to come and solve a problem for you. Choosing is having the presence of mind to allow your Feeling Nature a safe way to express a feeling as part of your healing process.

6. Break something.

Inform anyone in your space what you are about to do. Then, CHOOSE to break something as a piece of cardboard or a dead tree branch. Tear up an old phone book or magazine.

7. Pull on a towel.

Roll up a towel and pull it horizontally. Add a growl.

Releasing anger.

8. Kick it out.

a. Kick a soft object like a pillow.

b. Lie on your back on a bed and kick downward one leg at a time with your knees bent. Add your fists, swinging your same side arm and leg together. Turn your head toward the active arm and leg.

c. Stand in a box and fuss when you feel like you have something to fuss about. Protect your feet with shoes. Have a box large enough to swing your legs, and shallow enough that you can step out easily. If the box is too deep, you may fall forward and harm your arms as you seek to break your fall, or hit your head on something. Fuss until you experience a shift of energy. Then take some constructive action.

9. Throw something.

If you want to throw something, follow ALL of the above rules for safety.

10. Listen inwardly.

Listen to what your body wants to do and find a safe way to do it. When you are fearful you will want to run away, or perhaps, scream. When you are angry you will want to attack one way or another. Usually this will be a desire to tell someone off, hit, bite, kick, strangle, or chop someone's head off. Imagine that someone as being present and tell them off; hit a bed; bite a towel or eat grape nuts, corn nuts, or corn chips (that is, if you don't use this as a rationale to support abuse of food); kick a pillow or a cardboard box; strangle a pillow; and chop carrots or wood. There is always a safe and constructive way to express anger.

Now remember to give Love and protection to your inner child. That is what your child needed and that is what you were mad about not receiving in the first place. When you heal your inner separation you will no longer be angry.

TEARS: *RELEASING LOSS*

One day a client called me because she had just had a "panic attack" while driving. I suggested that she put the phone down and shake her body to help it do what it wanted to do. After doing that she told me she felt like screaming. I suggested that she put the phone down and scream. After doing this she said she felt like running away. We had quite a bit of snow on the ground at the time, so I asked if she had a basement. She did, so I suggested that she run in place for a while down there and then call me back. After running, she asked to come to see me (my office is in my home). Once she was in my home, she wept for over 3 hours. Under all these other emotions was a genuine grief for her father who was ill with cancer. She had told me at an earlier session that she had no feelings for her father because of the way he had treated her. Her feelings were there. She had denied them all, including her Love and longing to be Loved by her father. Sadness, being a tender emotion, is often hidden behind anger. And, if we have repressed anger to *try to get* Love, fear will be closest to the surface. Her fear expressed itself in the "panic attack."

When someone is crying with ego intent, their energy is irritating and we want to tell them, "Knock it off already!" They are manipulating for us to be their Greater Being. And, believing that we could make them happy, they are blaming us for their unhappiness. It is an invitation to enter a "special relationship" with them in which we act as the strong one while they act like the poor victim.

Tears of healing are experienced very differently. They are a genuine expression of our Feeling Nature when we are touched by Spirit/Love. Such tears call another to move in gently and tend us. They call out compassion in others who understand our "growing pains."

There are always tears at the point of healing. This is where **we shift our stance of being abandoned and separated from a Greater Being, to seeing one as present for us. This heals our sense of loss.** We may experience Spirit coming through our own inner Nurturer, as in the Healing Methods described in Chapter 5. We may also be receiving Love extended from the Nurturer of another. For the other person to be a healing force for us, they must be connected between their own Thinking Nature and Feeling Nature. Only then can they facilitate the forming of a holy relationship. Put more simply, **only those who have healed themselves can be healing to others.**

SIGH: *RELEASING FEAR*

A sigh marks the point where we release fear. There are so many times in life when we are frightened and we take a quick in-breath. We tense our whole system and block feelings in the process. When we feel safe to feel these feelings, we are also safe to do the out-breath which releases this tension. Become aware of how you and others sigh when you hear the words you need to hear, or see what you need to see in order to feel safe. I call awareness to the sigh in our groups. We actually make an exercise of it. When someone sighs, we all sigh with them and say, "The crisis is over." We usually do this three times in a row. When I first learned about doing this, I went around the house for quite a while sighing and saying, "The crisis is over." Sweet relief! There were many times when I had forgotten to tell my body the danger was over. You might want to sing "Sigh, the Crisis is Over" on the audio tape *Musical Companion to Sharing the Course.*

ENLIGHTENED WITNESS: *RELEASING LONELINESS*

At every point where we defend, we see some harm as present with no protector who sees the need to protect; or in seeing it, the protector does not respond effectively. These memories accumulate and **we secretly long for someone to see that the harm we experienced was done to us.** I like the term Enlightened Witness used by Alice Miller in *Banished Knowledge.* **The Enlightened Witness is the person who not only sees, but also names the harm done to us, or that we experienced as done to us.** I share an example from my own life to show you what I mean. This also illustrates why I say we have experienced harm as having been done to us. Remember that when we defend, we never see our part in any of the pain that results from our separating. It is in joining in our healing process that we acknowledge the results of our own defending.

By the time I was a teenager, I made myself invisible to avoid harm to myself. This showed up when I got overlooked when it came to giving recognition at the church I attended. The day I was to read the prayer, the minister forgot and went directly from his sermon into his prayer. I was never asked to take a route for collecting pledge cards as other kids were. I was overlooked at every election for Fellowship officers. The final blow came at the end of my Senior year.

I attended Sunday School every Sunday for twelve years. This was so important to me that, even on days when my family went to visit relatives in a distant city, we got up very early to arrive in time for me to be a guest there. I got a certificate of attendance to take back to my church. When the day came to give awards, there were two of us with perfect attendance. You guessed it, they forgot to call my name. I was as voiceless as I was invisible, so I said nothing. No one else spoke up for me, either. I watched my best friend take all the honors.

Some years later I visited his mother. She told me she often thought about how I was overlooked at church. My heart leaped with freedom when she named it. She let me know she saw what I experienced as so hurtful at the time. She was my Enlightened Witness. Of course, over the years I awoke to see how I had made myself invisible and voiceless, believing *that* would save me from harm. I needed to forgive myself and all that I held against those at church. Note that making myself invisible and voiceless were idols which I thought would save me.

In group, we often serve as the Enlightened Witness for others as we hear them speak. We name what hurt them. The ultimate Enlightened Witness, of course, is the Holy Spirit, the part of our Self that remembers everything that has ever happened to us. And, when we remember the Holy Spirit, we heal our loneliness.

A Note on Healing:
The first changes we make in life are to restrict and limit our Life expression. While we deny and numb the results for a while, we intuitively know we moved to unhappiness. When called to change again in our healing process, we may find ourselves resisting more change. Know that changes involved in healing release or undo the early life changes that led us to restrict and limit our experience of Life. These healing changes miraculously bring us what we long to receive by switching our polarity from being resistant to being receptive. To heal is to Be happy.

PART II

Joining with
A Course in Miracles

7

WHAT IS *A Course in Miracles*?

In this chapter I share thoughts on *A Course in Miracles* itself. *A Course in Miracles* is a book, a hand, a guide, and a Voice that receives us as we take our journey Home. Home is the end of our journey where we have relinquished attack in favor of extending Love. Home is where we are fully alive, innocent, peaceful, and happy. This is Atonement, oneness with God.

PHYSICALLY SPEAKING

Physically speaking, *A Course in Miracles* is a book. It consists of a text, a workbook for students, and a manual for teachers. These were all scribed by Helen Schucman with the assistance of William Thetford between 1965 and 1972. Helen was in her fifties at the time, and William in his forties. Both have since died.

Fascinating accounts of the scribing process are available to readers in *Journey Without Distance* by Robert Skutch, and *Absence from Felicity* by Kenneth Wapnick. Judith Skutch was guided to establish a foundation and in 1975 accepted both the Course and its copyright to be tended by Foundation for Inner Peace. The Preface to *A Course in Miracles* also gives an account of how it came, what it is, and what it says.

The text gives us theory on universal spiritual truths. It makes the distinction between what God created and what we made in our defending process. The Course therefore tells us what is real and what is unreal. This distinction is also known as knowledge and perception.

The workbook gives us 365 lessons to apply universal spiritual truths. Its focus is on living the message. It provides a step-by-step curriculum for us to follow to undo the separation we made in defending. These lessons may be done daily. Their life changing nature requires growing in awareness, however, and readiness may not coordinate with a daily time schedule. The lessons provide a lifetime of learning, so when one reaches the last lesson, it is appropriate to begin again.

The manual for teachers gives additional information to those who choose to teach, or demonstrate that they trust the way of thinking presented in the Course. The manual includes characteristics of those who have connected their thinking with God and live with a healed mind.

EMOTIONALLY SPEAKING

Emotionally speaking, *A Course in Miracles* **is a hand we take to comfort us as we switch our thought system from ego to God.** Workbook p. 119/120 says, "If it helps you, think of me holding your hand and leading you. And I assure you this will be no idle fantasy." Helen knew the voice speaking to her as Jesus. When we transform our thinking from the physical realm to the spiritual realm, we know the presence of Spirit assisting us. We know we are not alone.

Knowing the comfort of a companion on our course is critical to our willingness to transform our thought system. Reversing thought means reversing energy and identity. This requires intervention from the Holy. Once we choose survival thinking we are stuck cycling within it. To let go of survival thinking feels like dying for we only know ourselves as an ego. As the ego "dies out" we become radiant for we no longer block the energy of Life flowing through us.

MENTALLY SPEAKING

Mentally speaking, *A Course in Miracles* **is a guide for transforming thought.** It presents Thoughts of God to us in the poetical rhythm of iambic pentameter. It is pure mental energy that invites us to undo, or outgrow willful ego thinking and join the Will of God. It calls us to awaken and know that we are as God created us and not as we made ourselves as egos. It invites us to realize the power of our thoughts and the intent with which we use them.

Thoughts of ego survival project fear/guilt with them. This is natural Life energy reversed. Therefore, it is not in harmony with God and it curses, or offers harm to receivers. It invites others to separate from God, also. We are taught to undo this process, and once again extend Love that is in harmony with God. That which is in harmony with God can only bless. As Love flows through us we are blessed, and Love naturally extends to all around us blessing them, too. Love invites others to unite with God, also.

Terms are presented in a circular fashion. Each time a theme is represented it is related more deeply to other terms. Therefore, we are invited to understand terms and concepts ever more deeply as we read.

Theory within the book gives us the information we need to feel safe to apply the message. Only in applying the message do we learn the truth of it. We are taught to choose to extend Love rather than project attack. This is known as Forgiving.

SPIRITUALLY SPEAKING

Spiritually speaking, *A Course in Miracles* is the Voice that receives us as we walk the path from body identity to Soul identity. When we make the inner connection with the Holy, we have Love to give. We are then in Heaven. Our identity is Beloved. The Course calls us Beloved and welcomes us Home.

Spiritually we approach the Course with humility realizing we do not know Truth, for we have all adapted to survive. Humility allows us to listen and to learn anew. The Course inspires us to choose union and Peace and therein know Love. Its words are meant to touch our hearts and stimulate us to remember our wholeness/holiness.

Accepting the new way brings us to Reverence, which is how we see things when we identify as a Soul. Our attitude is one of living harmlessly, honoring all of Life. The reverent view all with compassion and caring. To be reverent is to know the Peace of God and experience Joy which is Justice for our *seeming* difficult journey Home. At the end of our journey we know only Life, and are free to release our physical body to be one with the pure energy of God.

8

WHY STUDY
A Course In Miracles?

In this chapter I share benefits of using *A Course in Miracles* as a book, a hand, a guide, and a Voice. *A Course in Miracles* views us as Spiritual Beings, or as Souls with bodies, rather than the reverse. Pain and suffering come from viewing ourselves as bodies and disregarding our Souls. *A Course in Miracles* teaches Laws or Principles for our whole Being and welcomes us as we awaken.

AS A BOOK

When I first read *A Course in Miracles*, much of it was beyond my ability to understand. What I did understand, I read over and over. I found other books like *Sharing the Course* which helped by explaining terms to me. Over time I expanded what I read with pleasure. I used Sondra Ray's *Drinking the Divine* workbook to relate *A Course in Miracles* to my life. I read one sentence at a time in the workbook asking myself over and over, "What is this saying to me about me?" I did learn to HEAR. I also learned to SEE. I learned to LIVE. I also learned to LOVE.

Through study of *A Course in Miracles* we take ourselves to a higher vibration. The book is written as poetry, somewhere between speech and music. It has the soothing effect of a lullaby. Its simple, direct rhythm pulls us to a higher vibration. Its rhythm opens our higher mental processes. It aims at reorganizing our thinking and revitalizing our lives.

As we accept this shift in energy, we let go of pain we have been holding. Pain is the tension that we use to *try to get* Love from others. The ego is tenacious. Since we never *get* Love through ego means, we are always building more tension and then use that to *try* again.

Behind all intent to change others is a need to cry. As we learn to join with the Holy Spirit aspect of ourselves, we surrender to this tender emotion and release the frustration of *trying* to change others. As we *accept* the idea of making our own inner shift, guided by *A Course in Miracles*, we move to the vibration of Joy.

Through study of *A Course in Miracles* we learn to live miraculously. Miracles are natural, and take place with each inner shift. Each inner shift is a correction of some error we hold in our minds that separates us from God or the flow of Life. We live miraculously when we gain knowledge, understanding, and awareness of Laws involved. *A Course in Miracles* teaches us those Laws.

AS A HAND

Through study of *A Course in Miracles* we learn our true nature is a Child of God, free and unlimited. It teaches us that we removed ourselves from Love and Harmony. It helps us open ourselves again to *accept* Peace and Joy. *A Course in Miracles* tells us there is no need to blame, and no one to blame. We simply need to awaken to how we use fear beliefs to keep ourselves deprived.

It is Spirit that heals us. Our comfort comes in taking the hand of Spirit. By following the model laid out in the Course, we open the door so Spirit can reach our Feeling Nature.

Through study of *A Course in Miracles* we learn to value our own Being and nurture our own Life. It teaches us to connect and attune with the Will of God which is our own true will. Free Will doesn't mean we can do whatever we want. It means that we only want to do what is natural, and that is to Love and be Loved.

We choose again. We choose to open and receive Love from Spirit rather than close and project pain to parents or others. In *A Course in Miracles*, those of us who allow Spirit to flow through us and extend Love are called "brothers." God is Light. We have accepted God and become radiant beings. The ego is that part of us that lives darkened as the moon is darkened when the earth is between it and the source of light. Some of us live our lives in eclipse!

AS A GUIDE

Through study of *A Course in Miracles* we learn ideas for us to *accept* at our own time, when ready. All problems reflect spiritual immaturity. As we learn to Love ourselves, we stop creating more problems and heal those from our past. Until we reach spiritual maturity, we continue to follow our personal laws. Personal laws are those we impose on ourselves in surviving. They always restrict us. They reflect ways we believed we could save ourselves as a child. When we continue to follow personal laws we are allowing that child part of us to run our lives.

In an early chapter I told you that as a child I believed I could save myself by keeping my mouth shut. The ways I carried that out in my life reflect personal laws. As a spiritually mature person I use my voice to share understanding. I speak, write, and demonstrate the healing of those personal laws.

Through study of *A Course in Miracles* we learn to look at relationships from a perspective of wholeness. When we remain a receiver from God we are free to receive Love extended by others. The problem is that we have learned everything based on being a partial/separated self. "Special relationships," as defined by *A Course in Miracles*, are those in which we believe another person saves us. We believe they are the one from whom we can *get* Love. Holy relationships are those in which each person heals their separation and extends Love for the other to receive. Since both have reversed their survival intent, each is a receiver of the Love extended.

In "special relationships" we are functioning as a separated self. When doing this, we either view ourselves as the strong one and the other as weaker, or we see ourselves as the weak one and the other as the strong one. Notice what is going on here. Each person holds one pole. One is viewed as *giver*, and one as *receiver*. Since each holds to a pole, there is no connection within, and therefore no flow of Love. When living with ego intention, we hold opposite poles. The experience of either pole, however, is fear and guilt.

In "special relationships" we believe we could *get* Love from the other "if only." This implies, "If only I were to be good enough; good enough, long enough; the other would do it right"; or "If only I could *get* the other to do it right." From our ego intention, none of these conditions are ever met so we never receive Love. We continue, as in all ego patterns, to *try to get* and in the process build pain and suffering. We never "feel" good enough. (This is a belief, not a feeling, and is to be corrected.)

We misname things in this situation. It is not true that the one who looks strong, is strong; or that the one who looks weak, is weak. Nor is it true that what the strong one gives is Love, or that what the weak one wants is truly Love. Both of their actions are masquerades as they project attack. Both are *trying to get* Love.

In "special relationships," neither person is functioning with their own inner battery connected. Both are living in ego intent and suffer accordingly. Neither realizes the intensity of pain they inflict on themselves and then project to the other in this process.

Only recently has the term co-dependent become popular. The one who has held the pole as *giver* in a "special relationship" had previously been viewed as okay while the one viewed as *receiver* had been seen as the one needing help. In defining co-dependency, the true pattern was revealed.

To take the Course is to be guided to let go of the whole pattern of *trying to get* from another and Be a generator of Love. We do this one lesson at a time. If you happen to be one who reads books from the front cover to the back (not everyone does!), start over when you reach the back of *A Course in Miracles.* This is a lifelong process that doesn't end when we reach the back cover.

AS A VOICE

Through study of *A Course in Miracles* we know Grace. When we are willing to silence the ego voice and hear the Voice of God we move to the state of Grace. In Grace we know we have errors to correct and welcome the Voice which guides us to Love. It is in acknowledging that we are all souls with bodies that we look on each other as Children of God. We see that all of us are living out our uncorrected errors, and therefore we choose to be helpful to each other. Listening to the Voice that guides allows us to give Loving responses that invite correction.

Through study of *A Course in Miracles* we give our Life meaning. Meaning comes from spiritual awareness. This means we are aware of the Voice that inspires us personally. Following this Voice allows us to live consciously based on Principle rather than live unconsciously by habit. Studying allows us to incorporate the holy message and hear the words as we live our lives. When aware, we choose to follow this Voice, giving sacred responses in everyday events. This gives our life meaning.

With Grace we accept the Love of God. With this we gain certainty of God's presence. Only that which is of God is real, and only that which is real can be shared. In sharing the Love of God our Life has meaning. It is our willingness to know and share Truth that brings us the experience of Pure Joy.

9

JOINING WITH THE LANGUAGE

In this chapter I share ways to join with the language in *A Course in Miracles*. There is an aspect of ourselves that always identifies with Truth. *A Course in Miracles* is a book of Universal Truth. It is written in masculine gender with Christian symbols. If we do not identify with one or both of these, the part of us that hungers to receive Truth naturally rebels. It is as though at a time when we are most hungry, a delicious meal is placed in front of us packaged with someone else's name on it.

Some years ago I participated in a ukulele band while on a cruise of the Hawaiian Islands. On the last evening our band played to entertain others on the ship. Afterward, our leader handed me a certificate. I quickly looked at it, saw the name was not mine, and handed it back to him telling him he had made a mistake. He then told me that he was not mistaken, and that Noelani is my Hawaiian name.

I had very quickly made him wrong, declared the certificate not mine, and excluded myself. If I had not been open to learn more about the name, I would never have known that it means "Beautiful girl from Heaven." Interestingly, this event happened shortly after I took a major step in spiritual growth, committing myself to teach only Love. I had prayed for a name to be revealed to me to represent this new identity. If I had not gone beyond making him wrong, I would never have known that my prayer was answered. Nor would I have known the Joy of Noelani Publishing Company.

In the same way, **the only essential for beginning to grow with *A Course in Miracles* is that we *accept* that we are receiving something good from a Force that offers it freely to us, and that we deserve this gift. Recognize this as the Law of Being.**

We all want to end our sense of being incomplete and lonely. I have known people to express anger and frustration at both the gender and symbols used in this book. I believe their anger shows their hurt at feeling excluded from something they see as valuable toward achieving their goal.

The words and symbols are not meant to exclude any of us. Just as I needed to change my approach to the certificate that I believed had someone else's name on it, any of us can change the way we view the language of *A Course in Miracles*. We defeat ourselves when we rebel against it for we separate ourselves from the valuable message. Making it wrong does no good. Fighting against it does no good. I recommend "translating" words so they allow us to feel included. Our hearts sing and leap with pleasure when we include ourselves, which surely is better than that old feeling of being left out.

Most people find it difficult to read *A Course in Miracles*. There are several reasons for this. The first is not due to the language itself, but the poetical rhythm. **The rhythm calls us to a higher vibration, a whole brain function which is new to us.** Wholeness is also Holiness. Since we aren't used to this vibration we tend to tune out what we are reading. It is not uncommon to read a page, and when getting ready to turn to the next page suddenly saying, "Wait a minute, I've just read this page and I don't remember what I read. I don't even remember reading it!" This effect passes with time as we expand to join with the higher vibration.

From years of teaching I have learned that I must meet students where they are if I am to help them grow. ***A Course in Miracles* is a written message to us, so it doesn't bridge the language gap to us as individuals. We need to do this ourselves.** Knowing that we cannot diminish God, I invite students to change the language wherever they need in order to begin to join with the Universal message of Love. I have no intent of making the language in *A Course Miracles* wrong. **The problem is in our understanding.**

Truth is written elsewhere using different pronouns and symbols. I speak here to those called to use this resource and find themselves rejecting the language, not the message. *Sharing the Course* is to help you receive the message. Throughout this book I explain some of the more difficult concepts as simply as I can to help you with that aspect. On Text p. 263/283, *A Course in Miracles* says Peace is a state from which no one is excluded. Here are some ways to include yourself. Find a starting point.

THE TERM "GOD"

It is natural in our growing process to confuse our parents with God. So, most of us transfer to our view of God any un-healed pain associated with their inability to Love us. We end up uncomfortable with the term, "God," and certainly don't associate God with Love.

Rather than resist, use any of the following terms instead: Nature, Life, Life Force, Love, Light, Inner Guide, Intuition, Truth, Peace, Principle, Universal Mind, Master Mind, Intelligence, Uni-versal Law, Universal Energy, Mother/Father God, Mother Earth, Father Heaven, Goddess, Great Spirit, Spirit, or Source. **All of these terms have in common our ability to view them as a Force greater than ourselves that *gives* to us.** I found that af-ter substituting for a while I became comfortable with the term "God," for I had expanded my awareness.

Here is an example of substituting in reading *A Course in Miracles:*
Text p. 268/289, "God has one Purpose which He shares with you." Use your preferred word ---

"Nature has one Purpose which it shares with you."

"Peace has one Purpose which it shares with you."

"Inner Guidance has one Purpose which it shares with you."

"Mother Earth has one Purpose which she shares with you."

"Great Spirit has one Purpose which it shares with you."

THE TERM "SON OF GOD"

Now we need to think of ourselves as *receivers* from this Greater Force. The term Son of God really becomes a problem if we object to masculine language and are uncomfortable with the term God. God's Son means who I am when I know I am worthy, receive Love, and extend Love to others. This is who I am in Truth. **Until I identify as Son of God I identify as the sepa-rated and wounded one I came to identify with in my adapting.**

Rather than resist, use any of the following terms instead: Me, Self, Natural Self, Loving Self, Healed Self, Whole Self, Holy

Self, Innocent Self, Feeling Nature, Natural Child, Child I am created to Be, or Beloved Child.

Sonship is our state of Love, our state of Being rather than doing. As a "human doing," we identify as separated from Love and are forever *trying to get* it from others by doing. We *do* what we think will please others to win their Love, or we demand it one way or another. None of this works. As a human Being we are expressing Love we receive by the conditions of identifying as the worthy receiver of this Love from a Greater Being. We are like Jesus Christ in this identity.

Here is an example of substituting in reading *A Course in Miracles*:
Workbook p. 354/364, "... let the Son of God awaken from his sleep...." Use your preferred word ---
"Let Me awaken from my sleep."
"Let my Natural Self awaken from its sleep."
"Let my Healed Self awaken from its sleep."
"Let my Innocent Self awaken from its sleep."
"Let the Child I AM created to Be awaken from its sleep."

THE TERM "HOLY SPIRIT"

The Holy Spirit is the part of us that remembers all that we deny about ourselves as we defend in adapting to survive. It is the sane voice that speaks to us and allows us to reverse the insanity of the ego. The Holy Spirit remembers our past decisions, brings them to the present to release them, and in doing so, releases our future. We move from what *A Course in Miracles* calls "time," to eternity. The Holy Spirit speaks *for* us. **Since Holy Spirit thoughts are true to the Universal flow of Life, what is *for* us is not *against* anyone else.**

Rather than resist, use any of the following terms instead: intuition, inner guide, inner healer, inner comforter, quiet voice inside, Voice for God, Nurturing Parent, or Higher Self.

Here is an example of substituting in reading *A Course in Miracles*:
Text p. 501/539, "Be certain any answer to a problem the Holy Spirit solves will always be one in which no one loses."

Use your preferred word ---

"Be certain any answer to a problem intuition solves will always be one in which no one loses."

"Be certain any answer to a problem your inner healer solves will always be one in which no one loses."

"Be certain any answer to a problem your inner comforter solves will always be one in which no one loses."

"Be certain any answer to a problem the Voice for God solves will always be one in which no one loses."

"Be certain any answer to a problem your Higher Self solves will always be one in which no one loses."

THE TERM "CHRIST"

Christ, or our Christ Self, is our state of Being. This is the state of Love when we are free of illusions about who we are. It is our state of radiance after releasing our restrictions to energy of Life flowing through us. Jesus, the man, is called Christ because he fully demonstrated Oneness with the energy of God in transcending his ego. Witnesses saw his radiant Being after his resurrection. We, too, take on radiance as we transcend our ego.

Rather than resist, use any of the following terms instead: Light, Higher Self, Love, Loving Self, Enlightened Self, Awakened Self, Transformed Self, Healed Self, or Radiant Self.

Here is an example of substituting in reading *A Course in Miracles*:

Text p. 187/202, "Christ is the extension of the Love and the Loveliness of God...." Use your preferred word ---

"My Light is the extension of the Love and the Loveliness of God."

"My Higher Self is the extension of the Love and the Loveliness of God."

"My Awakened Self is the extension of the Love and the Loveliness of God."

"My Healed Self is the extension of the Love and the Loveliness of God."

"My Radiant Self is the extension of the Love and
the Loveliness of God."

THE TERM "BROTHER"

The term "brother" in *A Course in Miracles* can be read differently in various passages. It may simply refer to another person. At other times it refers to the other person while they are
identifying as a Beloved Child of God and therefore extending
Love rather than projecting guilt as an attack. Many passages
take on additional meaning when we read the term "brother" to
refer to the other or holy side of ourselves. Therefore, when we
read a passage that addresses us while we are identified in our
ego, it is the other side of ourselves. Brother may also refer to
Jesus Christ as the one who walks beside us to assist in our
spiritual journey.

**As a spiritual reality, "brother" is the energy that exists
in Truth and allows us to join and be one with others.
Whether it refers to another person, or to another aspect of
ourselves, it refers to that energy that includes rather than
separates.** The phrase, "turn your other cheek," tells us to respond with Love rather than fear when someone sends an attack
which invites us to separate. By turning our cheek we invite the
other to join rather than separate.

Rather than resist, use any of the following terms instead:
another person, another Son of God (true friend), yourself or
other as Beloved, other side of yourself (your Christ Self), your
Light side, your holiness, your sane side, or your healed self.
"Jesus Christ" is also an appropriate substitute.

Here is an example showing various ways of reading "brother" in
A Course in Miracles:
Text p. 59/65 "You and your brother will yet come together in my
name, and your sanity will be restored."
> "You and another Son of God (one choosing to ex-
> tend Love) will yet come together in my name,
> and your sanity will be restored."
> "You and your friend will yet come together in my
> name, and your sanity will be restored."
> "You and your Light side will yet come together in
> my name, and your sanity will be restored."
> "You and I (Jesus Christ) will yet come together
> and your sanity will be restored."

THE PHRASE "IN THE NAME OF"

Using capital letters refers to the spiritual level of vibration, or the vibration of Love as opposed to fear. "In my Name," or "In the Name of Jesus Christ" refer to the same thing. Both of these mean, in the vibration of Love. So, when we read a capitalized word our mind is drawn to the higher vibration. Several Workbook lessons refer to this higher energy. Workbook Lesson #67 says, "Love created me like Itself." Workbook Lesson #110 says, "I am as God created me." And, Workbook Lesson #184 says, "The Name of God is my inheritance."

A COMMENT ON GENDER

Speaking from a point of spiritual understanding, one of the saddest things about language use is its polarizing of things to masculine or feminine. This truly does not apply to the spiritual in any sense other than when related to being masculine meaning the active pole and feminine meaning the receptive pole. If we consider God as male, we deny the female. If we use the term Goddess to rebel against using God as male, we have still denied a pole. **Life energy flows based on recognizing both poles, active and receptive, masculine and feminine. God, as Life, is the creative flow between these two poles everywhere. Christ is the radiant Life we express when Life flows freely through us.** Our language itself traps us, making higher understanding difficult. We can rise above this. Happiness requires understanding this Law of Life and the limitations of our language.

For years I have listened to students share by reading *A Course in Miracles* aloud. I find that as each person translates to terms that are personally acceptable, resistance lessens. In this way of sharing, everyone's understanding broadens and all of us are assisted to embrace the message we so long to receive.

Be willing to include yourself. I welcome you. In a later chapter I share other benefits of reading with each other and give some suggestions for how to do this. First, I discuss personalizing pronouns as an additional way to include ourselves and therefore empower our receiving.

10

PERSONALIZING THE MESSAGE

In this chapter I share ways to read *A Course in Miracles* in its most personal form. Authors speak to readers either using the impersonal third person (he/she, they), second person (you, and the collective you), or first person (I, we). **I find that my joining with messages in *A Course in Miracles* deepens as I re-read passages in their most personal form.**

In the last chapter we looked at using terms that feel comfortable to us as one way to include ourselves. Personalizing symbols and pronouns as we read *A Course in Miracles* is another. Here is an example taken from the Manual p. 3/3: "Its (*A Course in Miracles*) central theme is always, God's Son is guiltless..." I may choose to personalize and read this as, "Its central theme is always that I am guiltless." This sentence continues using masculine pronouns. "Its central theme is always, God's Son is guiltless, and in his innocence is his salvation." I may choose to read this in first person as, "Its central theme is always, I am guiltless, and in knowing my innocence I am saved."

Another way to make the message personal is to first read a passage written with a second person "you" and then read it using first person "I." Here is an example using the first paragraph of Workbook Lesson #24:

In no situation that arises do you realize the outcome that would make you happy. Therefore, you have no guide to appropriate action, and no way of judging the result. What you do is determined by your perception of the situation, and that perception is wrong. It is inevitable, then, that you will not serve your own best interests. Yet they are your only goal in any situation which is correctly perceived. Otherwise, you will not recognize what they are.

Now read and listen to this passage this way:

> In no situation that arises do I realize the outcome that would make me happy. Therefore, I have no guide to appropriate action and no way of judging the result. What I do is determined by my perception of the situation, and that perception is wrong. It is inevitable, then, that I will not serve my own best interests. Yet, they are my only goal in any situation which is correctly perceived. Otherwise, I will not recognize what they are.

Do you feel the difference? This passage speaks to me in my identity as wounded child (ego), separated from a source of Love. **Personalizing it lets me truly know the message speaks to me and not just others.**

One of my favorite passages is from Text p. 12/15 "Child of God, you were created to create the good, the beautiful and holy. Do not forget this." I remember that I am to create the good, the beautiful and the holy!

Here is another example of personalizing a message by changing from collective to personal pronouns. The first paragraph of Workbook Lesson #105 reads:

> God's peace and joy are yours. Today we will accept them, knowing they belong to us. And we will try to understand these gifts increase as we receive them.

This certainly feels different to me when I read it,

> God's peace and joy are mine. Today I accept them knowing they belong to me. And I understand these gifts increase as I receive them.

You may notice two other changes in this message. **I read A Course in Miracles with conviction. Therefore, I make a firm statement omitting the word "try."** Instead of saying "I will try to understand," I say, "I understand these gifts increase as I receive them." We so often allow the word "try" to be a cop-out word. Whether we are *trying to get* to New York, or *trying to get* to understanding, we are using ego intent in either case, and defeat ourselves with the reversal of our magnetism (intent). I either do as suggested, or decide not to. I don't "try" to do it!

The other change is reading the passage in present tense, saying I understand (now) rather than that I "will" at some future time. Our subconscious creates whatever we affirm. The stronger our affirmation, the stronger our results. I address affirmations at length in Chapter 15. For now, know that when we put something in the future in our minds, we may also put our desired results in the future as well. It is in the present that we receive and enjoy.

11

READING WITH OTHERS

In this chapter I share ways to read with others. Reading *A Course in Miracles* when alone fulfills the need for quiet time, solitude, and rest from our hectic worldly existence. There is also something in us that seeks to share with others that which is meaningful to us. Reading *A Course in Miracles* with others provides this quiet, restful, and meaningful time.

Reading with others calls our attention to a single task and focus. Universal Law shows us that what we focus on increases. Stated another way, we might say energy follows thought. As we think together, we grow together. Reading together gives us an opportunity to raise our vibration by speaking words of Truth. It also gives us an opportunity to hear Truth spoken. The more we hear these words, the further they sink into our subconscious. **Our subconscious creates our life experience based on what is impressed on it. Therefore, choose your impressions wisely and freeingly.**

Here is an example from Text p. 83/90. First, read it as it is. Then listen as Joe reads it to Bob.

> Decision cannot be difficult. This is obvious, if you realize that you must already have decided not to be wholly joyous if that is how you feel. Therefore, the first step in the undoing is to recognize that you actively decided wrongly, but can as actively decide otherwise. Be very firm with yourself in this, and keep yourself fully aware that the undoing process, which does not come from you, is nevertheless within you because God placed it there. Your part is merely to return your thinking to the point at which the error was made, and give it over to the Atonement in peace. Say this to yourself as sincerely as you can, remember-

ing that the Holy Spirit will respond fully to your slightest invitation:

I must have decided wrongly, because I am not at peace.

I made the decision myself, but I can also decide otherwise.

I want to decide otherwise, because I want to be at peace.

I do not feel guilty, because the Holy Spirit will undo all the consequences of my wrong decision if I will let Him.

I choose to let Him, by allowing Him to decide for God for me.

Here are some points of explanation on this passage before Joe reads it to Bob. This passage says that the undoing process does not come from us. It speaks to us in our ego adaptation. Returning to the point of error means remembering the early life scene which once overwhelmed us. As in the metaphor given early in this book, this means to return to the point that we squeezed the balloon. That was where we chose denial as a way of dealing with what overwhelmed us. To give it over to the Atonement means to see the whole picture now. That means we accept what went to the other part of the balloon. That is what the Holy Spirit remembers for us. The holding of this scene for us until we are ready to solve the problem with our own Love is God's plan for our salvation.

Giving the process, or solution over to the Atonement means we recognize our restricting and choose its release. This means we are ready to receive into our awareness that which we put on hold. The Atonement process includes acknowledging the presence of a Greater Being beyond the parent or care giver who failed us in our early scene. The Holy Spirit is your own Loving response to the child who was so frightened at the time. **We make life very complex looking for solutions outside ourselves. Universal Law is always simple.**

When we read a passage personalized to one other person, we deepen our sense of connection with that person. Life energies are raised in both of us. In this example I also change the word "but" to "and." Notice it. I address this after you read the passage. Joe starts by calling Bob's name.

Bob, decision cannot be difficult. This is obvious if you realize that you must already have decided not to be wholly joyous if that is how you feel. Therefore, Bob, the first step in the undoing is to recognize that you actively decided wrongly, AND can as actively decide otherwise. Bob, be very firm with yourself in this, and keep yourself fully aware that the undoing process, which does not come from you, is nevertheless within you because God placed it there. Bob, your part is merely to return your thinking to the point at which the error was made, and give it over to the Atonement in peace. Listen as sincerely as you can, Bob, remembering that the Holy Spirit will respond fully to your slightest invitation:

Bob, you must have decided wrongly, because you are not at peace.

You made the decision yourself, AND you can also decide otherwise.

Bob, I know you want to decide otherwise, because you want to be at peace.

You do not need to feel guilty, because the Holy Spirit, your own voice of Loving-kindness, will undo all the consequences of your wrong decision if you will let it.

And, Bob, do choose to let this loving voice decide for Love for you.

Bob says, "Thank you, Joe."

In our use of language, the word "but" is most often used to bridge from Love's way of thinking to fear's way of thinking. This is undoubtedly an abuse we have built into our language from living in our egos. We want to read with others as a way of joining. I find it helps to join when I correct this abuse of language in my mind by noticing the word "but" everywhere, including when reading *A Course in Miracles*. By replacing it with "and" I learn to intend my thoughts Love's way and keep them going in that direction. Look at these examples. Feel the difference in your gut.

Example one:
> "You made an error *but* you can correct it."
> "You made an error *and* you can correct it."

You may not feel much here. What about this one?

Example two:
> "You've followed my directions well *but* there's more to learn."
> "You've followed my directions well *and* there's more to learn."

When we have not healed our sense of separation (which means all of us), any comment that implies we are inadequate calls out guilt. The first statement in each example tends to call for guilt in response. Do you feel this? Remember, guilt is our state when we believe we have no Greater Being to Love us and we are unworthy of receiving Love. The word "but" calls out this guilt. This means we feel our guilt at these times.

When people speak this way to us, we always have the opportunity to view this with gratitude, of course, and correct the error in our mind (the belief that there is no Greater Being to Love us and we are unworthy of receiving Love). To release the guilt we connect with the Loving voice within us.

The second statement in each example indicates you've done well so far and I'm going to give you help. Using the word "and" instead of "but" is inspiring. You are offered an opportunity to sense that a Loving person is there for you and you deserve to be treated Lovingly.

The first statement in each example indicates that the other person addresses us from their ego and, therefore, is not extending Love. Having to constantly be called to find Love within because the other addresses us from their ego gets tiring. I personally prefer correcting the use of the word so I don't go around calling out guilt in people. I believe we can learn our lessons in Loving ways. I'd rather extend Love and call people to heal by joining with the energy of Love.

Using "and" is a more Loving way to speak. This is the Holy Spirit's way of giving a call to awaken and see once again what we denied. As we become aware of our language usage, we speak from our higher voice and offer the call to others to awaken. When we invite others up instead of down, any resistance to waking that they have comes to their awareness from within. With it they receive the opportunity to listen to the Holy Spirit.

We will not have projected another attack at them to encourage ego resistance.

And, one more example:

> "I'd love to take a bike trip in Europe *but* I don't
> have anyone to go with me."
> "I'd love to take a bike trip in Europe *and* I don't
> have anyone to go with me."

In the first statement you can hear that the person has quickly put a stop to the idea of taking the trip. It sounds like a dead issue. Fear's way won. In the second statement the person sounds open to finding someone and would probably welcome your accepting the statement as an invitation to be the one to join in on the fun. Also, note that if you were to suggest a mutual friend who might be interested, the response in the first case would be "Yes, but ____." In the second case your suggestion would more likely be welcomed, accepted as helpful, and likely be pursued.

It is in actually taking the steps that heal our separation from Love that the principles and concepts in *A Course in Miracles* take on meaning for us. This includes learning to join with the language and with others in our reading of the Course content.

I share with you an extensive list of Practice Exercises in Chapter 25 to use to join with others. First, I address the process of changing our minds. *A Course in Miracles* is about changing our minds from fear's way of thinking to Love's way of thinking. Give thought to this.

Reading together.

PART III

Changing Our Minds

12

THOUGHT

In this chapter I share information about thought as our spiritual connection with Life. As human beings, under proper conditions we can go forty days or more without food, several days without water, and a few minutes without oxygen. How long do you think you could go without thinking?

It is through our thoughts that we stay connected with guidance at all times. We have two systems of thought for doing this and we are using one or the other at all times. These two systems of thought are called altars. **We either kneel at the altar of the ego, or the Altar of God.** When kneeling at the altar of the ego we believe that defending and manipulating *gets* us what we want. When kneeling at the Altar of God we know that awareness and truthful expression bring us what we want.

We go inward to decide which system to use in the present. We either call out images that remind us that there is no Love for us, or remember there is a Greater Being for us and respond to that Voice of Love. When we believe no Love is available, we feel fear and call out critical or controlling voices that tell us what we should do to *try to get* Love and approval. This is our ego substitute for a Loving guide. Since ego energy is resistance against the flow of Life, we never *get* Love by responding to a critical guide. **When we become aware of which thought system we are using, we are then free to change our minds.**

Every thought we have "intends" energy to fear or Love. To intend energy is to direct it and we either direct it to resist God (anti-God) or to flow with God. Fear is willful resistance against the flow of Life, and separates us from God. Love is willingness to align with the Will of God and this willingness opens us to God. **Our spiritual journey is one of reversing intent by reversing all thoughts directed to fear or resistance.** This is also known as undoing the ego, forgiving, accepting, and saving ourselves.

Transforming a thought, or reversing intent, has several parts to it.

1. We change the image we hold which calls out fear.
2. In releasing fear, we expand and receive information.
3. The expanded image and information call for a new response.
4. Our new response brings the miracle of Love.
5. We live with understanding and faith.

Here is an example of updating a thought. I learned not to put my hand on the stove because I knew my mother or father would respond in a frightening way. I held an image in my mind of their reaction the time I got near the flame. The image was a constant reminder to restrict my behavior. I learned not to touch the stove out of fear of being harmed by, or abandoned by the parent that I saw as my Greater Being at the time.

As an updated and complete thought, I know how to use a stove for cooking food. I am grateful to have such a wonderful and convenient appliance to serve me. I also realize that my flesh will burn, which is painful to me. I know that the stove has no intent to harm me. It is there only to help me. I choose to use the flame for cooking and keep my flesh clear of the flames on a stove out of Love and protection of myself.

I now understand why my parents responded as they did. I am grateful that they kept me physically safe when I didn't know how to do that myself. I have also kept young ones away from flames to protect them until they were mature enough to understand and keep themselves safe. I no longer hold images of fear of my parents. My original behavior was held by an ego thought pattern and my release came in expanding information and switching my intent from fear to Love.

During our phase of physical survival we take in thoughts of others like a sponge. We do not have the ability to discern what is true and what is false. We believe that what our models do is what we are to do. We believe that all we hear is true. We believe that all we are asked to do is right to do. Advertisers take advantage of this level of thinking when implying that we will be happy if we buy and use their products.

It is important to realize that we have been provided a way to always have a voice that guides us (critical ego or protective Holy Spirit). The difficulty is that we continue living in our survival mode long beyond its appropriate time.

Usually, around our late twenties, our Thinking Nature is ready to begin the natural process of updating thoughts and switching intention. **Every thought we took in from others must be reviewed. Typically we feel betrayed by God as we take this step to awaken.** After having done our very best to do everything we thought would bring us Love and approval from our external authorities, we feel unhappy, at best, and miserable, at worst. We feel like we wasted all those formative years in pursuit of happiness only to journey down the road to despair.

It is in realizing the marvelousness of God's plan for us that we release our anger at God. *A Course in Miracles* says it is the Holy Spirit that remembers who we are as innocent Beings. We know this part of ourselves. It is our own remembering of every scene in our earlier life where we needed something and didn't receive it. We also know what we needed. Life is so marvelous that it gives us the ability to meet that need for our own inner child now. To do so, we need to switch intent from blaming the one who did not meet our need for Love, to being a Loving grown-up to our inner child. We cannot do both of these at one time. **To chose to blame is to choose to continue to see ourselves as separated from Love and deprive ourselves. To give ourselves what we need now is to know Love and also realize that no time has been wasted.**

Sorting through all these thoughts comes during our phase of spiritual development which is the process of growing in awareness. The most pervasive and harmful enemy is our own ego thinking, which is our intent to make ourselves wrong and unworthy of God's Love. The closer we come to accepting Love, the stronger our ego will seek to keep us "surviving" in the ways we once decided. I choose to think of this as part of the magnificence of Life. We were created to survive almost anything. Our survival mechanism continues its function until we are willing to release it. Its function was to assure that a parent was there for us. **When we are willing to be that parent to our inner child, we no longer need that function. Our spiritual process is the undoing of this survival function.**

Every problem we have is a thought seeking to be updated. We awaken to see that others do not consciously intend to hurt or deceive us. When they are still living on ego thinking themselves, they are hurt and deceived. We pass on to others what we believe. **To bring our thoughts to completion is to accept all that is there to see, and to no longer see things as there that are not there. This includes seeing that others are functioning on fear and realizing that** *trying* **to change them keeps**

US in our ego, also. Choosing to function on Love resolves thoughts to Peace and Joy and invites others to follow.

Here are several examples of resolving thoughts. First, a learning from my own life. When I first began seeing clients in the office I had made from the smallest bedroom in our home, I did what I had been told was right to do to protect myself and carried liability insurance. The fee was $25 a year. Then one day I received a bill for $465 for a year of coverage. This came with a notice that the rate would be much higher the next year. I immediately felt resentful, for this was a large percentage of my income at the time.

I knew that if I paid this bill, my resentment would pull my energies down to the ego level. I would greet each client at the door with resentment, saying to myself, "Are you the _____ that is going to sue me that makes this insurance necessary?" To function at the ego level is to expect and invite "punishment." I knew I would no longer buy into a thought system that says I deserve to be punished. My goal was to give Love and receive only its rewards. I knew that if I could not greet clients with Love there would be no growth. I sat the bill on my kitchen table knowing I would not pay it. I knew there had to be a better way. Within a few days I knew the better way.

I went to a workshop on tithing and realized that this was my answer. By definition, tithing is giving ten percent of our income in gratitude to God. To me, tithing means seeing Goodness anywhere and acknowledging this presence of Love by giving money to support it. The moment I accepted the idea I felt free (of resentment). I knew that in acknowledging the world as a friendly rather than a hostile place I would deepen my ability to give Love to others.

Instead of paying for liability insurance, I thought back through my life and recalled people who had offered Love to me that allowed me to grow to where I was in life at the time. I divided up the $465 and sent checks with letters of gratitude. These went mostly to teachers, authors, and musicians. The results were truly miraculous. Since then I have continued to see things everywhere which nurture me and help me grow. I respond with a tithe in gratitude.

We live in a culture so indoctrinated with the belief that we will be harmed and that attorneys and insurance will save us. Everything about this is based on fear thinking. The more we narrow our thinking, the more we put ourselves in positions which jeopardize us. This thinking cycles to greater intensity like all addictions.

Hopefully there will be a time when we have *assurance* that God is a Loving God, and ask, "What is insurance?" Do we really want sickness, injuries, revenge, and a view of the world as being against us? Do we really believe that insurance saves us? These are ego ideas that have no place in Love. We receive much misguidance from the insurance and legal industries which have selfish purposes in mind.

We are just as misguided to believe that gambling or winning the lottery will save us. Both are based on *trying to get*. In either case we do not truly believe abundance is ours. It is in giving that we receive and know the richness of Life.

Another area in which we need to rethink relates to sickness and its prevention. All sickness exists in fear and there is no better way to assure against sickness than to expand awareness of ways we contribute to sickness and stop harming ourselves. Sickness comes from opposing the flow of Life (which is fear), and wellness comes from aligning with the flow of Life (which is faith).

There are terrifying advertisements on television sponsored by agencies which think they are being helpful in preventing sickness. They tell us what to do to "save ourselves." They do not realize that in *trying* to scare us into "prevention" they call our energy to that of the sickness they purport to prevent by scaring us. X-rays and physicians do not save us. **Transforming thought saves us by opening us to the healing energy of Love. When open to learn, we are individually guided as to what we need to do to be safe and well at all times. Until we transform our thinking, we depend on external sources to support us when sick. They are meant to serve like our baby teeth. Our own higher thought supports our being well.**

We are always rethinking relationships. Daily we can listen to people on television, or read books by people telling how badly they have been hurt by others. Coming out of our numbness and learning to name things is a step in our transformation. If we go no further, however, we still do not find happiness. Blame itself is the intent of revenge, and revenge never brings happiness.

Life gives us an inner guide which is the perfect complement to the injured child. We can either continue to blame those who injured us and perpetuate our injury, or use our inner resources to join our Feeling Nature and create happiness. **We need to become aware of the power of our thoughts to miscreate or create depending on our intent.**

For years I led workshops at a local university. One day, at the end of a workshop on anger, my boss came to check in on

things. She was carrying a popular book on Love which she had
been reading. She said, "We ought to offer a workshop on Love."
I, in all my naiveté, replied, "If you want a workshop on Love, I'll
teach it." Little did I know where that would lead me. I set out in
my usual way to "study" Love.

I looked for it everywhere. As a measuring stick, I used the
thought that where there is Love there is growth. So, all day long
for six months or so, I asked myself if I was experiencing growth
from what I thought, said, and did. Was there growth in my in-
teractions with others? The more I questioned, the deeper I sank
into despair until I had what is sometimes called a "Dark Night of
the Soul" experience.

I allowed myself to see that I had never known Love. This
meant that nothing I had given was Love, either. About then I
was fully aware of the enormity of the challenge I had accepted
with that simple "I'll teach it." And, I was about to find out what
the "it" was. I had agreed to teach (live and demonstrate) Love.
To know Love is also to find ourselves, and that is also to know
God.

GUILT

About the same time, and not surprising as I look back on it,
I had another major realization. It was about the nature of guilt.
I thought guilt was related to those times when I made mistakes,
did something bad or wrong, and needed to apologize. Since I
had always been such a Good Girl, I thought there were only a
few of these. I figured I had apologized and set things right.
What I didn't know was that my whole Good Girl adaptation was
guilt. As long as I was being so good to *try to get* Love, I was not
in a state of Love. I was not creating Love. I was not giving Love.
All I knew was guilt. That was surely news to me. I would say I
was living and giving guilt if this were true. It isn't, though.
**Guilt is not something that can be shared. It is our private
hell.**

Here are some signs of guilt:
All addictions.
Health, relationship, or money problems.
Fear of rejection - "What will others think?"
Self-rejection - not liking parts of my body, my be-
    havior, my abilities, my income, etc.
"I'd like to _____, but _____."
"If it weren't for you _____."

"I'll show you _____ (if it kills me)."

"I'd rather die than _____."

Attitude of scarcity - not enough for everyone.

Comparisons. "You are so smart." (This has an implied, "and I am so stupid.")

Competition - the need to win over another.

Believe that things happen to me that cause me suffering and misery.

Believe I deserve to be punished.

Believe I owe someone or they owe me.

Believe someday I will be loved or appreciated.

Believe I need to get rid of someone to be safe.

Believe I am unsafe to express spontaneously.

Believe I am wrong to ask for things for myself.

Believe if I have a party no one will come.

Believe I always have to be setting an example.

Don't know what I want, think, or feel.

"Feel" doubtful, needy, inadequate, overwhelmed, hopeless, helpless, envious, jealous, suspicious, chronic grief, hateful, lonely, uncertain, confused, vengeful, regretful, or that I don't belong anywhere.

Turn away praise.

Give with strings attached.

Keep peace at any price.

Afraid to say "No." Afraid to say "Yes."

Keep secrets, live a pretense, deceive, lie, cheat, sneak, hide things, snoop, act, or *try* to make a good impression.

Do things I do not want to do because I believe I should, and feel burdened.

Never good enough, have never done enough.

On a treadmill, never rest, and get sick on vacations.

Fighting against anything, including illness is opposition and resistance.

Holding back what wants to express through me.

Things don't feel right or make sense.

Inner dialog which is *trying to get*, *trying* to change another, *trying* to talk another into or out of something, justifying attack.

Criticism of self or others.

Feel "unfaired against."

Feel limited, or in a self-imposed silence.

Disorder, clutter, constipation, hoarding.
Feel angry or self-righteous.
Fear dying, terror, anxiety, panic attacks, numb.
"Over-react"
Feel stuck in life, like going nowhere.
Avoiding things.
Rigid with daily habits.
Mishandle money and credit.
Chronically late or absent.
Drive a faulty car, fear flying.
Always have to be good, look good, be nice and polite.
Feel overly responsible - "I have to fix others."
Do more than my share of any work to be done.
Read minds, anticipate, *try* to please.
Make my own feeling responses wrong.
"Feel" dirty, damaged, or ugly because of what others have done to me.
Let others harm me, or want others to sacrifice for me.
Apologize for choices and expressions.
Lack faith in my own hunches.
Fear being a fool, humiliated, or embarrassed.
Insensitive, cold, or lacking in compassion.
Intimidation, disgust, dread, revulsion.
Eyes fixed in a watchful stare.
Eyes that look dull or empty.
Don't want to be seen or known.
Tense and push with sexual or vocal expression.
Don't want people to come to my home. Don't want to be alone. Can't stand to say "Good-bye."
Feel like I am going crazy or living in a fantasy world.
Eat fast and wash food down.
Voice harsh or too quiet. Mumble. Always asking questions.
Feel like a failure or afraid to succeed.
Don't trust anyone. Feel like I am in someone's shadow.
Make fun of people, or enjoy comedies that attack people.
Life doesn't feel worth living, want to kill myself or someone else.

So, I realized I was living the dark experience of guilt. I wasn't truly living as a Soul. My body was going through an act. **Perhaps you know that sense of not really being alive. With it goes the worry that we will die before we truly live.**

As far as our Souls are concerned, guilt has nothing to do with being bad. **Guilt is our sense of the void where we have not as yet accepted Love and Life. It is darkness in our Souls which turns to radiance when we accept Love.** What Love touches becomes beautiful. If we *think* we are bad we will continue to resist Love and Light. Isn't it ironic that all the while we are being a Good Girl or Nice Guy we truly believe we are bad.

THOUGHT-STOPPING

> To switch from what never makes us happy (blaming and seeking revenge) to what does make us happy (knowing our innocence and receiving), we need to learn to thought-stop. This requires willingness to consciously choose to stop all thinking about what the other person did or didn't do that hurt us; what we'd like to do to them; and, our persistent inner chatter about how damaged we are.
> Thought-stopping does not deny what is happening (or has happened). In thought-stopping we consciously deny that intending our thoughts to blame, self-pity, or revenge ever brings us happiness.

I call the switching of intent forgiving or accepting. Neither of these says that what the other person did was right, or that it was proper for them to do (or not do, in cases of omission) what they did to us. I included the preceding "guilt" list which shows us what we need to eliminate in order to allow space for higher thought. Everything on that list indicates we are using the ego thought system.

Thought-stopping requires:
a. *discerning* ego thoughts from higher thoughts.
b. *stopping* thoughts that go with ego thinking (blame).
c. *allowing* higher thoughts which come from the Holy Spirit.

A higher thought is the opposite of a lower thought. For example, instead of believing people will reject me, I accept myself.

There are a couple reversals here. First I reverse the focus from others to myself. I look at what I am doing instead of what I think they are, or will do to me. I realize that in fearing rejection by others I am in truth rejecting myself. Secondly, I shift the idea from one of rejecting myself to one of accepting myself. When I accept myself I become likable to others and my experiences teach me that I need not fear rejection.

If we lived with harsh punishment and took on the belief that we deserve to be punished, we must reverse this to know that we only deserve help to grow. Another part of this reversal is changing the harsh and punitive way we think about ourselves, talk to ourselves, and treat ourselves. As we become gentle with ourselves we no longer condone abuse from others. We leave abusive situations and choose to not live or work with people who are abusive. **When we forgive our past we no longer fall prey, in the present, to anyone seeking to abuse us for their own selfish purposes.**

Ultimately we need to learn to catch the first thought that leads us into the ego thought system. That is our point of refusal. When I recognize the image I hold, I say, "I know where you lead and I'm not going that way! I choose _____." When we stop a thought, we need to replace it with a higher thought. I will talk about affirmations soon. We affirm to make firm for ourselves the opposite of our ego thought and this includes the reversals of which I spoke earlier.

The whole of *A Course in Miracles* is to lead us from our thought system made during survival, to thought which is one with God. This is called the Atonement. Happiness comes from changing our minds. While changing our minds is not easy, if we want to be happy, there is a plan.

God does not impose on us or take our survival plan from us. God does want us to be happy. **When we are ready to release our survival mode, we ask for release of our ego thought by maintaining a higher thought for three days.** It is something no one can do for us. "Thou shalt not steal" means we cannot steal from others what they have gained by right of consciousness. This means we cannot steal the miraculous results of someone else's courage to transform their thought.

This three day period is our period of temptation. It is when our ego beats us up and others escalate with their manipulations. Anyone who has tried to give up any addiction knows this well. Those who have stuck to the new way know the power which comes in on the third day.

Asking for release of the lower thought opens the door for God, Love, and Life. Life is a process, so this transforming goes on continuously. **Our entire thought system is meant to be transformed. We do not rest from the process, we rest in the results of our discipline to stick with it.**

The reason we fall back into ego habits once we have made it through the three days is because there are many, many thoughts that need to be uplifted and held for three days. Our ego thought system is a whole system of thoughts. This is a lifelong healing process. To hold the energy of Love is to know Freedom, Happiness, and God. We awaken to see our defense system for what it is, our baby teeth in terms of our connection with Life. Something much more secure and permanent awaits our willingness. Next I share what *A Course in Miracles* says about thought.

13

WHAT *A Course In Miracles* SAYS ABOUT THOUGHT

In this chapter I share key points from *A Course in Miracles* on changing our mind. The entire Course is about retraining our thought from that which separates us from God to that which joins us. Therefore, what I have selected to use in this chapter represents only a few selections from the whole. **All suffering comes from being stuck in ego thinking. Freedom is freedom to give a new response. It comes from changing our mind, both intent and content.**

A Course in Miracles begins by telling us in the Introduction, "Nothing real can be threatened. Nothing unreal exists." This means that ego thoughts have no Life of their own and exist only if we give energy to them. That which is of God is true and always will be true. This is what is real. While our ego thoughts seem real to us, when we realize our errors and undo them, we know what has been there all along - not threatened by our non-readiness to see truly.

On Manual p. 1 we read, "To teach is to demonstrate. There are only two thought systems, and you demonstrate that you believe one or the other is true all the time. From your demonstration others learn, and so do you. The question is not whether you will teach, for in that there is no choice. The purpose of the course might be said to provide you with a means of choosing what you want to teach on the basis of what you want to learn. You cannot give to someone else but only to yourself, and this you learn through teaching. Teaching is but a call to witness to attest to what you believe." The Course goes on to say that we set up our life based on what we think we are and what we believe the relationship of others is to us.

Workbook Lesson #285 speaks of waking with joy expecting only happy things to come to us because we ask only for them. For example, upon first awakening we may choose to open our arms, and with palms up, accept the gift of peace. It requires both awareness and discipline to realize that we set our intention for the day with our first thought. When you first awaken in the morning, do you scan your mind and day to pick up the worries and scares of the day before? Do you awaken hearing words of the Higher Self affirming you? Do you hear Spirit guiding you with new directions for your day? Worry is a habit of thought in which we entertain worst possible scenarios and worst possible outcomes. Give yourself space for Higher Thought through a continuous practice of refusing to fill your mind with worry.

Workbook Lesson #5 says we are never upset for the reason we think. Regardless what upset we bring into our thought, the reason we are upset is because we have intended or directed our mind to ego thinking. and therefore have chosen to think upsetting thoughts.

Text p. 77/84 says, "Whatever you accept into your mind has reality for you. It is your acceptance of it that makes it real. If you enthrone the ego in your mind, your allowing it to enter makes it your reality. This is because the mind is capable of creating reality or making illusions." And, since the ego consists of illusions, "Whenever you respond to your ego you will experience guilt, and you will fear punishment."

On Text p. 91/98-9 we are told that our part is only to allow no darkness to abide in our minds. We need to take note of two words here. Guilt is the darkness. To abide means to reside, to remain in a place. We are not to allow guilt-producing thought to remain in our minds. We need to hear these thoughts only to recognize the need to correct them.

Text p. 78/84 says we are to learn to think with God and like God, for this engenders Joy, not guilt. "Guilt is a sure sign that your thinking is unnatural." It is only in entertaining ego thoughts that we suffer, for "The guiltless mind cannot suffer. Being sane, the mind heals the body because *it* has been healed." **To heal is to correct our thinking: undoing all intent to use our ego thought system, and undoing errors contained within content of our ego thoughts.**

Life is only and always a process of growth. Growth includes breaking down of the old to allow for the new. We grow as individuals, we grow in relationships, we grow as families, we grow as nations, and we grow as a world community. The planet itself is changing. Growing includes finding Truth which means connecting with God. We do this by listening for our individual guidance and accepting the new. To feel safe we must accept that changes, including planetary changes, will be good for the whole. **Accepting and cooperating with this process allows us to know the glory of Life which is God.**

On Text p. 353/378 we read, "As the light comes nearer you will rush to darkness, shrinking from the truth, sometimes retreating to the lesser forms of fear, and sometimes to stark terror." As we grow, and things around us change, thoughts and images emerge from our subconscious. These were the scenes in which we experienced the absence of a Greater Being. We feel the feelings that we once repressed. These include intense terror, rage, and grief which clear in our healing. We once again experience our perceived state of separation which we numbed from awareness. This will be fleeting when we remember that Life is gentle and good for these images, and feelings do not come up to clear until we have grown the ability to tend them. It helps to remember that we lived through the events which are clearing in our minds, and at this time our thoughts and feelings about the events are healing because we have reached a level of understanding which allows for this.

On Text p. 166/179 we are told that littleness and Truth are denials of each other. *A Course in Miracles* asks us directly on Text p. 184/198, "Would you be hostage to the ego or host to God?" Text p. 78/85 says, "... the question, 'What do you want?' must be answered. You are answering it every minute and every second, and each moment of decision is a judgment that is anything but ineffectual. Its effects will follow automatically until the decision is changed."

On Text p. 56/62 we are told to, "Watch carefully and see what it is you are really asking for. Be very honest with yourself in this...." We choose guilt or Love, darkness or Light. We use our thought to remind us to blame, or we use it to tell us where we defended and therefore where we need to heal. We use our thought to remind us that we are not safe to grow, or we use it to tell ourselves we are protected and safe to grow under Loving guidance.

Again, on Text p. 285/306 we are told that littleness or glory are our choices and that we will always choose one at the expense of the other. Text p. 22/26 says, "Corrective learning always begins with the awakening of spirit, and the turning away from the belief in physical sight." Physical sight is what we perceived with our eyesight and awakening means to understand what was there, "Oh, I see!" I will explain perception and Vision in a later chapter.

Usually when we hear the word "disciplined," we think of something rigid or restrictive. In truth, a disciplined mind is a free mind. When we have learned to be vigilant for ego thoughts and choose to use them only as indicators of what we need to correct, we are free. Maybe it would be helpful to relate the word disciplined to disciple. A disciple accepts the teachings of a master and teaches them. A healed mind is free of ego process, free to teach Love. To accept healing means we are willing to listen to the Holy Spirit voice, the Loving voice within us, and therefore know Love's presence. This is conscious choice. This is using thought mindfully. Text p. 183/197 says, "The Holy Spirit cannot speak to an unwelcoming host, because He will not be heard." And, Text p. 103/111 says, "Your vigilance is the sign that you *want* Him to guide you."

Now, suppose we've decided to start listening to our own inner guide. We make a major decision on our own. (I'll tell you how one of these went for me in a minute.) Most likely it will not be long until we are into a confrontation with either a parent, a teacher, a mate, or our boss. It will be someone who seemingly had power over us. This person, whom we were perceiving as our Greater Being, will feel abandoned in the relationship. This is "specialness," for we have been seeing them as the one who has decided for us until taking this step in our growth. Feeling abandoned themselves, they will most likely respond with an attack from fear. Attack is the way our ego seeks to connect with others, insane as it may seem. They are *trying* to keep a connection with us using ego level thoughts and behaviors.

At the Soul level we grow in awareness. This lets us see that behind every attack is a person needing to connect with Love. It is self-defeating to attack, of course, if our goal is Love. It is just as self-defeating to respond with an attack if *our* goal is Love. Spiritual maturity brings awareness, and with it freedom. When we are aware that the real need behind attack is the need to connect with Love, we can choose to respond to that need, and not the attack. **Freedom is freedom to give a new response, and this comes from awareness of choice.**

Some time ago I was working through issues of a lifelong pattern of living with secondhand and hand-me-down goods. So many times they were not really me. I was beginning to believe I deserved more and better than this. Then Spirit tested me. Spirit guided me to purchase a specific new car. I was afraid to even bring up the issue with my husband. I anticipated a rejecting response. (This is what I received as a child, and reflects my parents' fear of not having enough money to survive. This is part of what I am healing here.)

When I did bring up the subject, my husband responded resolutely that we didn't have money in the budget for a new car. Issue closed! I felt frightened. Spirit was saying one thing and my husband was saying another. It seemed like he was opposing my own Life Force.

My husband's relationship with me had nearly always been supportive of my growth, so I looked at things from his perspective. He knew me as one who had a new tree planted in the front yard less than an hour after first having the idea. Believing he would be unsafe should I act so quickly on the idea of getting this car, he became fearful and sought to stop the idea. I experienced this as an attack.

I chose to respond with Love to my husband, so I contemplated for a while. This is what *A Course in Miracles* says. Text p. 200/215, "Every loving thought is true. Everything else is an appeal for healing and help regardless of the form it takes. Can anyone be justified in responding with anger to a brother's plea for help? No response can be appropriate except the willingness to give it to him, for this and only this is what he is asking for." I realized his intent was not to harm me. I decided to be helpful by giving him more information so he could deal with his fear.

I made a list for my husband of all the reasons why I didn't need a new car. This included his having just put all kinds of new parts on the car that I had purchased secondhand from a client a few years earlier. I then listed my spiritual needs. Among them was my need to be willing to follow Spirit's guidance to be true to myself. Of course, one of my greatest needs here was to update my self-concept of what I deserved.

In a very gentle way I shared my listings. My voice was shaking with fear as I remembered results of asserting myself as a child. Yet I knew I was going to follow Spirit. This was going to be the first major decision that I was making whether he approved or not. His response was tearfully Loving. He was moved by my growing awareness of spiritual guidance and my courage to act on it. I offered him the option, and he chose to go with me while I made the purchase.

This story has a miraculous outcome. Miracle principle #36, Text p. 3/5 says, "Miracles are examples of right thinking, aligning your perceptions with truth as God created it." I had decided to follow the voice of Spirit as to my worth rather than the level of worth I assumed from living with hand-me-downs.

Soon after I purchased the car, I received a totally unexpected check in the mail. It was more than enough to pay for the car. It came from a woman who had been a student of mine for a few years. She said she was expressing gratitude to me for my teachings which she said had led her to God. She had not known of my purchase at the time that she arranged for the money to be sent. We were both intrigued by how Spirit had worked through us. I experienced Spirit's seal of approval for my higher choices.

I'll summarize about thought before going on.

1. It is likely that we have never known Love and don't realize that.
2. Guilt is far more than the feeling we get when we do something that breaks a law or moral code. Guilt is where we still live in darkness.
3. Guilt has many ways of showing itself. (See list in Chapter 12.)
4. Becoming aware of our illusion of what Love is and where it comes from can be traumatic. We may feel betrayed by God and have a strong urge to strike out.
5. We intend our energy to fear or Love with each thought. Our energy is always anti-God or aligned with God.
6. We must learn to discern the two thought systems. Fear thinking has errors in its content. Love thinking is aligned with Truth.
7. It is in realizing that we have not known Love that we can make the necessary transfer from fear thinking to Love thinking. We connect with God through Loving thought.
8. Transforming thought is a constant process which requires vigilant monitoring of all thoughts. To heal our separation we both switch our *intent*, and correct errors in the *content* of our thoughts. We are told in *A Course in Miracles* that our task is to simply correct our errors, bringing all thoughts to Truth.

A Course in Miracles tells us on Text p. 27/31 that, "The mind is very powerful, and never loses its creative force. It never sleeps. Every instant it is creating....There *are* no idle thoughts. All thinking produces form at some level."

A Course in Miracles says on Text p. 195/210, "Every loving thought that the Son of God ever had is eternal....they are eternal because they are loving. And being loving they are like the Father and therefore cannot die." **Thoughts are vibrations that either pollute or purify the planetary pool.** One agitated person can disturb a crowd. One peaceful person can calm a crowd. I choose to think responsibly. I choose to bring my thoughts to Peace and extend them to fulfill my part in bringing Peace to our planet. Join me and we are closer to Peace on Earth.

Changing our minds requires that we change the way we see things. This change is from ego perception to Vision. We also must consciously choose to deny errors in our thinking, and affirm Truth. I explain these changes in the next two chapters, "Perceiving and Seeing," and "Denying and Affirming."

14

PERCEIVING AND SEEING

In this chapter I share the transforming of thought from perceiving to seeing truly. **Perception is every thought we make about ourselves, others, and the world while we view our life with no Greater Being. Vision is our corrected view. We live the results of our seeing. Therefore, we choose our results in choosing how we see.** We were created to know Love. Everything else is ours to correct.

A couple years ago I was wondering whether I wanted to write a book or not. A student asked me a wise question, "What needs to come to completion for you in writing a book?" While I wrote down her question to contemplate the answer, I heard a flip inner response, "Nothing, I'm just fine as I am." I look back now and see the humor in that inner response. It could only have come from the ego voice that wanted to avoid seeing and feeling, for the process of writing has been a process of bringing one fear thought after another to awareness for completion.

This chapter is no exception. And, if you believe like I used to that authors write a book from front to back, that is not always true. With most of *Sharing the Course* completed, I realized I omitted this important point. Realizing this was also realizing I had another thought to bring to completion. I knew that in clearly discerning the difference between perceiving and seeing for you, I would also clear my error. This is how I made a correction.

Before teaching a class on the other side of our city I stopped for a salad. As I was leaving the restaurant I bought a piece of cheesecake to eat after class. Upon returning home I ate the whole piece while sharing the delight of my day with my husband. Before finishing the cheesecake I was nauseated, finished eating it anyway, and went to bed feeling sick and miserable. The voice that said, "You should know better," was no consolation.

The next day I experienced inner turmoil and my mind searched for someone or something to blame. That evening we had a group meeting in which we did Practice Exercise No. 57, "SEE ME." I was not able to identify a feeling or complete the exercise. The day after that I went through hours of mental confusion and disorder. I even felt disoriented and needed to remember the month and if I had paid bills that were due. As the day went on I began to remember eating the cheesecake and felt shame. I didn't even want to admit to myself that I had once again poisoned myself. I realized I poisoned myself in *deciding* to eat it. This took me to lower thought. And then, with conviction I set out to solve the problem once and for all.

I decided to look *with willingness to truly see* what was going on with me. To *ask* for increased awareness is to pray. These thoughts came to my awareness in answer to my prayer. Over Thanksgiving I spent a delightful two days at Nemacolin Woodlands, a resort in southern Pennsylvania. I felt so good about the way I was treated that I wrote to the owner saying, "I know my preciousness from the way you treated me." For three days after this I lived with the glow from this brief vacation, feeling the sweetness of life. People even told me I looked sweet. I sensed I was living with grace. And then I ate the cheesecake.

Note that I held the higher thought (that Life itself is sweet) for three days, therein *asking* for that to be true for me now. My ego became threatened of dying out and tempted me to darkness with cheesecake. I bought the idea and gave up delight. I have had enough of these "cheesecake scenes" in my life to know they serve the ego, keep me asleep, unaware, guilty, hating, and resenting.

As I thought back I realized other things. The day after returning from vacation we had a group meeting in which we were preparing for Christmas. Our Practice Exercise was to identify a feeling that would help us know what urges were being born in us. Though I knew that what was birthing in me and would come to fruition in the next year was being an author, I didn't mention it at the next group meetings. (This was the first group doing Exercise No. 57 and since I teach four classes a week, I do each exercise four times.)

I was aware of a nagging fear of gaining weight. It was an old fear that I had not felt for a long time. Prayer brings new information, and I realized that the real fear was *fear of delight*. For me, being delighted as a child was not safe, and my ego solution was to eat sweets. Substituting desserts for delight was what set up weight gain and the fear of gaining weight. I had accepted

112

"heaviness" as safer than "lightness." I could then see that if I resolved the *fear of delight* I would not need to be concerned about gaining weight.

I gave attention to my thoughts for further awareness on the "delight" issue, and realized my mind was preoccupied with resentment about Christmas. I had begun dwelling on my need to make every family member happy. That set up hopelessness, of course.

I spent the next two days resisting rereading references on perception and Vision in *A Course in Miracles,* and resisting writing. Working on this chapter I told myself that if I reveal myself, people won't like me. I told myself my book was no good. I began to hate the book and hate myself. I felt trapped for I knew that the only way I could be true to myself was to teach as I always have, which is to give examples from my own healing. Being truthful has delighted people.

Then I had a dream in which I woke to find a shiny silver ring on my finger. It had an angel etched on it and the word, "seraph." In researching this I found it is singular for "seraphim" associated with the Presence of God. Seraphim are guardians of the divine throne. In this dream my immediate delight turned to fear as I believed I had stolen the ring while asleep. Obviously I believed I was not entitled to the holy gift of delight associated with knowing the Presence of God.

I also looked up the word "delight" in the dictionary. It means to take joy, to rejoice in the fulfillment of a desire, and to feel grateful. I reflected back. My first visit to this same Nemacolin Woodlands was in May of that year after having been called to go apart to listen for guidance. It was then that I was told the time was right for writing this book and was given its title. I was truly delighted with myself when I returned only six months later knowing the book was written and the content editing nearly completed.

I share this story to illustrate the dynamics between ego perception, and Vision. Perception is every thought we make about ourselves, others, and the world while we view our life with no Greater Being. My mother was not free to receive my delight, and I had decided delight itself was not a safe expression. Our struggle is to awaken and "see." What we always need to see is that we are safe to be who we truly are, Children of God. All else is error and is ours to correct on our spiritual journey.

The misperception that I am not delightful, that I am not sweet, that I am not safe to experience these natural qualities in myself, leads me to choose sweets in an effort to make true what is already the Truth. In truth, I am a delightful Being and so are you. Join me.

The first step is willingness to acknowledge that unhappiness in any form comes from holding errors in mind, which are illusions rather than Vision. Vision, which comes from the Mind of God, is always reaching to us. We put a lot of energy into blinding ourselves to it. Vision is truth which is there for us to see and all we need to do is acknowledge it. Instead, we look for reasons to fear and reconvince ourselves by finding things all around us that prove we are right to fear.

Perception (hell) is the world we make as we stay preoccupied with the past, remembering no Love. We want to not see so we do not feel the separation we set up in shifting thought to darkness, devoid of Light. We believe we are separated from Love, we perceive ourselves as unworthy of it. **Vision (Heaven) is the world God created which we only know in remembering the presence of Love.** When willing to see truly, we know there is no separation and live in grace receiving all the gifts that Life has for us.

Having recognized what is behind my justifying eating of sweets and fear of gaining weight, I use any thoughts about either as clues to ego perception. I look for beliefs that declare I am unsafe to experience delight as an author, and change them. Just as I was delighted to know my preciousness by the way I was treated at Nemacolin Woodlands, I now know my preciousness by the way I treat myself.

Changing our minds requires shifting from listening to the voice of the ego to listening to that of the Holy Spirit. We undo what never was true. I list the characteristics of each way of seeing to assist us in recognizing our errors, and their corrections.

PERCEPTION	VISION
Serving ego - hell	Serving God - Heaven
Anti-Life/Anti-God	Power to heal
Guide is ego	Guide is Holy Spirit
Author is ego	Author is God
The world I make	The world God created
Identity I choose	Beloved Child of God
Incomplete past	Complete present
Preoccupied with past	Present
Remember no Love	Remember God
Remember only separation	Remember union

Want to not feel separation and terror	Acknowledge union and feel good
Fear seeing/feeling	Willing to see/feel
Value not seeing	Value seeing and healing
Value illusions	See truth, fear disappears
Add something not there	Accept reality
Not see all that is there	Not deceived
Give illusions reality	Know oneness with God
Blind to maintain illusions	Shares Mind of God
Live results of illusions	Live miraculously
Cost is limitation	Gift is expansion
See reasons for fear	See reasons for Peace
Don't know afraid of Love	Desire Love
Try to get Love	Extend Love
Interpretation brings guilt	Interpretation brings forgiveness
Condemn self	Love self
Hold grievances	Accept miracles
Justify attack	Protect preciousness
Want revenge	Want Peace
Want the problem	Want the answer
Don't see real problem	Understand
Diminishing self-worth (See less and less Love)	Define self in greater reality (See more and more Love)
Idols to *try to get* sweetness	Give sweetness
Defend, cannot receive	Receive sweetness
Hopeless	Hopeful
Private hell - sacrifice, loss, deprived, guilty	Share gentleness, kindness, peacefulness, Joy
Accept suffering	Awaken to Grace
Asking for what hurts	Asking for what heals
Horizontal axis	Vertical axis
See Spirit as threat	See Spirit as guide to salvation
Block knowledge of Joy	Know Joy
Believe all alone	One with God
Not whole, feel needy	Extend holiness
Project pain	Extend Loving thought
Special relationships	Holy relationships
Idol substitutes for Love	No attraction to idols
Faith in idols	Faith in God/Sharing
Act on "shoulds"	True to self, bless others
Conceal desire to kill	Commitment to nurture
Fear dying	Love living

As we realize we have been under the influence of ego thinking, our next step is to take charge of our thinking. We do this by denying perceptions as true for us and affirming what is true. I address this next.

15

DENYING AND AFFIRMING

In this chapter I share how to redirect thoughts that we once misdirected. **We are meant to use our mind aligned *with* the energy of Life so that our thoughts expand our experience of life.** Thoughts aligned with Spirit know the presence of Love, receive Life energy and allow us to grow. Meanwhile, ego thoughts distort energy of Spirit. In ego perception, we declare the absence of Love and separation from God. In our resistance to seeing truly, we stay stuck in self-defeating patterns. All such use of thought is misuse and fosters destruction.

To deny is to declare not true and to affirm is to declare as true. We are denying or affirming our connection with God/Love with every thought. In perception, we deny the presence of Love and affirm its absence. This is known as defense. We make this choice unknowingly. In Vision, we affirm the presence of Love and deny its absence. This is known as correction. We make this choice knowingly.

To affirm is to make firm in our mind. Every time we say the words, "I am" we are affirming or stating something as true for ourselves and denying its opposite. Our subconscious mind is such that it believes whatever we *consistently* say about ourselves, others, and our world. When we use denial as a defense, and choose perception, we set a belief in mind which we may not reconsider for many years. Therefore, our subconscious mind continues to create results from what we declare defensively even though we don't remember that we chose to defend.

With our very first thought in the morning we set the tone for our day. Do you begin your day by scanning your mind

117

to pick up on worries and scares of the day before? Or, do you awaken speaking and hearing words that encourage you to grow? We are given the freedom to reconsider at every moment and correct the choice we make.

Having no ability of its own to discern or decide against harmfulness, our subconscious simply creates what we declare as true in our perception, **Worry is imagining the worst and therefore setting up the very conditions we most fear. A continuous practice of refusing to fill our mind with worry allows space for Higher Thought.** A continuous practice of affirmative thinking gives us a supply of nourishment. Every time we affirm Love's presence we prepare our mind to welcome it.

In the previous chapter I shared my process of awakening from a denial I used as a defense. Without remembering that I had done so, I denied my natural delight when I was not received with Love. Without delight, life isn't sweet. So I also chose a substitute, sweet desserts. This idol set up the fear of gaining weight which masked the true fear, that of expressing delight. While I then feared rejection associated with being overweight, this rejection was aimed at my false ego expression, not my true delightful tender self. At the level of perception, I believed I was saving myself by hiding myself.

When I use the word "affirmation," I mean the conscious use of a statement of that we *do* **want to acknowledge and bring into our life experience.** Here are some examples based on information from the previous chapter. "I am a delightful Being." "I am safe to express my delight." "I (my book) am received with delight." "I am delighted by how I am received." "God is delighted with my willingness to convey this message to you."

In order to make a proper affirmative statement, we first need to gain understanding of what we want to bring into our life. As in my example, I first declared a willingness to see what I needed to see. When we habitually declare Love's absence and our perceptions as true for us, we do not at first believe what we choose to affirm.

After seeing what we need to affirm, we integrate our new beliefs into our Feeling Nature. This means we begin to *feel* them as true for us by repeating the statements many times, and in many ways. As we repeat them, we also change the pictures we hold in our mind. Pictures we use to remember Love's absence must give way to pictures in which we see Love's presence. These corrected pictures allow us to know we are safe to give and receive what we once denied.

118

Fear thinking holds images of destruction. **Love thinking holds images of safe fulfillment of desired outcomes.** At the point that we accept truth instead of perception, our energy shifts. That which we have been repelling is now attracted to us.

Since the term "denial" is used both to indicate a defensive move, and to indicate the correction of that move, the term may be confusing. The following contrasts denial as defense and denial as correction.

DENIAL AS DEFENSE	DENIAL AS CORRECTION
Concealing device	Corrective device
Sets up perception, deception, illusion	Allows for Vision, Truth, clarity
Decision to forget	Decision to remember
Directs thought to confusion	Directs thought to awareness
Denial of knowledge	Denial of error
View self as guilty	View self as innocent
Isolated and alone	Wholeness and Oneness
Darkness	Light
Littleness	Magnitude
Disruption of Life flow	Communication and healing

Consciously used as a tool, denial is the correction of ego errors and affirmation of truth which brings miracles. A typical denial statement used to correct errors is, "I no longer need to believe _____." This means I now longer need to believe that the ego thought I was holding will save me or bring me desired Love.

For example, I decided as a young one that the way to make sure that I would be loved was to never say what I wanted. I believed at the time that this would please my parents and bring safety to me. Of course, as the years went by I didn't even know what I wanted, and my life became influenced more and more by what others demanded of me. I ended up only knowing what I didn't want others to do to me.

I began reversing this pattern by correcting my thinking. I consciously used denial statements.

119

"I no longer need to believe that I keep myself safe
by not knowing what I want."
"I no longer need to believe that I keep myself safe
by not saying what I want."

I followed these with affirmations.

"I am safe to know what I want."
"I am safe to say what I want."

At first, I didn't know what I wanted. I made an exercise of writing a want list. I included things I wanted to have, do, and be. (See Practice Exercise No. 36. I included this among the Practice Exercises because sharing in a group helps overcome defensive denial of our hearts' desires.)

When I first began realizing what I wanted, I was still unaware that I, too, was demanding of others. I would state a want, and expect someone else to act on it to fulfill me. I was wanting the other to change in a way that I was still too fearful to change. There were more steps to take. **I needed to see myself safely having, being, or expressing what I had denied.** This meant that I needed to consciously deny the old pictures of disaster that I held in my mind and replace them with pictures of safe outcomes.

The other side of expressing myself was to no longer go along with the pattern in which I automatically did what others demanded of me. Since I had adapted to an entire cultural pattern, this was a fearful process and required much courage. I had to see myself living through and safely reaching the other side as I reversed the direction of my refusal. I switched the pattern from refusing to know and express myself, to refusing to act based on external demands.

To this day I continue to awaken. My process is one of listening to the Voice that calls me to express as I am guided from inside rather than react to that which happens around me. Every step calls for a change of mind. Each change includes beliefs that I state in words, and the mental pictures that accompany them.

We grow by *seeing* more and more that the expressing of our true self *IS* the presence of God, or Spirit flowing through us. To bring a Peaceful existence onto earth, we realize that we must make the inner connection that brings us to Peace. Only then do we extend Peace rather than look with animosity on all that isn't Peace. We deny that we need to wait to get holy qualities from other people, and express them through ourselves. Then others reflect them back to us.

It is through the words, "I am," that we connect with God in our mind and heart and are guided truly. Therefore, in denying our separation and affirming our right to be guided by Spirit, we heal our separation from God. Since the Spirit of God is always lifeward, no harm is done by following inner guidance. Refusal to follow any other guidance corrects all misguidance of ego perception.

USING AFFIRMATIONS IN A GROUP SETTING

Here are some ways to use affirmations in group:

a. Going around the circle, one member of the group repeats the same affirmation to each person around the circle. They call each person by name, maintain eye contact, and state their affirmation. They continue around the circle until their energy shifts. This is accompanied by tears of release and Joy. There is also a sigh (the crisis is over). If I were going around the circle I might say, "Karen, *I* know what *I* want." I am sure that Karen would give a response like, "Yes, Nancy, you do." Then I would go to Kay and say, "Kay, I know what I want." I can see Kay smiling now. Her smile says, "Of course." I would continue on around the circle.

b. Do this process in reverse. Each member of the group takes their turn, calls the person's name, maintains eye contact, and states the affirmation using "You." "Judy, *you* know what *you* want." After many say this to her, she may have a shift of energy. This may be followed by Judy stating the affirmation as in "a." above.

c. Group members "gossip" among themselves while the person overhears the conversation in third person. "Judy knows what *she* wants." "Isn't it great that she knows what she wants."

Things to know in order to state affirmations properly include:

a. <u>Make a corrective denial statement first.</u> "I no longer need to believe (the old belief, perhaps that eating sweets brings sweetness to my Life)."

b. <u>State the new belief as true now.</u> (Perhaps, "I nourish myself with sweet thoughts." "My life feels sweet." "I express delight.")

c. <u>Keep statements short.</u> Split them if necessary. ("I have all the courage I need and I approach job interviews with confidence" easily splits into "I am courageous," and "I am confident at job interviews.")

d. <u>Vividly picture the positive statement as true for you to evoke feelings that accompany the new message.</u>

e. <u>It is best to *not* use negatives in an affirmation.</u> Consider the following: "I will not wet my bed." "I will not eat ice cream at bedtime." In both cases, the mental picture called out is of that which you do not want. Therefore, while you may believe you are saying you will not do these things, you have instructed your subconscious to create them by giving it the picture. It is more powerful to say, "I choose to have a dry bed." "I eat fresh fruit at bedtime." Now your subconscious has pictures of a dry bed and fresh fruit.

f. <u>Watch for words that include subtle denial.</u> Example, "I can have a relationship that nurtures me." "Can" is the word of denial. Just because we "can" have something doesn't mean we will or do. Omit the word and hold an image of your being safe in a relationship. State, "I have nurturing relationships."

g. <u>Eliminate modifiers as "more" or "pretty."</u> Instead of "I am more peaceful," say "I am peaceful." Instead of "I have a pretty good salary," say "I have a good salary."

h. <u>The word "will" can be very powerful and can also be used by the ego.</u> "I am willing to stop all self-criticism." "I am willing to Love myself." Used as statements to reverse our intent from willfulness to willingness, these are powerful statements. They would be followed by, "I speak lovingly to myself." "I Love myself." Note how fear sneaks in to make sure things always stay in the future as in these examples: "I will have an intimate relationship." "I will find the right career for me." By seeing them in the future, our subconscious finds ways to keep them in our future. Correct these to something like: "I am intimate in relationships." "I enjoy my true expression."

i. We are always doing what we are doing because one way or another we believe it will keep us safe. This is true no matter how destructive our behavior may be. Therefore, to do the opposite seems unsafe, to our ego, of course. For this reason, I like to <u>add the phrase, "and I am safe," after any affirmative statement.</u> "I say what I want and I am safe." "My life is sweet and I am safe." "I am intimate in relationships and I am safe."

The old saying, "Things are worst just before the dawn" is true when we are doing affirmations. The more safe we feel in our true self, the more unsafe our ego will become. The increase of resistance is a sign of our effectiveness. And we need to be even more persistent to continue affirming. Ego thoughts cannot persist if we choose to give energy to affirming truth, and not to them.

There are many ways to use affirmations in spiritual growth. We can think them, say them, write them, sing them, dance them, draw them, etc. The important thing is continuing until our energy shifts from resisting our Good to receiving our Good. As you go through your day, look for things that confirm your affirmation. Do not *dwell* on anything else. Know that any hounding thought is coming from ego resistance. See it as informing you of what you need to consciously deny or thought-stop.

Denise, a member of one of my groups, really means business with her affirmation process. She sits in front of a mirror and plays the audio tape, *"Feeling Fine Affirmations"* by Louise Hay. As Louise states affirmations with the "you" voice, Denise repeats them speaking as her grown up self to her feeling child in the mirror. When Louise speaks with the "I" voice, Denise repeats and hears the child's response to her. Louise Hay and Sondra Ray are both excellent author resources for affirmations.

PART IV

Meeting in Groups

16

WHY MEET IN A GROUP?

In this chapter I give you a model of a group purpose and share the benefits I see in being "On Purpose." **Those of us who have allowed ourselves to be truly honest know that we are lonely no matter how many people surround us.** Rather than lament our loneliness, we need to learn to be in community. At the Soul level, our urge is to join and share, and only fear has separated us. All meaning in Life lies in sharing.

I met with five others on October 2, 1988 to decide whether we would start a group to study *A Course in Miracles*. We first defined our purpose as individuals and then as a group.

My purpose was to:

    a. bring together all my skills in one expression, and,

    b. Teach Love to all who would seek Love with me and be open to receive.

The group purpose was to:

    a. multiply the power of healing Love by gathering together in Love.

    b. allow this energy to dissolve and release fear.

    c. learn under guidance of *A Course in Miracles*, from wisdom through me as leader, and from others within the group.

    d. heighten discernment and empower choice.

I am the only member of the original group that stayed devoted to my purpose in the group setting. More than one hundred fifty people have attended group since then as regular members and guests. We did not have instant happiness. Trust grew slowly. There was a definite period of shifting when people began to meet outside of group in a way that expanded energy of the group rather than being divisive. Typically someone would say, "I'm going to _____, would anyone like to go with me?"

Groups of all sizes began doing things together. Everyone was included and we all gained from opportunities offered by others. No one needed to be without companions when they wanted them.

We began to celebrate each other. We became community. We became the Loving family for which we all longed. A most wonderful aspect of our community has been its openness to integrate new students. Our attitude is one of welcoming the unique gifts that each person brings to us. Our desire to expand our Loving circle has prompted some members to become leaders themselves.

Currently, I have set a limit for myself of forty regular students who meet in groups of ten. I repeat each lesson four times a week which allows students to make up a class if they are unable to attend their assigned group. We meet throughout the year with an occasional break. Each class is two hours, either 7:00 P.M. to 9:00 P.M. or 10:00 A.M. to 12 Noon. I remember the days when people were so fearful that they watched the clock and ran out the door when the meeting was over. Things changed, of course. Students now hang around chatting and hugging, and my husband and I joke about the last one out needing to lock up.

Here are some things I've learned about the value of meeting in a group. **Our life issue is always one of feeling separated from Love.** The process of group itself gives us a sense of union and wholeness which is holiness. This comes from joining the circle, singing together, rocking together, and sharing experiences which have a continuity encouraged by homework. Our ego intent to separate is reinforced by our whole society. We need some place where we can gather to experience Love in action, often for the first time.

We all want to be happy yet we follow laws that separate us. **A group dedicated to joining gives us permission and support to live by Laws which govern joining.** Since these are the opposite of those we have learned, group support becomes essential to accepting the new way.

To illustrate the pervasiveness of thinking that separates, I use an example from my life right now. As I write this book I hear my ego voice telling me I ought to be using more religious terms. It says, "People won't believe you are writing about *A Course in Miracles* if you don't use the language in the Course." I have learned from experience that we can only apply a message when we understand it, and most of us do not understand holy words well enough to live them. So I continue to use terms everyone can understand. The voice that remembers "church" says I am not doing it right. It says, "You ought to spend all your group time reading and talking about *A Course in Miracles*." This voice denies that applying the message in order to join is what the Course is all about.

My whole life experience has shown me that we can read holy books and never live the lessons. Though we live the holy message in my groups with miraculous results, I still hear the voice that tells me others will make me wrong if they find out how little time we spend reading from the book. To keep me true to my recent learnings and not fall back to old ways, I remember how group members have transformed their lives by understanding the holy message given them in clear, simple language which allows them to immediately apply what they hear. This focus allows me to stay true to my new learnings which support joining.

Spiritual Truths are very difficult to comprehend and put into practice because they go against all that we have learned. We must remember that in living what we learned in the past we still feel unhappy, deprived, lonely, anxious, angry, and sick. **Sometimes when things aren't working for us we need to do just the opposite.** It takes time for new thoughts to ripen. It also takes extended practice to transform our ways.

Group is a place where we can explore and practice being truthful and without pretense. I purposely do not have anyone introduce themselves with any social roles or factors. Each new person coming into group is invited to ask a question of other members, and answer it for them first. The most often asked question is, "What brought you to group?" We all reveal our true selves as we answer this and tell how we have met our needs within group.

Groups are ongoing and provide us a continuing opportunity to practice and strengthen our skills. We use our highest qualities here so we build our ability to express them. **Soon we find ourselves "slipping" and giving Loving responses elsewhere.** We gain support for our newly emerging energies before going out into the "cruel" world. We begin to impress the world with Love instead of the world impressing us with fear.

In a group dedicated to sharing Love, we have others who believe in us and reinforce our ability to do well in Life rather than support our fears of failing. Those who have been part of our growing know our goals and encourage us. They receive us with Love as we expand. We learn to Love ourselves by being Loved. **We learn courage by being encouraged.**

Society teaches us to prepare for instantaneous illness, disaster, law suits, and death. **We must make a deliberate choice to cultivate our faith and initiate Goodness rather than respond to Life with fear.** Proper group experiences affirm our innate Goodness and the preciousness of our lives. This multiplies our Goodness. It is a fact of life that because we are defended we do not see ourselves truly. We will begin to see ego patterns in others first. This is a critical point in the learning process. If we judge what we see in others, we stay in our own state of denial about ourselves. To truly learn is to see how each of us carries out the same pattern we see in anyone else.

In group we see others go through healing processes and learn to not fear healing. Remember, our greatest fear is of opening to Love. We closed because we were totally convinced that there was no Love for us. While we hold that belief we find plenty of "proof" in our daily life. In group we begin to recognize our own defeating beliefs as we hear others express theirs. As we change our thinking, we become just as aware of wonderful things we were ignoring and denying.

Learning to name things is essential to growth and change. Many of us have been subject to cruelties all our lives that no one has ever named. Until they are named we cannot heal them. I remember a time when I was in so much emotional pain that I took a few days to go off alone and journal. I went to the home of a friend. One morning she made the simple comment, "You seem so troubled." A voice in me got very excited and began saying over and over, "Yes, I am troubled." Then the dam broke and I wrote for hours on what was troubling me. **Cruelties we experience on a daily basis are so ingrained in social patterns, so justified within ego thinking patterns, that we live with violence disguised as utopia.**

As an example, nothing is more pervasive right now than surgery to alter the appearances of bodies. It is an idol. It plays into ego thinking. "If only I change my physical form I will *get* the Love I long to *get*." It is violence. I have lived as a woman, with women, and watched women. Because we believed that our *trying to get* Love, is Love, we have lived without Love that would nurture our Life. In denying the most basic need of Life, nurturing, we have had our wombs removed, our ovaries, our breasts. We are now having our breasts altered in such ways that we will be denied sexual pleasure that comes from touch to our nipples. We are being denied the bonding experience of nursing our own babies. We are having facial surgery that leaves us unable to feel a touch to our faces.

We could add eating disorders and obsessive body building as idols. They, too, seek to alter the body as a way of *trying to get* Love. It is Love we want, not mutilation, starvation, or masochism. Spiritual maturity, not denial, brings Love and youthfulness. Growing spiritually requires attention to our Souls, not just our bodies. May God help us see and properly name these idols.

In group we use repetition to reverse our investments in fear thinking. We read and reread the same ideas from *A Course in Miracles*. We speak higher words, share higher thoughts, sing affirmations and build these ideas into our Souls. Only these activate our heart center and invite every cell in our body to explode with light like an acorn bursting to become an oak.

We repeat Loving messages we give to others, for they do not believe us at first. We use repetition to reverse our investment in fear thinking just as we used repetition to build it. Commercial advertisers know just how many times to repeat a message to convince our subconscious that we have to have their product. If I need to be convinced this way, I am sure that they are hoping to sell me on the belief that their product will bring me Love and Happiness. These, too, are idols. The process is the same, however, and we need to become aware of what we already have had impressed on our subconscious, and what we choose to impress on our subconscious. We experience the results of our choices.

We are impressed by more than words. The energy of each person vibrates out like a tuning fork and we all tend to tune to it. When we truly realize this, we will select our "company" wisely. In an effective group our strengths vibrate. One gentle person in a group activates gentleness in all. One creative thinker inspires all to think creatively. One courageous person gives hope to all that they, too, can overcome fear. For all this, we give thanks.

Happiness comes from meeting our spiritual need to join. We may first need to acknowledge that we have never known Love. This includes awakening to See that all we have given for years was really our attempt to *get* and what we received was someone else's attempt to *get*. With this realization comes despair. When clients or students morosely report to me that they are in despair, I excitedly respond "Great!" This usually shocks them. Then I explain that despair is our point of crossing over from unhappiness to happiness. It is the ego that despairs of ever finding happiness. Then we are ready for a new way.

If we think of our body as a cross, our arms reach out on a horizontal axis. This represents our attempt to *get* Love from other people under ego rule. Here, each person functions as half a person and feels justified in doing anything to *get* the other to function as their other half. This includes killing oneself or the other in its most extreme manipulation. When we shift focus to the vertical axis on the cross, we connect our own Thinking Nature with our Feeling Nature. Only then is energy free to flow through us from Heaven to Earth.

A Course in Miracles **invites us to declare our true identity, our right relationship with God, our holy nature. "I am as God created me."** I am innocent and Beloved. This is our starting point which declares who we are on the vertical axis. The horizontal axis is all I made with my ego thinking, separated from any realization of God's presence.

In Twelve Step programs, one begins by declaring one's identity on the horizontal axis, and the powerlessness that accompanies this. The idol or addiction used to *try* to save oneself is named. The program also asks participants to then acknowledge a Power greater than themselves that restores them to sanity. **Everything in our horizontal axis identity is insane. It is devoid of Love. We awaken to Love which is the vertical axis. When we realize our past impression of Love is an illusion, being in a Loving group affirms the truth that Love does exist. We also remember that we desire it and that it is a gift to us available through following the Law of Being.**

In summary, when our purpose as an individual and the purpose of our group are one, every need we personally meet enhances our group and every group need we fulfill enhances ourselves. Effective group experiences live in our minds and allow us to make new decisions, go new ways, and experience new results in our lives. **It is our most precious gifts that we have repressed and kept hidden to preserve them from violence. In a safe place we birth and nurture them.**

Each person in the group graces everyone. I remember attending a group therapy session many years ago where we set goals. The leader asked me how I would know when I reached my goal. Seemingly from nowhere a voice declared, "My presence will grace your life." My life was anything but graceful at the time. I say with conviction now that my presence graces your life. There is no greater gift I would choose to give to you.

132

17

WHERE TO FIND A GROUP

In this chapter I share places where you can find people who share your interest. Whether you choose to start your own group or join an existing group, I am sure you will appreciate knowing about other groups.

Perhaps you have led groups of various kinds and have already gained skill in leadership. Now you are learning about *A Course in Miracles*. You may then choose to use your skills with *A Course in Miracles* as a new focus like I did. This book is full of ideas to help you. If you are looking for a group led by someone else, the following places are sources of information for you.

Miracle Distribution Center, 1141 East Ash Avenue, Fullerton, CA, 92631, (714)738-8380, offers a full range of services for students of *A Course in Miracles*. This includes a newsletter, "The Holy Encounter." For finding a study group, they offer national and international group listings. Call or write to them and they will inform you of groups that meet in your area. The Center also offers a free catalog of books and tapes related to the Course and a brochure of spiritual counseling services available. They have an 800 number for placing credit card orders only, (800)359-2246.

Foundation for Inner Peace holds the copyright to *A Course in Miracles*. They also have materials related to the Course available for purchase. Contact them at P.O. Box 1104, Glen Ellen, CA, 95442, (707)939-0200.

Churches most likely to have Course study groups are Unity, and United Church of Religious Science. You will find them listed in your local phone books. For area listings, contact Unity School of Christianity, Unity Village, MO, 64065, (816)524-3550, and United Church of Religious Science, 3251 West 6th Street, P.O. Box 75127, Los Angeles, CA, 90075.

Word of mouth has carried *A Course in Miracles* around the world. All of my students found me that way. People who attend classes or workshops on any kind of personal growth may know a contact person for you. This includes Twelve Step programs, and Gestalt or Transactional Analysis institutes. Those interested in Native American practices often realize their shared goal with the Course.

Another source would be a metaphysical bookstore or a store with a metaphysical section. Libraries often know of groups meeting in their community. Food cooperatives often have bulletin boards used for connecting people with similar interests. If there are no notices posted by people looking for you, post a notice to look for them!

Here are a couple of suggestions from one of my students. Keep your eyes open for very happy, loving, fun, sparkly-eyed people who are not drinking or taking drugs to *try* to have fun and feel wonderful. Ask them their secret. Pick the most mellow radio station in your town, the one that plays quiet, peaceful, soothing music. Call in and ask the disc jockey to help you find a Course in Miracles group by asking listeners to phone in if they know of a group.

You may be the one who is called to start a group. In the next chapter I tell you how to establish a safe space to hold a group meeting.

18

CREATING A SACRED SPACE

In this chapter I share guidelines for creating a space which supports remembering our spiritual connection. Usually we are so defended by the time we reach adulthood that it takes some life event to hurt us deeply before we surrender to our tenderness. Until then we believe our walls of defense are necessary to tough out life while we picture ourselves living in a space with no comforter. We harden our bodies and store our tears. We forget who we are as tender, innocent Beings, deserving only help to grow. In a sacred space we remember our true identity. A sacred space is a safe place to grow. To grow is to relax our bodies, feel our feelings, cry our tears, and expand our lives.

CHARACTERISTICS OF A SACRED SPACE

A sacred space is where we risk seeing that we chose to hide ourselves and *that* is why we do not have the Love we need now. Our defenses are all disruptions of our connection with Life/God. We carry out these disruptions inside ourselves, and in relationships with others. Every kind of disruption will show up in a group setting. Our ego choice is to continue disrupting and blaming. Each disruption is a point of learning where we have an opportunity to reclaim those aspects of ourselves which have not as yet received Love and affection.

A sacred space is where we are willing to see our own ways of disrupting and risk letting them go. It is a space where we are willing to see that we blame, and how we blame others. We learn to tend our precious Feeling Nature that deeply longs to know our own comforting presence. It is where we learn that in giving and receiving, no one loses. It is where we welcome true expressions from others and learn that our contributions are valuable to them.

All present in a sacred space must be there with the intent to grow. This means that each of us is willing to feel our

135

feelings rather than disrupt their healing process. Compassion comes from having felt that fresh little flower feeling that accompanies our defensive wall being shattered by some life event. **In knowing our own tenderness, we naturally choose to respond gently and kindly to others.**

Tender expression is so different from our usual way of living in which we wear masks, act, compete, and *try* to change others without looking at ourselves. We come to a sacred space to give by listening, and to express harmlessly with reverence for the Life of every individual. We all grow at our own level and on our own time schedule. With persistence we transform our patterns of disrupting and blaming. We join the Will of God which supports all Life. Then we truly know we Belong.

A sacred space provides structure for each of us to tend our own growing. Here, we make no one wrong. Disagreeing and arguing only serve to further convince us that Love is not available. These patterns further convince us that we need to keep our precious selves hidden.

Openings and Practice Exercises in *Sharing the Course* provide abundant opportunities to share in ways that make no one wrong. Through the continuous experience of being safe, we grow to trust that Love is there for us and overcome constraints imposed on us from both outside and inside ourselves. Our growth reflects that we have given and received Love.

ENVIRONMENT

Because we do not open emotionally until we feel physically safe, we must first make the environment comfortable. The group must know that someone is tending the space. For example, if water is boiling on a stove, someone needs to be responsible for turning off the flame. This may or may not be the leader of the group. I both teach in my home where I tend the space, and I teach at the home of another where she tends the space. Ultimately, as leader, I pay attention to all needs for safety of the group.

Physical comfort is fostered by a place that is visually aesthetic. Other physical comforts include proper seating, lighting, heat and ventilation, and a bathroom nearby.

People need to know ahead of time what the rules are for using the space. I have a written handout called "Rules and Courtesies for Attending ACIM" which I give out periodically. For example, my classroom tables jiggle easily and beverages spill.

My rule is to place cups on napkins. I also ask for a courtesy. If they are fortunate enough to end up with a dry napkin, they are to leave it on the table for someone else to use. This is to conserve paper and eliminate waste. People need to know where bathrooms are located and appreciate an invitation to meet their own needs in classes that do not take breaks.

There really is no separation between physical needs and emotional needs. This is clear when we consider the size of group and seating arrangement. A circle allows everyone to be seen and feel included. A space that is too large feels separating. A space that is too confining calls us to put walls up and that is equally separating.

For emotional comfort, an ideal group size is six to ten people. When a group is smaller than this we may feel unsafe to share. Even in sacred space there is safety in numbers! If there are more than ten, it doesn't feel emotionally safe to feel young and tender. It is like a mother goose with too many goslings. The quieter and more hesitant ones in group may get left behind or hurt.

To create a sacred space, it is essential to minimize interruptions from the environment. This includes ringing phones, door bells, beepers, chiming watches, and children. I have learned over the years that meetings of this nature cannot be held where there are young children in the home whose parents participate in group. If you want to see how persistent and ingenious human survival mechanisms are at getting attention, just watch a child whose parents have turned their attention inward or elsewhere!

IDOLS

Idols are all the things we do defensively to keep ourselves from feeling when we believe Love is not present for us. The *intent* in using any idol is to not feel terror of separation. The *result* of using any idol *is* separation and denial of the terror that accompanies it. Idols choose death rather than Life. By their nature, idols keep us from seeing Truth, so we do not see them for what they are. We always choose an idol because we are afraid of Love and idols direct our energy against Love (anti-God). It is never the idol that we truly want. We want Love. We take a substitute which is to avoid feeling terror of its absence. Idols are the addictions that enslave us and keep us feeling unfulfilled as long as we believe there is no Love available to us.

For readings on idols, see Text p. 573-75/617-19, "Seek Not Outside Yourself"; Text p. 575-777/619-21, "The Anti-Christ"; Text p. 577-80/622-24, "The Forgiving Dream"; and Text p. 586-88/630-33, "Beyond All Idols."

The opposite of choosing an idol is choosing to share. Idols separate. Sharing joins. We share to accept Love and be happy. The choice to share is a conscious choice we make to undo earlier choices for idols.

Idols disrupt inwardly and outwardly. Idols oppose our own growth and seek to disrupt the growth of others. For example, I know that when I eat sugar (sucrose), I will also be in ego thinking and living out addictions which deny my tender feelings. Therefore sugar is an idol for me. When under the influence of sucrose, I don't want anyone to touch my tender feelings. I look serious, withdrawn, or fierce. This lets others know they are not safe to be tender around me. This is not what I really want, of course. I defeat myself every time I take this substitute and eat sugar when I want sweetness in my life. When I eat sugar I think ego thoughts. When I think ego thoughts I eat sugar. I can decide to stop either of these to reverse the process. **We release our idols to reclaim our tender selves and accept the Love we truly want.**

The leader of a sacred space sees to conditions necessary for growth. This means both providing what supports growth, and excluding what hampers the process. Recognizing idols, properly naming them, and setting up conditions to minimize them is a task of leading. Knowing what I know about sugar, I do not serve any sweets at a meeting where our intent is to reclaim our inner child. If anyone were to arrive with food to be used to avoid feeling, I would consider it my job to address the issue.

While safety requires a leader to name and not support disruption of feeling expression, it is equally true that every group member is responsible for choosing harmlessness. When a member is not willing to give up using an idol on group time, they are saying they do not want to give or receive Love. Therefore, they are not ready to be in the sacred space. While saying "You are not ready to be here" is hard to do, Love must say "No" to harm's way. Harm can come from within ourselves, within the space, or from outside the space. We monitor all of these to choose what is sacred.

Chemicals As Idols

For beverages, I provide water, sun brewed ice tea, or herb tea at my meetings. These do not alter natural expression. Many chemicals we use daily keep our bodies intended in ego ways. They deaden our feelings and indicate that we are not wanting to grow. While we are choosing to emotionally deaden our feelings, we may also drink caffeine as a stimulant. Caffeine will stimulate, and perhaps agitate, both of which will counteract some of the results of our depressing ourselves. Caffeine does not release our emotional restrictions or bring us to Joy.

While smoking would not be appropriate in a sacred space, there is more than the usual reason for this. Nicotine counteracts our body's response to anger. This means that blood vessels which usually expand when we "get hot under the collar" constrict with nicotine in our system. Nicotine does not eliminate or heal the anger, it only helps to hide it from our awareness which is what our ego wants. To heal, we need to listen to the anger of our inner child. That is the only way we find out what our little one is angry about and what we need to change to be safe and happy.

Alcohol masks fear, bringing a false sense of safety. Marijuana masks sadness, bringing a false sense of euphoria. All of these chemicals are idols which we think will save us. Use of chemicals interrupts sharing by deadening our feelings and inviting others to do likewise. Chemicals only harm and are sure signs that we aren't ready and willing to accept and Love our Feeling Nature.

Prescription drugs often serve the same purpose of deadening feelings. As long as we see no safe place to feel and be comforted, we continue with our idols. I choose to share with you as much as I can about creating a safe space, for **I have learned from my own experience that idols are no longer needed when we feel safe to share.**

Disruptions As Idols

Anything that disrupts group process needs to be considered as an idol. These disruptions include all the things we learned to do as children to get attention when we believed we weren't valued. They include competition, comparisons, cold silence, criticism, sulking, cutting up, and arguing to keep heat going where we anticipate no warmth. As we open to receive Loving attention that we truly desire, these give way to sharing.

To eliminate disruptions which are simply due to lack of information, be clear about procedures for creating your sacred space. Tell new students how long you believe it will take for them to get from where they are to your meeting place. Tell them what time to arrive and where to park. Tell all participants to arrive early to prepare beverages, give hugs, and be seated ready to start on time. Each person can help maintain order by being responsible about bringing their book, a notebook, and a pen.

Time structure must meet our internal sense of Divine Order for us to feel safe. This includes starting and ending at stated times. The leader has a time structure in mind and stays aware of this to see to fulfillment of the group's purpose. I call group time "sacred time" for we honor every level of our Being.

Recently I agreed to present a workshop at a church. At the time I was to begin, only one of the twenty-five registered participants was present. That challenged me! I decided to wait no more than five minutes. After delaying the start of the workshop by five minutes, I started a question around the circle of those present. By the time we finished that, all participants were present. Social time disregards feelings, and therefore Divine Order. Such disregard is separating.

When a group member does not show up, thoughts of other group members will be called to worry about them. So, my rule is that anyone who expects to miss will report to me ahead of time. This behavior is an idol like the many I have already addressed. It calls for fear energy from the group. Only someone who believes Love is not available would accept worry on the part of others as its substitute.

Money easily becomes an idol. I have known people to skip meetings to "save" money, refuse to pay what is due, and drop out owing money. I do my work to prepare for students. I also provide four opportunities a week for them to attend class. Therefore, my rule is that once they are a group member, payment is due whether they are present or not. I honor choices to "rest" for a week or vacation and send class notes so students can stay current with homework assignments.

The above rule is my rule for winter. In the summer I allow for everyone to expand and enjoy. Those who are free to come in the summer do so, and pay accordingly. My experience has been that stopping all disruptions, including abuse of money, is directly proportional to committing energy to sharing.

Bringing guests into a sacred space requires care. Entering a Loving space when we are not used to it can be very frightening. And, of course, this would call out disruptive behaviors. I have sought to eliminate as much of this as possible by seeing that the person has adequate information ahead of time. Guests are always informed that they must be willing to participate as a group member in Practice Exercises and not just observe our being open and tender. Students either pay the fee for their guests, or inform their guests of the fee.

Time Violations As Idols

It is essential to sacred space that meetings not be interrupted by late comers. Some years ago I belonged to a group in which two of the six were habitually late. I was privileged to have an experience with these women in which we all became truthful about time. I learned something valuable that day. One woman shared with us that she experienced separation anxiety whenever she left one place to go to another, so she would linger as long as possible and then rush to the next place. Of course, before our talk, she wasn't aware of the separation anxiety, only that she was always rushing and always late. Once aware of her pattern, she changed it. The other woman shared that she was always fearful that she would not be accepted where she was going so she waited as long as possible before going there. So always arriving when things were well under way, she never felt a part of things. Others in the group were irritated by her lateness and were not feeling kind toward her when she arrived.

Do these patterns sound familiar? Both women had found ways of defending which they believed would save them from the terror of feeling separated. **The result of defending is always to create the conditions we intend to avoid.**

A member consistently leaving before the completion of a meeting is equally disrupting. Their leaving interferes with the circle coming to completion. Usually when examined, their reason is one of fear also. **Proper naming of the behavior invites a higher response.**

I do not speak here of occasional lateness due to accidents or road construction on a freeway. Nor do I speak of the occasional time when someone needs to leave early. Such events that occur occasionally call out compassion whereas habitual abuse calls out anger. Habitual time violations, properly named, are

141

idols not to be tolerated. They must be seen for what they are - interruptions of the process of Love by fear.

A Course in Miracles says what isn't love is murder (Text p. 461/496). **Disruption is an invitation for everyone to go to their ego and separate from Love. Yes, it is Loving to stop harmfulness.** Love does not go along with and support that which is destructive. A skilled leader masters the art of being firm in not allowing ego disruptions while being gentle and kind to receive new Spirit that births when ego patterns are released. We have rules to assist in eliminating things that call us to our ego. Only then are we free to go the way of God.

I realize that I speak here from a high level of mastery of group leadership. I also work with a group that has been refined down from the masses. These are the committed ones willing to share. **I have told you the ideal, first of all, to let you know it is possible, and secondly, because I know that the closer you follow this model, the deeper your healing will be.**

SHARING

Clearly stated rules help shift energy from using idols to sharing. We stay hardened until we know we will be safe to express tenderly. When our environment is safe enough, we begin healing. **I follow a rule of no tape recording (audio or video) within a sacred space. With this rule we know our tender expressions do not go beyond the space where we feel safe to share them.**

Healing is accompanied by tears of release. Typically, new people in my groups spend two to three months crying a lot. Having Kleenex readily available says this is "normal." It is my preference to not hand Kleenex to someone who is crying. Doing this can interrupt and give them the message to stop crying and dry their tears. My rule is to encourage tears, and assist with tissues when someone begins to look or search for them.

I am sure you wonder how anyone could enjoy a place where despair is necessary to healing and tears are so plentiful. **It is only the ego that despairs as we share in a sacred space.** I tell people we are like a bottle of soap. We start putting clear water in and lots of soap bubbles spill out. Eventually, if we are persistent and patient, we will have a bottle full of clear water. Water represents our Feeling Nature. Clear water is Happiness. We must feel and release our pain in a space where we know a comforter. The group itself serves as a comforter.

Sharing requires Good Will toward others. This rule is usually called confidentiality, I prefer to call it Good Will. Littleness involves talking about other people in judgmental ways. ("Did you hear that Julie had another abortion!") Good Will says it is wonderful to share *ideas* learned at group. This includes processes and things learned from what is shared by others. Extending Good Will is how we Teach Love in the world. We do not "talk about" other people in ways that would further their identity as anything other than fully worthy of Love. When we know the difference between fear and Love, we talk about people sharing with others the miraculous changes we have witnessed, and in doing so we multiply everyone's Joy.

Our family members so often do not celebrate our growth because they are invested in ego patterns with us (special relationships), and they experience our shifts as threats. Instead of responding with Joy to our most courageous steps, they respond with fear calling us to return to the way they want us to be. They are not ready and willing to share with us.

Participating within a safe group setting gives us a feeling of belonging to and with something greater than ourselves that supports our life. The group becomes our family, our community. Those growing with us know our courage and welcome our changes. Successes inspire hope within the group. The group celebrates our changes.

Members of my groups have been "accused" of participating in a cult by those who know little about these groups. These "accusers" have received information that *A Course in Miracles* is something other than holy. I assure you that cults are based on fear and authority as control. **There is no better way to assure against cult activity than to learn to share feelings and develop inner Authority. The only way anyone can have power over us is for us to choose to stay deadened to our own feelings.** (See Chapter 20, Accepting True Authority, which contrasts authority as control and inner Authority.)

LEAVING GROUP

When the time comes for you to leave a group, there is a Loving way to do this. I ask group members to inform me ahead of time when they know they are leaving so I arrange time for the group to say their good-byes. Times of parting serve as opportunities to heal as well as everything we do in group. It takes us a long time to realize that we are important to those around us and to realize how much our behavior affects them. A time of proper parting is a time to hear of our importance to others. It is a time to give and receive gratitude and blessings as we continue our journey.

In my experience, most people do not leave group Lovingly. More frequently they just don't show up and leave people wondering what has happened to them. This way of leaving, as well as expressing anger at the leader or a group member and then not coming back, both set up unresolved "special relationships." They tie up energy at the ego level. Therefore, paradoxically, **people who leave non-Lovingly seek to tie themselves to the group with "unfinished business." It is a sure sign of other unresolved partings. For those who remain in group, the bind is released by forgiving.** This involves healing scenes in our own past when people disappeared uncaringly or hurtfully.

Leaving group Lovingly allows hearts to stay open and Love to be extended by all who have shared growing experiences in the sacred space.

19

STUDENTS SHARE

In this chapter I share impressions from students who have participated in group from four weeks to four years. When I invited my students to share their experiences in group with you in the form of a letter, their responses delighted me. These letters reflect initial fears and discomforts. Most meaningfully, they reflect the empowering effect of participation within a sacred space.

✻

Dear Reader,

I have been to four meetings. I am the newest member of the Community and I want Nancy's book to have the perspective of the beginning by someone still at the beginning.

The first night I parked at the school nearby. When I told Nancy that I had parked there because I was afraid and would leave if it became too much, Nancy smiled her soft smile and commented that most people were terrified when they first came and that I should feel free to park in the driveway if I wanted.

At my first meeting, I was the only one who cried. I appreciated the loving gentleness of those who reassured me that my tears were as welcome as my laughter. I appreciated the person who shared my dismay at the thought of all that stuff hanging off the end of my nose and not being aware of it. She also shared that Nancy and she had agreed that this was the worst part of crying. I appreciated the wastebasket Nancy put beside me so I didn't keep holding all that wet tissue.

In a short time, I've learned to "hate" mirror work and learned that this is normal. I've also learned that hate violates a Universal Law.

I've learned to hold hands (left hand on the bottom) and to do "the Scrunch" during closing. [She is referring to being the person caught in the middle when the group gets off rhythm where half of the group is swaying to the right and half to the left.] I'm just beginning to learn to look people in the eye, smile, and not become afraid when we are in our circle. Hopefully, soon I'll be able to find things in the ACIM book, remember everyone by name, and write my own affirmations.

I thank Nancy for this gift.

Kay T.

*

Dear Reader,

In the Spring of 1991 I made a pivotal decision in my life. A decision to be happy, a decision to put myself first in my life, a decision to take control of **my** life, which up until then just seemed like a series of things happening **to** me. It was then that I decided to divorce my husband of over 13 years. I made it through those difficult times with the help of a wide support group of friends and family, and also a deep seated belief that "things would be OK." I was, and still am, an eternal optimist - not believing I had a spiritual side at all. I now see this as the Basis of my Spiritual Self - the belief that a Higher Being gently guides me and watches over me. There is no need to *fear*.

In the Fall of 1991 a co-worker and good friend started ACIM. Every weekend at work I'd ask her, "So what was class about this week?" And she'd talk with great enthusiasm. I would listen mostly, because self-examination and groups of people scared me to death! Especially groups of people sharing, hugging, and crying together (who ever heard of such a thing!). My friend gave me Nancy Glende's card and lovingly encouraged me to try ACIM. That card stayed on my bulletin board from October until April. During that time, every other piece of information on that board came down except Nancy's card. And I thought, "Somebody up there wants me to call Nancy." And I did. So began the Miracle.

The tremendous changes I saw in my friend during those months were my impetus to desire change in my life. If she could be happy, so could I. If she could be so enlightened, so could I. If she could be at peace, so could I. If she could be such a positive light in this world, so could I.

Since I started in the Course In Miracles group, I've become all the above. Through the total acceptance of who I am by others in the group, and their never ending positive energies, the changes have been extraordinarily rapid. I understand my fears,

146

my inner child's needs. I don't ignore my feelings, fears, or needs anymore. I've learned that spirituality is not an intangible thing - it **is** me! It is my every word and deed. I pay attention to my life now. I make changes and decisions purposefully. I know how to forgive, and I don't need to place blame on others anymore. I have developed strong personal affirmations, which I repeat to myself every day - I see bold signs that I am truly internalizing these beliefs. What I need, I receive. The less I worry about money, the more I have! The more I believe I'm perfect just the way I am, the more I attract others to me. I see results every day, and others see the changes in me. Since I've joined the group, I've found that the group energies and Nancy's energies support me throughout the week ahead.

Good luck to you in your Spiritual Journey.

Katherine S.

✳

Dear Reader,

I have had some remarkable changes in my life since starting *A Course In Miracles.* I guess you could say I have had some miracles of my own.

I had been in therapy with various psychologists for five years, because of panic attacks and a fear of traveling alone in my car, especially on freeways, and had not made any progress. When I joined the Course In Miracles group in January, 1991, I was still plagued by some fears and panic attacks. I am happy to say I have not had a panic attack in over fifteen months, and I have been driving on the freeway for the past ten months without that fear that kept me chained to my own neighborhood.

Some other more subtle rewards have been the genuine friendships I have realized from the group members - most noticeably since the group retreat one month ago. The support and strength and love I received has been so helpful in my day to day life. Since I have learned to open to others and extend myself in a loving way, it has returned to me many times more.

I am thankful for being directed to the group and for guidance to go love's way when all I knew how to do was isolate and continue to operate out of what I now know was my ego state.

Lil W.

✳

Dear Reader,

The first course I ever had with Nancy was a course on anger that was offered in the evening at a local high school. I arrived late and angry, and stood around outside a while wondering if I should go in. I entered and stayed angry for about the first hour or so of the class. I mention this because the two greatest elements of my life - anger and a belief that I was not worthy - have diminished to such a great extent that they are now oddities in my life, whereas before these feelings were pervasive.

The weekly meetings with the Course In Miracles group have to a great extent replaced the private sessions I had with Nancy. (I do occasionally have private therapy sessions, and they are far less frequent than before. It is unusual for me to return about the same problem.)

When I first started with the Course In Miracles group, I found a lot of the things we did to be strange and uncomfortable for me. I often worried about the cost, and I used to dread when we sang together. I hated to look other people in the eye during the singing, and was always relieved when it was over. I used to dislike going to group. In the beginning, I would think how nice it would be to stay home, and more than a few times I called Nancy to tell here I wasn't coming, and ended up deciding to come anyways. I was late often, at least as often as I felt I could get away with it.

I used to rarely cry during the group talk - I felt very uncomfortable about crying, and if by chance I did cry one week, the next week I was terrified to even show up. I think one reason that I stuck to it was that I always felt better when I left than when I came in, though in the beginning not for very long. I used to really feel relief when we would have a break for a week or two, because then I didn't have to attend and tie up my evenings.

There was an intermediate stage that gradually evolved where the above changed for me. I began to look forward to the weekly meetings, and was usually on time. At this stage I remember dreading the few breaks we would have, because while I was feeling good when I left the meetings, in a week or two I was miserable again. I felt like a bad battery that couldn't hold a charge; if I didn't return weekly to get my dose, I would soon be back to zero. At this stage - after about a year or two, I found myself crying often, and was more comfortable sharing my feelings with others. When I first started many of the concepts that Nancy was talking about were a complete mystery to me. She would ask a simple question about something we had learned and I could never answer. I can't even count the number of times I just sat wondering. I was beginning to get a feel for some of the ideas, though I did not often try to integrate them into my life.

Where I am today, I find that my moods are quite even, so much so that even small disturbances stand out and I am moved to take care of them quickly. I have the tools and experience to resolve most of my problems, and many friends to turn to for wisdom. I do not cry so much in group at this point, unless I am healing something in my life, and my emotions do not relate to how long I have been away. In fact the breaks that we have are important times for me to grow and process on my own, and I look forward to them for that reason. My calmness and gentleness is greatly in evidence, and other people in the group trust me, and when beginners enter the group I am able to make the transition more comfortable for them.

Today I am eager and excited about the changes I have made in my life. I now see the things I want to manifest, instead of the blocks to fulfillment. I have reached a point where I now take for granted that I will come upon what I need easily. Over the last two years I have grown to become a leader in the group. Last year and this year I led the men's retreat, and many of the men and women in the group have come to me to ask suggestions concerning problems they are having. I wouldn't have predicted it four years ago - life was such a mystery to me then. It is a mystery to me still - the Divine Mystery, of which I am a part and with which I flow.

I see in the near future the fruiting of my years of patient effort in the art of stained glass. I have no doubt that I will establish myself as one of the premier studios in Cleveland, at least. My earliest ambitions were to be a writer, and I know that I will fulfill that dream too.

I am continually challenged by life, and my rewards for meeting that challenge are all around me and growing: an orderly home and life, peace of mind, a loving relationship with someone who supports by growth and whose growth I am supported by, and a circle of close friends who mirror to me the true beauty of myself, and are thus inspired to see and demonstrate their own beauty. This is an ideal setting: a circle of forgiveness, of permission, and of acceptance.

The group has grown and evolved too. I have seen great changes in many of the people in group. We have matured a great deal, and in the last year or so begun really reaching out to each other. We started as a group of students learning from one person - one leader and many followers. We have evolved from this to a true spiritual community that cares for and looks after its members. Many of us have taken leadership roles in group. That would have been unthinkable even a year ago.

Bill G.

*

Dear Reader,

When I first joined ACIM in 1989 I was someone who always wanted everybody to like me. I dealt with life by being very nice and very strong and if being nice and strong didn't work, I somehow managed to hide or escape from the situation. I found it was useful to be on guard and to censor myself. I feared that if people found out about the not-good-enough parts of me, I'd be totally abandoned. I didn't tell anybody anything and on the outside, I probably appeared to be a very nice, somewhat secretive person. On the inside I had no idea how to relate to people and I had no idea how I needed to relate to myself.

In ACIM we talk about feelings openly. Throughout my life I have never allowed myself to talk about my feelings and it was very difficult for me to figure out what feeling I was feeling. Then to verbalize my feelings in front of people was very new and awkward for me. The most difficult part was trying to hold back tears as I talked about feelings. For me, crying in front of people meant failure. In ACIM I learned crying and tears mean healing. When I first allowed the group to see my tears, I remember having mixed feelings. I was extremely angry that I wasn't strong enough to hold these tears in anymore. I was also extremely relieved, relieved that I didn't need to keep up my false front anymore. After that, my life changed and I opened.

Through ACIM I've discovered that emotional and spiritual growth and healing is an ongoing process and I am making choices about which direction I want to go, every minute of the day. The first thing I needed to do as a member in ACIM was to make a commitment to always attend even though I was resistant and afraid. That was a difficult step for me. Through that commitment I've learned a new way of doing things and a new way of being. The group experience provides a safe place for me to proc-

150

ess situations where in the past I would have fled. The group provides a safe place to learn how to express all my feelings and to learn how to listen non-judgmentally to others express their feelings. The group provides a safe place for me to see others in their growth and I learn from their growing. I have learned that I'm not the only one who feels the way I feel. I no longer need to be nice, or be strong, or to run away like I did before joining ACIM. I now choose to go the way of *A Course In Miracles*.

Roz K.

✳

Dear Reader,

Why the Course In Miracles group? Although there were several reasons why I joined the Course In Miracles group, they all related to one emotion - Confusion. I was confused not only about who I was emotionally, but also where I belonged. For many years I tried to make myself fit into what I believed was the ideal person, choosing friends and paths of life toward this goal. I was so sure that people would not accept me for myself, that I tried to make myself into someone I wasn't. I surrounded myself with those I perceived to be the right type of people and right things. Without regard to, or knowing how I was damaging my true self, I turned my life into the one goal of being an ideal person.

My first major step was modeling school. Then because of my limited circumstances, I joined the military. Although both were valuable learning experiences, neither path was correct for me. Realizing I would need to support myself, I joined the working world. Again, I felt I did not fit in and was not satisfied. I was still searching to make myself more ideal. Having seen the effect of education on many of my peers, I elected to go to college. While obtaining a four year degree, I began to take an interest in politics.

It was after I became involved in politics that I realized something was still missing. Although I had surrounded myself with many associates, no one knew the real me, including myself. I began worrying about my future; I was afraid I would be left alone without friends, loved ones or money. I started reading self-help books and listening to self-help tapes. Neither gave me the support I needed. Thereafter, a friend mentioned a Course In Miracles group. Reluctantly I attended a class entitled, "Learning to Love Yourself," taught by Nancy. Although I enjoyed the class, I was not yet motivated to join the Course. About six months later I ended a traumatic personal relationship and was searching for solace. Remembering Nancy and her lecture, I joined the Course In Miracles group.

During my time with the Course In Miracles group, I have come to know that peace and acceptance come from within. I have stopped questioning who I am and am now accepting the person that I am. I have learned to use the various tools and techniques, presented in the Course to help me further my internal educational discovery of me.

I realize that I no longer have to fear a lonely future. As I continue to grow, my ability to come to terms with myself strengthens. I realize loneliness is a state of mind. I plan to continue my study in the Course In Miracles group. I also plan to continue my personal and spiritual growth in other ways. I am currently expanding into newer horizons by taking singing lessons.

I strongly recommend joining a Course In Miracles group for those who are searching to know themselves and who are ready to make this personal discovery.

Carolyn J.

✳

Dear Reader,

I got married "late in life" (age 38) because it took me that long to find the right person and be ready emotionally for him. Mickey and I were both ready to start a family and began trying soon after our wedding. After six months of no success, we started extensive medical workups to determine the cause of our infertility, which took another six months. The specialists could find no cause - just the general low chances of getting pregnant in the over 35 age group, which is less than 8% each month. I pursued infertility treatments intensively and had four in vitro attempts in two years. Two of these attempts resulted in pregnancies, both of which miscarried after just several weeks.

After four years of infertility, I met Nancy and started participating in ACIM. This experience was essential in expanding my mind, achieving peace and becoming receptive to the flow of events in the Universe. I scheduled my 5th in vitro attempt for early December, 1991, and in spiritual preparation, I scheduled an individual session with Nancy.

[Joan describes here scenes and dialogues from her visualization.] We began to explore past relationships in my childhood and I began to let go of the burdensome, entangling parts of relationships of people I loved. I visualized the entanglement as an umbilical cord from me to them and from them to me. Some cords were thin and I could easily cut them with a knife. Others were very thick and gnarly, requiring a very sharp knife, great concentration and effort to cut. With Nancy's guidance, I was able to tell each of these people how much I loved them and that I wanted us both to be free.

I visualized my two miscarried fetuses. The first was a girl and I told her how disappointed I was that she didn't make it because I had so many dreams and plans for her. I loved her dearly and really wanted her to be a part of my life. She comforted me and told me that her physical body wasn't perfect this time. The time wasn't right for her to come into our lives and that God wanted everything to be right for us. "Let me go now," she said. "I will be back when everything is right for us." I reluctantly, but lovingly cut the cord, and cleansed my womb to make room for the next baby. I did the same with the second miscarried fetus.

I was the oldest of four children and the "apple of my parents' eyes" until my brother was born three years after me. He was mentally retarded and had associated medical and physical problems. My parents were totally unprepared and devastated by this tragedy. I felt the need to protect my parents by becoming wise and responsible beyond my years - making sure the house ran smoothly, taking care of my brother and making sure my younger sisters behaved well when they came along. I gave up my "special position" in the family and gave it to my brother.

At this individual session, I realized something I had never realized before: There was no room in my spiritual womb for my own children since I had taken on this other role. When I visualized the umbilical cord attaching my brother and me, it was very, very thick, like a huge tree trunk. When I told my brother about this attachment, he was surprised because he was not aware that it was there. He encouraged me to cut this cord because he wanted me to go free. He felt no need for the attachment created by such negative emotions as guilt and false sense of responsibility. When I went to cut this cord I found that no knife could cut it. I had to get a saw like two huge lumberjacks use to cut a tree. I needed help to use this saw, so I got my parents, relatives and friends from ACIM to help. My brother even helped. I cried painful and joyful tears and when this cord was finally cut, we all celebrated the joyful occasion. [End of visualization.]

153

I had my 5th in vitro procedure in December, 1991. I produced six eggs and all fertilized, which is unusual. Usually 50-80% make it. I knew immediately that I was pregnant and that there was more than one baby. Ultrasound confirmed my intuition. I knew there was a male and a female. This was confirmed by amniocentesis. The amniocentesis also confirmed that the babies were genetically and physically perfect! My pregnancy progressed without complication and was quite enjoyable. Our two precious babies were both seven weeks early - tiny, secure individuals who know they are very loved and wanted! I love each moment I am with them and look forward to the years ahead. These babies are truly Miracle babies!

Joan M.

✳

Dear Reader,

When I first entered the ACIM group three years ago I was terrified. My boyfriend and I had been seeing Nancy privately for nearly a year, the results of which were both positive and productive. The prospect, however, of revealing myself to a group was the most terrifying of my life.

I had a history of panic attacks that literally paralyzed me whenever I attempted to speak publicly. A milder, less noticeable version plagued me daily when interacting on a one-to-one basis.

My voice quivered uncontrollably, even when reading prepared materials from a book or paper. My thought processes shut down so that I literally could not think straight, making an extemporaneous presentation or discussion impossible. Although I know it handicapped my career and social life, I avoided public speech at all costs.

As one might expect, I did not endure the weekly Course meetings for long. During the six days between meetings, I suffered constant fears of attack and humiliation. Although intellectually, I could see that the group was loving and supportive, emotionally I felt debased by my performance there. Finally, after eight months, although I felt miserable, I had a good knowledge of the Course principles and I was incorporating them into my life. I could see that my growth was important and the group had a lot to offer in that regard, but I could not enjoy those benefits until I faced my fears and released them by whatever means were right for me. I left the group.

Nancy had been taking voice lessons for a couple of years at that time, and freely shared her progress with us during our sessions. Her experiences encouraged me and I decided to begin voice instruction.

The first six months of work were a veritable catalog of resistance behaviors. I felt like I was holding together the jaws of an alligator. The consequences of quitting seemed worse than the terror of going on. Then, slowly, I began to see some changes. I had begun singing and the encouragement I received from unexpected sources was a real miracle to me. I experienced a new confidence and I felt good.

A year and a half after I had begun my first voice lesson, Nancy gently urged me to return to group. I agreed to try a few sessions to see how I felt. I was still apprehensive.

That was eleven months ago. I am presently an active, contributing member in the ACIM community. I now speak with authority and grace to the extent that those who did not know me prior to my rejoining the group are mystified to hear my story. I am now enjoying the love, support, and true friendships I have always desired. The boyfriend with whom I began my journey four years ago is now my life's partner and during that period we have grown together and nurtured a truly loving relationship - one that I never thought possible.

Today, I accept real joy and abundance into my life, knowing that I am worthy and deserving of the very best. I am still singing and developing a strength and beauty that projects my personal power. I shall be forever grateful for the gifts God offers me every day of my life and for the courage to reach out and accept them.

                                                        Nancy B.

                                    *

Dear Reader,

I came to the group feeling very devastated and unlovable. My third marriage was in ruins, and I despaired of ever finding another relationship with a woman.

My first meeting in the group was initially frightening. However, the openness of some of the other people about "things that I could never talk about" surprised me, and somehow was comforting to me. It was obvious that they were being accepted despite their "faults." The focus of this first meeting was on our relationship with our mothers. I was paired off with an older woman who hadn't had very many good experiences with men.

We each role played each other's mother. We each wept. We have felt close to each other since.

Many things happened since that first meeting. I went through a lengthy period of forcing myself to go to the meetings - despite the fact that **after** each meeting, I was glad that I had attended it. I came to view the other people as loving human beings. I came to view other men as **true** friends - not rivals. I had a number of women friends outside the group, but I'd had very few men friends with whom I could really be myself.

The group has provided true, unconditional love - more than I've ever had in a romantic relationship with a woman. It has greatly increased my self love. I no longer "need" to have a woman in my life (as a source of love). Having a romantic relationship is now a desirable "extra" element in my life - it is not necessary for my happiness. And, the hugs and human connection that it has provided me has given me a "family" life that I had never experienced - I now have a spiritual family.

Monte B.

✳

Dear Reader,

Over the years I'd find references to ACIM. I'd make half-hearted attempts to obtain more information, but to no avail. Last October I found myself in what is commonly referred to as the "empty nest syndrome." I was feeling lonely and alone. One day I called a friend to invite her to lunch - this was a call I'd normally procrastinate about, but not today. In our conversation my friend Suzanne mentioned a course she was taking that was changing her life. You guessed it - ACIM. Just that week I'd again been seeking out information concerning ACIM and here that information came to me. Suzanne gave me Nancy's phone number. Again I'd usually procrastinate, but not this day. I immediately called and made an appointment with Nancy. When I first met Nancy she asked why was I here. My answer was plain and simple - I was led. I attended my first ACIM class that night and I immediately knew I was where I belonged. Here was acceptance, support, unconditional love. I realized very early on that I'd been living my life through blame, judgment, and criticism. Nancy, always being able to pinpoint what each class member needs, pointed out that when I stopped blaming, judging, and criticizing myself I'd have no need to do the same to others. For

156

me it comes down to loving and accepting myself first. Then all good will follow. Through Nancy I'm learning what is ACIM's major point - I can live my life through love or through fear. I'm choosing love's way. I'm more and more aware of my perception in life - in any given situation I have the choice to see my own life through love always. There is an overwhelming supply of love, acceptance, comfort, nurturing, and support within my class. Furthermore, the energy for growth is awesome and I know I'm home ....

Karen K.

✳

Dear Reader,

I attended Nancy Glende's class on "Loving Oneself." It was a two-part class. Shortly after I attended the first class my grandmother died. I had to miss the second class to attend the funeral. I called Nancy at home to tell her I wouldn't be there and I wanted the information so I could learn to love myself. She invited me to come to ACIM group. Four years later I am still learning to love myself.

Being a part of the Course In Miracles group has been a life changing experience for me. When I joined the group, I had been on my own for six months. I was a very scared individual. I came from an environment in which people around me took care of me and I had no idea how to take care of myself. Through the group experiences I developed the courage, confidence, and strength needed to bring into my life nurturing relationships, loving environments, and a job I truly love doing. I developed friendships with people where I find Trust, Encouragement, Support, and Love. I experience Peace and Joy in my life because I have learned how to take care of myself. I Love Myself. And this I learned by participating in the Course In Miracles study group led by Nancy Glende, who I am grateful for, and Love Dearly.

Denise S.

✳

157

Dear Reader,

My introduction to *A Course In Miracles* was in 1983, it was by reading *Teach Only Love* by Dr. Jampolsky (which gave me tears of Joy!!!). That brought me to a study of *A Course In Miracles*. At the time I was experiencing a personal crisis from the break up of a long term (five year) relationship! I just knew the Course was for me! So much so, when I received the Course books, I read through the Text in about a week!! (About 625 pages - whew!!!). I was empty and yearned for a way out of what I felt was spiritual and emotional barrenness - the Course and its wonderfully comforting messages nurtures me! The Course throughout the years has given me a new (a much healthier) outlook on life - providing dynamic relationships with my friends and co-workers and most importantly, a feeling of well-being about myself I had never experienced before. I trust those readers that are drawn to Nancy's book will find answers to questions asked for too long a time, and most certainly will be led to study *A Course In Miracles* - in *that* they will be blessed!!! It is with great certainty of healing that I recommend Nancy's book and, of course, the personal study of *A Course In Miracles*.

Joe G.

＊

Dear Reader,

I am grateful to have this opportunity to share my experiences being ACIM student:

I. Identification and discernment about my resistance:

One of the most powerful ways I have grown as a sharing student has been through honoring the rules for participation. That is, that I am committed to being present, to growing, and that I do not want to miss a class because I benefit immensely from attending.

I have learned to discern:
* when I need to rest or process information or pain.
* when I need to take a break for an extended period of time.
* when it is for my highest good to be present when I feel terror, scare, tender, or pain.

* when I am wanting to gain approval from "the teacher" or fellow students.

Throughout my three years as a sharing student I have practiced with right use of my will. I have become aware at a deep level, the feelings of doubt amid chaos that rise when I've chosen from my ego. I have also experienced the rapture of following my intuition or God's direction. The sensation of having my thinking and feeling nature connected is one of profound peace and safety to be in the world.

The way I learned is by practicing making choices, having a wise sharing teacher to guide me, forgiving myself for any mistakes I have made, being willing to make corrections, and being willing to experience all my feelings.

II. The right "to pass."

When given *permission* to pass on participation, I consciously chose to partake in group work. When I first began sharing, I said little, said it quickly, and experienced shortness of breath! In time, sharing myself became easier.

Risking to reveal myself consistently gifted me and others. Experiencing myself in a group that lovingly receives me is very safe and affirming.

I also came to realize how much I gain from what others share and that we as people share many of the same scares. By sharing who I am, I contribute to the group's energy and they contribute to my energy field.

By accepting the freedom to say "No" I received the freedom to say "Yes." There is no sense of obligation, only one of choice. I have chosen to expand and raise my energy.

By experimenting with "No" and "Yes," I experience the different feelings and energies each brings me. I simply choose. No one judges that. Only love is extended to me. And love draws me out and up.

Marianne T.

✳

Dear Reader,

This is a small part of my perspective as a student in the Course In Miracles group. This Course and it's teacher, Nancy Glende, have changed my life. I now know infinite love, peace and the importance of living each moment. I am guided by lifeward thoughts. These thoughts have replaced my old, cyclical, patterned, lifeless rules which only moved me from one day to the next.

Before I met Nancy Glende and studied *A Course In Miracles* with Nancy, I knew patterns of pleasing, self-criticism, helplessness and being the victim. Everything always had to be better or was never good enough. The love I gave was often connected to thoughts of receiving something back, although I wasn't aware of this expectation consciously. My awareness came as resentment, anger and withdrawal from my friends. Any goodness offered to me was accepted with the thought of owing the giver something.

Studying and living by the principles of *A Course In Miracles* has opened my life to love, peace, happiness and knowing that I am worthy of all that life has to offer. I am good enough. I now know a new way of thinking which changes self-criticism to self-acceptance. I now experience life by extending love. The gifts in my life are peace, love and happiness which multiply every time I extend love, accept my goodness, and take care of my inner voice calling me to remember that I am a delightful child of God.

Paula S.

✳

Dear Reader,

One year's expansion -   I have been a student of ACIM for nearly a year, and my greatest gain has been self-awareness. I can distinguish more readily between my ego/fear and love/truth behaviors, as well as those of the people around me. With this awareness, I've experienced a shift in behavior. My ego directed actions are no longer so enjoyable, and many have been replaced with behaviors that honor myself and those around me.

The ACIM classes provide a safe haven to learn and practice these new behaviors in the company of others also looking to enrich their lives. Interaction with classmates outside the classroom setting reinforces our lessons.

I'm not sure that I notice personal growth from day to day, but I can certainly appreciate favorable changes over the past year. I have especially enjoyed those "holy instants," situations that allow me to see that I've grown, and I delight in my inner knowing. Even my moments of frustration are tempered by an awareness that I am being presented with another opportunity to learn self-love.

This is by no means a process that will occur overnight. Nonetheless, I have experienced a clear improvement in the quality of my relationships with my parents, friends, and co-workers. I feel more at peace with my life, and look forward to new challenges with less anxiety and more excitement.

Bruce S.

＊

Dear Reader,

The Course In Miracles group has been a rich enhancement to my life. It's funny to say that now, when seven months ago I was resistant to ever being involved in the group. I think people are all much the same, we're looking for love, connectedness, purpose, and fulfillment. The Course In Miracles group has helped me with my much needed process of accepting and loving myself as I am, tuning into a Higher Energy that guides and pro-tects me, and knowing that love attracts - and if I put love out there, like a magnet - it comes back to me. The people in Group have been loving to me, and Nancy's guidance has opened me to worlds I never knew existed and now, can't imagine not being a part of me. *A Course In Miracles* talks about the two very clear directions we can follow - love and fear. I never realized before now, how ruled by fear I'd been. I was almost always focusing on negative outcome, on pain and scarcity. The simple, loving, good things in my life were never enough. I was always searching outside of myself for the answers, for my sense of safety and love. I never realized, before studying *A Course In Miracles*, that safety, love and peace stem from within...from unifying within my higher and worldly self. There are no saviors. There's assistance, guid-ance, nurturing, support and love out there - but no saviors.

At first when I joined the Course In Miracles group, I felt like I didn't really "need" it, things were going along well in my life. Then, about two months later, I felt like my entire world crum-bled. A lot of big changes faced me at that point in my life, too. I felt like I was dying. I didn't fit in anymore. I felt different and depressed. In retrospect, I realize my ego was battling inside me as I began the process of drowning out its voice with the voice of positive, loving thoughts. I wasn't dying, my ego had begun to die. I still endure battles inside when I feel struggle, separation, and fear. At the time of each battle I am closer to the truth, more at one with myself and the world around me. I remember that feeling whole is thinking and seeing whole. The Course helps me connect within, and with the world.

I'm still at a place where not all of me is open, and pieces of me stay resisting and hoping for more, rather than being open to more. That's OK, that's the ebb and flow of being.

The Course In Miracles group allows me to remember to allow myself to be and to be all that I am. And to remember to be open to receive all the love, joy, peace, abundance and fulfillment possible. I thank the Universe for providing the possibility to see life clearer, through Nancy, *A Course In Miracles*, the group, and myself.

Laura K.

*

Dear Reader,

When I met Nancy, I was sober through a 12-Step program. This program helped me to stop an addiction that would certainly end my life and any chance of my developing spiritually. I reached a point in my sobriety where I needed more understanding of myself. I walked through the 12 steps with my sponsor, I went to more meetings and I helped as many people as I could.

There was still a part of me that was saying I needed more. I prayed to God and through a friend I was introduced to Nancy. I started to see Nancy in individual counseling every couple of months. She would have me sit in one chair and talk to my mother or father in another chair. They weren't there, of course, and at first I thought this was very strange and then she would have me tell the little child in me I loved him. This was the first step in recreating my parents, or creating a new parent inside of me. When I left the sessions I would be crying, only to be happy the next couple of days and not to return for several months. This went on for a couple of years.

When I met Nancy I smoked cigarettes and I drank gallons of coffee with plenty of sugar. I drove an old beat up Chevy and had grave emotional and mental disorders. I continued to see her, I would get myself into relationships that were unhealthy for me and I mean I would hook into women that would neglect me mentally, physically, and emotionally because this was all I believed I deserved. Nancy would always send me invitations in the mail about what kind of meeting she was having and where, and would invite me to them. I was still treating myself with disrespect and unworthiness and only looking out for what others wanted, in short, I was miserable.

Finally about two years ago I decided to attend a meeting of ACIM at Nancy's on a Sunday morning. The awareness of these people was very high. They listened to me, they didn't judge me, they hugged me, they were genuinely loving towards me. When they asked me how I was, they were prepared to listen to me for hours. I went only to a few sessions. The kindness and love was too much for me to handle all at once. I went back to my workaholic and "run from my feelings" routine and ignored my wants and needs and nearly self-destructed, sober. I went back in the winter of that same year. My second wife and I were separated, and I felt as though I was helpless. I made a decision to commit myself to receiving love from these people who are always aware of my presence. I am now separated ten months and believe that I am capable of loving my own self and nurturing my own feelings and caring for my own being.

I now accept love from others instead of trying to get love by being a certain way or acting a certain part or working hard at whatever the act might have been to get someone else to love me. I will be eternally grateful to Nancy for introducing me to ACIM. The way she teaches is as incredible as the Course itself. I am continuing on my journey and feel as though I am growing happier and more aware of the presence of God in my life on a daily basis. Life is good and that is what the Course is teaching me that I am worthy of all the good life has to offer and all the good life has to offer is for me.

P.S. I don't smoke anymore, I don't drink coffee anymore, or caffeine, and I have all but cut sugar from my diet. I've also met a person who is quite the opposite of any other women I have met in the past. She cares about and genuinely loves herself and that shows up in the way she is with me.

Bryan M.

*

Dear Reader,

I had never been involved in any kind of "group situation" that was remotely connected to spiritualism, nor was I on a spiritual or religious path...but if life's problems are the "sign posts" to God, then certainly I had been given the map to Nancy's house for class that first night.

I had seen Nancy once for counseling and had been invited to the Course by a friend in her group. It would be an understatement to say I was frightened. I resisted so that I found all kinds of excuses and ways to avoid attending. Looking back, I guess I expected to find pathetic people in bad polyester outfits sitting around sharing their skeletons and affirming each other's self-righteousness...not to mention how turned off I was by the strong "Christian flavor" the words in the text held. I had converted to Judaism, and was Bible-deprived as a child. But once I was exposed to the metaphysical, true meanings of words used both in the Bible and *A Course In Miracles*, everything started to make sense. And not only was I completely wrong about the "group's" members, I began to realize that by attending the classes, and applying the lessons, I was beginning to feel peace and harmony and wholeness in my life, for the very first time.

I was at such a low point in my life, that I began to believe in despair and hopelessness...somehow I had lost faith...mostly in myself. My life, I felt, was and had been a total waste! I was born the middle of three girls to a couple whose union was born out of lust and co-dependency to violent, abusive behavior and alcoholic rampages. It ended when I was twelve by my father's final act of violence in a homicide/suicide tragedy. My sisters and I went to live with my Grandmother - herself raised in an orphanage - unable to show love - cold, physically and emotionally abusive. I guarantee she was relieved to sign permission for me to marry when I was seventeen...and I thought I was gaining freedom and the family I so desperately wanted to recreate.

So here it is, four disastrous marriages, 3 children and 12 separate, unrelated surgeries later, when I realized...Hey! Maybe this is about me and what energy I've been drawing to myself, and perhaps it is time to slow down, stop denying and take time to explore who I am, what I want, and how I plan to get there.

I'd be lying if I said that starting in the group wasn't scary. It was. I was afraid I wouldn't know what to say, or that I would sit and cry like a blubbering idiot and everyone would think I was crazy. Yet everyone is there for the same reason...to unlearn the so-called "truths" we'd bought into over the years. And almost everyone starting out, cries. It's only natural as all that old painful garbage begins to surface...and yet no one thinks I'm crazy...there is so much love, support and encouragement in class. Affirmations and acceptance surround me in every way.

The Course itself is a structured learning tool to assist and guide us in this "unlearning" process. What we need to learn is simple and joyous...the recognition and acknowledgment that God (love, peace, harmony and freedom) is not outside of us, that in fact, it is our true inner self that is God, and always was...that we are all innocent and perfect, and that once aligned in our thinking and feeling nature, we will manifest only what is right for us, which is divine, universal law - and that is love's presence in everyone and everything. Nothing else is real, and anything but love's presence is ego/fear based and is simply an illusion. What is true about our genuine self, then, can also be said of the Course, and that is by building health, prosperity, harmony, good humor into your consciousness, the negative, unwanted things will disappear.

Our group has truly become an extension of family...a place when we're balanced and centered, feels warm, peaceful, and safe, inclusive and expansive, filled with beautiful, harmonious people...the way I always thought "Home" would be.

Suzanne D.

＊

Dear Reader,

I am excited to share with you my perspective of being a student in ACIM. I know I never would have learned to love myself and find inner peace without Nancy and ACIM. I had years of wonderful therapy prior to this and it was only able to take me so far. I still easily slipped into what I call my "gloom and doom syndrome." I felt unworthy, repressed, and unloved. I was a workaholic believing if I did everything perfectly I might be appreciated and noticed. My relationships were unsupportive. I was critical and judgmental, mostly of myself, and the fun in my life was definitely at a minimum.

During the three years I have been a student of ACIM this has gradually been changing, initially with a struggle and now more easily. As I look back I see the many steps I've taken in this transformation process.

I first learned how we get what we focus on and I started doing positive affirmations. I soon opened to new feelings and uncovered parts of myself that I never knew existed. At first many of the feelings that surfaced were painful and scary. I found myself resisting them. A huge step forward was when I realized that my resistance was more painful than the feelings I was holding back. I gradually let go of blaming and released judgments of myself and others. As I connected my thinking self with my feeling self it became easier to trust my own intuition and wisdom. My newest awareness and desire is to learn and love my own power. Just think of all I'll have to offer when I fully realize this! I am now even able to see each problem or difficult situation I encounter as an opportunity for growth. I feel grateful rather than fearful. Can you imagine this! There is so much more I have learned.

A few of the many blessing that have come to me because of my changes are:

*Finding *me* and liking what I found.
*Healing relationships with my mother and other family members.
*Developing healthy and freeing relationships with my children.
*Creating a loving, supportive circle of friends who celebrate me as I am.
*Peacefully releasing a marriage which was no longer right for me.
*Securing a fun, challenging, and financially rewarding job.

It was of utmost importance that Nancy made our group a safe place for sharing. I never wanted to miss class. I knew if I was hurting or struggling the group was the place to work through my process. I always made homework assignments a priority. I also quickly learned that it was vital to give myself times of stillness and solitude.

I am about to start my own beginning group and share my knowledge of ACIM. It has been an exciting journey for me. I know this is just the beginning and I have many new wonderful experiences ahead for me.

Beverly W.

✳

Dear Reader,

About three years ago I was feeling an urge to actively pursue spiritual growth again. At the same time my church was starting small home groups, Bev W. described to me the Miracles Sharing being held at her home and led by Nancy Glende. I wanted to be challenged to a deeper level of spirituality than I'd experienced. Somehow I felt drawn to the ACIM group. I have not been disappointed. My church affiliation continues as my ACIM group experience heals and enhances awareness. Concern that ACIM would conflict with religious beliefs is unfounded. I have experienced healing, particularly of a deep loneliness.

A Course In Miracles came alive for me and has become a part of me through Nancy Glende's skilled direction and through the group support made safe with Nancy's guidance. My life is peaceful, joyful and richly promising. I can't wait to buy this book - and share it!

Pat D.

✳

Dear Reader,

Being a student of *A Course In Miracles* simply means to practice meeting your Truth within and exercising it in your love-giving walk.

To personalize that statement, my inner knowing has always told me that God created me loved and loving. Yet, my life experiences left me with feelings of fear, helplessness, diminishment, deprivation, always wanting and empty. My behaviors and responses to these events were a slow and steady process of numbing myself through denial in an effort to reduce the pain AND grasping for answers in some church or in some other person.

The contrast between what I was experiencing and what my intuition told me was true eventually lead me to Nancy's classes on *A Course In Miracles.*

At first the information I was hearing and the thought processes required to understand them were so foreign to me my mind felt like a stale pretzel being asked to untwist and yet not break. It was difficult and scary because I didn't understand what I was hearing and my feelings of inadequacy heightened. I persevered because my spirit knew Truth and Love was being spoken.

It has been two years of self-discovery--discovering the wonder-filled child within; the not-so-wonderful critical parent within; and, now the nurturing/protective parent within who is wonderfully capable of responding Love's way.

I am experiencing my life's journey in a new way; truly fascinating and inspiring. The "Aha's!!!" are frequent; as frequent as the tenderizing tears of recognition that what I believed to be true was indeed an illusion and the explanation for my pain and deprivation. The release of my illusions is a continuing process and proportionate to my opening to receive Love and to GIVE Love with Integrity. My ego experiences the terror of this walk. I have learned how to walk through the fear and experience the Joy. The Joy is in the recognition that I am as God created me, a mirror image of loving creativity AND eternally alive. JOY is the experience of being fully alive, empowered, loving and loved.

This is testimony to a masterful teacher, committed to the focused gentleness of Love. Using the techniques and skills that Nancy offers to teach the principles of ACIM has brought me to the point where I can say it is possible to BE as God created me NOW.

Happiness is a choice. It is a choice to walk Love's way and accept the power to walk through the illusion of fear and receive the gift on the other side. Happiness is walking with this Vision.

Happiness is walking with like-minded souls who slay their own "dragons of fear" to walk in Beauty, grace and abundance. I see and experience the healing process of life in myself and others. That experience brings me Peace, Love and Joy. It is motivational.

Happiness is our birthright. It is in our joining that the walk is made easier and the earth is filled with creativity. Welcome friend!

Paulie A.

*

Dear Reader,

I have spent some time trying to set my thoughts down on paper for you. "What am I trying to say?" Not surprisingly I find it all keeps coming back to one thing - Love. I've reflected on the meaning of that word in my life and how it has transformed over the years. I've looked back to all the various displays of "love," the ideas of love promoted by society and the love exhibited by our society and the love exhibited by friends and family. I've thought back to all the times people told me they loved me, and, even though some of them meant it in a most heartfelt way, there was always something lacking in their words and actions. Something was missing.

As a young boy I had (an unrecognized) spiritual hunger and a sense of the miraculous unlike many of my peers. Not surprisingly Catholic school with all its disciplines, rituals, and religious hypocrisy did much to contradict or destroy those feelings. In the end though, their ignorance and cruelty only served to temporarily repress my truth; for even as they drove me away from God, the Creator was drawing me to him.

Many experiences have passed since then and through it all my awareness grew to include the realization that I was guided by a higher power.

When I reached the age of thirty my (past) life was cut away and I began to experience tremendous emotional upheaval as never before. On a daily basis I was having dreams and visions where information was being transmitted to me. So much of it was indecipherable at the time that I was constantly overwhelmed and often in terror.

By the end of 1991 I found myself at Nancy's door, not knowing what to expect anymore, and frankly, not caring. I felt no longer in control of my life, and totally submissive to whatever forces were ripping my life apart. I was very raw, or as she so aptly put it upon meeting me, very tender.

In a blessing beyond my wildest dreams I found the group to be a safe, loving vehicle which eventually served to transport me to a place where all my feelings, dreams, visions, and intuitions coalesced, and where, finally, the veil of illusion was lifted so that I might gaze upon the truth. That truth was love. Love. Love.

I have never cried for so long, with such depth, with such joy, as I did that day. I cry freely now, almost daily. It doesn't matter where I am or what I'm doing. I allow myself to receive information without fighting it, and, as the energy comes in, the years of accumulated fear and pain flow out of me like a river.

Currently I find it interesting to note that as I have become more connected to my feelings, my truth, that I have become increasingly disconnected with "old" people, "old" ways, and "old" ideas. The fine line between my greater good (love) or slavery (fear) is easier to recognize now and it is a simple choice for me.

David N.

✳

PART V

Sharing the Course

20

ACCEPTING TRUE AUTHORITY

In this chapter I contrast authority as control which is part of ego structure, with True Authority which is of God. I share that we may recognize our call to demonstrate True Authority as Teachers of God.

The question of authority is one of authorship. At all times we have faith in an authority. At all times we are committed to following an authority. At all times we are attending the rules or Laws of that authority. **The question is, to which do we give our faith, our commitment, and our attention? Do we accept the ego or God as author of our life?** Authority is something very different in our two ways of thinking.

Just as in the Law of Being where we are always receivers, we are responding at all times to an authority. First of all, it is essential for survival that we have some authority to follow until we are mature enough to be inner guided. Authority by control is that external control over us. When functioning in our survival mode we see ourselves as one-down to others. As we learn the role patterns, we also go to the other pole and exert control over others. We follow external control or exert control over others because we believe we will die if we don't. They both serve as a way for us to be connected to authority.

Our spiritual journey is one of acknowledging God as author of our lives by listening to and following inner guidance. We do not defy external authority in the process, we simply see it for what it is, our necessary first phase of development. We experience "seeming separations" as we make our transition from external to internal authority.

True Authority requires us to say, "I am ready and willing to know what I am to know, do what I am to do, say what I am to say, etc." As we follow these inner messages our stance with others is, "I am who I am, and I will be me whether you like me or not." There is no intent to harm here, only courage to be true to our inner Voice. **Higher guidance is always such that when we act on it we empower both ourselves and everyone ready to be empowered.** Those who aren't ready to be truly powerful continue to seek power over us by such things as expressing anger or distancing with cold silence. They may seek for us to have power over them by acting such ways as helpless, confused, poor, or sickly.

Authority as control is granted by role, title, license, education, or right of ownership. For example, We have authority because we are a parent, driver, policeman, minister, or property owner. This kind of authority does not require integrity. We can have a child and not know how to tend it even though as parent we have authority by control. We can have a license to drive a vehicle and not be a safe driver. We can be a policeman without having order in our own life. We can be a Reverend and live a life of despair. We can own property and not tend it Lovingly. **With authority as control, we have power over another whom we see as diminished in power, or we exaggerate the amount of power another has over us.**

True Authority is the expression of spiritual qualities. We may have gained the ability to nurture whether we have a child or not. We may be highly skilled at operating vehicles without being licensed to do so. We may have developed a high degree of order and awareness that allows us to administer situations, and not have a police badge. We may have made the inner connection with God that allows us to be a world server and not be ordained as a minister. And though we may not own property, we may recognize wholeness and live in a way that supports all of planetary life.

In summary, authority as control is granted from outside of us and we need not have integrity with our title. True Authority is the demonstration of spiritual qualities and we may not have social license or title to go with this. True Authority is power to create Goodness.

Following inner Authority is difficult in that we are all first programmed to respond to external control. External control does not give value to true Authority. We are only given credibility in society if paper work proves that conditions of authority have been met. As we demonstrate spiritual qualities gained by courage to listen inwardly, we long to be accepted by society. Instead, from society's viewpoint, we are either invisible or seen as a threat to be repressed. **Economic repression of the spiritual is maintained by societal acceptance of authority by control.**

Those who have True Authority are sought out as leaders because they are trusted due to their integrity. As we switch our authority, we go through a process like losing baby teeth. **When functioning on true Authority we live with an innate ethical sense that aligns with the Will of God. It is our permanent teeth. It is Home. To be Home is to be Happy.**

Teachers of God are those who live the message they speak. Their lives are characterized by integrity. Teachers of God who are to serve by leading groups are called and they respond to their call. They "do their homework." This means they are vigilant for fear thoughts and choose to hold Loving thoughts. In this holding, they demonstrate Love in their lives. Text p. 75/82 says, "Teaching is done in many ways, above all by example."

The exemplary life is characterized by growth. Leaders with True Authority go through the transformative process from ego to God. They realize it is an individual journey. They fully understand that growth takes place where a safe space is provided. They know they don't have to change anyone, fix anyone, or heal anyone. They know they don't have to be changed by, fixed by, or healed by anyone. They know to simply provide a space safe enough to share genuinely. Genuine sharing is "in the Name of God," or in the vibration of Love. Love heals.

I share with you my transition from external to internal authority to demonstrate this process. I began life as a daughter and added the roles of nurse, wife and mother to that. Each of these defined lines of authority. My first official counseling was as a psychiatric nurse. It was before I knew what healing was. It was part of my whole ego process. I had authority by my title as nurse. That was authority as control. I wore a uniform, carried keys, and was entitled to make decisions that involved patients. My job was my job. My home life was my home life. At my job, I looked strong and capable. My focus was on fixing others. In my home life I was breaking apart, separating from God.

As my husband's disease (and my addiction to "Be Good") advanced, I viewed his progressing disease as at fault for all the tension growing within our family. Near a breaking point, I spoke with a minister friend about what was going on in our home and he recommended a Transactional Analyst for counseling. My initial intent was to take my husband to see if he could be "fixed."

The counselors, a husband and wife team, saw through my strong act, my defense. It was a despairing moment. It was much later that I realized these moments bring the holy instant when we See truly. On the other side of despair I began to feel, to speak, and to heal. I am very grateful for my learnings through Transactional Analysis. I learned to identify ego patterns which they call games. By imagining an ideal parent, which they call a Nurturing Parent, I tended my Feeling Nature, which they call the Natural Child. I learned to monitor my language as clues to which energy system I was using, fear or Love, as *A Course in Miracles* would put it. The Healing Methods in Chapter 5 grew from my experiences of saving my Natural Child.

I became a Transactional Analyst, adding another authoritative sounding title to my name. At the same time, I entered a Master of Science in Nursing program specializing in mental health. As part of my schooling I developed a counseling program through a home care program at a local hospital. I was perfect for the job of supporting those who were home bound as caregivers to the chronically ill. I lived the life myself and had mastered many elements about it. I had compassion for those I tended.

After graduation I was Nancy with an RN, MSN, and CM (Clinical Member of the International Transactional Analysis Association) after my name. I continued on with the program I had developed in home care. Then the hospital went through a "reorganization" in which the new structure called for a social worker to do counseling and did not accept a nurse as a counselor. So I was fired from the job that I had so perfectly created and administered. I struggled inside myself and fought outside of myself until I finally released with courage. It was then that I declared myself in private practice as a Transactional Analyst.

With titles after my name giving me the authority, I counseled privately and taught in continuing education departments at schools and universities. Clients began to tell me about *A Course in Miracles*. Students began to call me spiritual. I didn't know about either. I started learning about *A Course in Miracles* and listed the book on a reference list for one of my classes. A student called to ask me if I would teach a six week course on *A Course in Miracles* as a Lenten series. It was spring and I was experiencing my usual midwinter fatigue. Not wanting to add anything to my schedule, I set conditions I was sure she would refuse. Instead, she accepted!

The first class was like nothing I had ever experienced. Our sharing and caring were immediate. I felt truly inspired. My fatigue lifted. And, teaching would never by the same for me. I grew more and more uncomfortable with constraints of public education institutions. For every contract I had with a school or university, I would do all my class planning and wait until the day before the class to know if registration was adequate. If the class was canceled I received no pay. I started each new class at the beginning and had no sense of growing myself. I had heard enough times that even though what I taught was valued, my classes didn't cover overhead for the institutions. Payment did not honor me as a teacher. While I wanted to use Healing Methods and teaching tools as in the Practice Exercises in this book, classes were subject to intrusion and I could not keep the space sacred. Then another person asked if I would teach *A Course in Miracles*. This time, I accepted!!

This came one year after the death of my first husband, and my dedication to go the way of Life. Shortly after accepting teaching *A Course in Miracles* as my life work, I resigned from all public teaching and built a classroom in my home. Here in a sacred space I could truly be healing in my teaching.

My work life and my home life became one over the years. Text p. 10/13 says, "To change your mind means to place it at the disposal of *true* Authority." As I corrected my thinking, I accepted true Authority. Until then, I was under authoritative control. I was giving authoritative control. This is characteristic in our survival mode which we are meant to outgrow.

The common element in my work life and home life in early times was that I lived with one-up, one-down authority as control. As I aligned myself with True Authority my life gained integrity. My strength became true strength, that of being true to my feelings rather than denying them and acting strong. True authority releases the restricted idea that I am only the son or daughter of human beings, and expands this to acknowledge my identity as Son (Beloved Child) of God.

Anyone who leads a group will do so with authority as control or with True Authority. They kneel at the altar of the ego or the Altar of God. Each altar is a belief system. Those who teach with control place themselves above the group and therefore stand apart from the group. Their intent is to separate. They do not demonstrate courage to accept God as Authority. Without realizing it they foster "special relationships" with students. Their words spoken from prepared lessons or read from the book, do not fit with their intention. They lack integrity.

Leaders functioning with authority as control believe they are giving Love to their students while, in truth, they are *trying to get* Love. They believe they know what is best for group members and resent students when they do not get the reward they expect from them. They justify anger and attack of students. Students who participate in such a class are also seeking to further a "special relationship," wanting to see the teacher as one-up, as the God they have not as yet had courage to know. They, too, will justify anger and attack on the leader.

As a group member you need to become aware of your own ego pattern of wanting your leader to enter a "special relationship" with you. This means you put them on a pedestal and think of them as your Greater Being. You believe they know what is right for you. You see it as their job to give Love to you. You carry over blame of parents to them and make them wrong. You justify being angry with them and attacking them.

Those who lead with True Authority are one with the group, growing with exercises to continue the process of choosing God as author of their lives. Like their students, they continue to release blame of parents, mates, teachers, religious leaders, medical professionals, and all other worldly authority figures for not fulfilling them. **As a member of their group, you feel invited and assisted to be more of who you are as an individual.** Leaders courageously continue to do their Spiritual Homework, ever deepening in accepting themselves, appreciating the gifts they give, and valuing the service they offer. They celebrate growth of their students.

Since all of life is a process, leaders need not be perfect, and won't see themselves as perfect. A true leader has gained understanding of the art of listening and responding to inner Authority moment by moment. They know grace, the willingness to learn. **Problems in group between the leader and students are due to unresolved "special relationships" on both parts. Therefore, every problem is an invitation to see where energy is still intended to external authority, and an invitation to know True Authority.** True leaders, who are happy to learn, look inwardly to resolve such problems. In doing so, they invite students to do the same. Only by going inward is the connection with God made that allows "specialness" to resolve. Happy learners are happy leaders and happy students.

For me, leading is a highly skilled and demanding service. I fully honor that I am giving my gift of leadership in its highest form. I charge a set fee for students to attend a group meeting which I lead. I encourage other leaders to charge a fee likewise. There have been those who wanted to *get* from me and give nothing. I refused these requests to enter a "special relationship" with me. There have been those who wanted to give a "Love offering." I believe the Love offering system would be proper for those who have attained spiritual maturity. For those who haven't, which is most of us, it serves the ego.

Those who lead with True Authority have become the one they were *trying* to find in another. Rather than feel rejected by the society which does not value the spiritual, they see God as their mirror. They know that "the smile of heaven is upon them." Because they are forgiving, they are giving to the world. They are the ones who initiate Love and Peace and make a difference in the world. They no longer identify as the titles after their name. As I gained True Authority, I once again became Nancy. I use no title to separate me from anyone else.

Recently I taught a lesson on Authority. Two students who are becoming leaders themselves, did homework related to this. I am sharing some of their work with you to show the difference in gaining authority by control, and True Authority. They are working on their belief system and their stance with God. They are forgiving and releasing beliefs that fit with authority as control. Their work is inspiring.

FROM PAULIE A.

[Paulie did "Father Affirmations." She spoke them to her mirror to see and experience her own Higher Self functioning with Authority.]

Paulie, I AM one with you. I see your willingness to surrender your fears and terror to ME. You are tender of heart and are discovering that surrender is your true strength. It is your teacher and I am proud of you for using that part of yourself so wisely and lovingly.

Your "strength" is awesome. I see you focusing your energy on being responsible for your Self; letting the darkness be "out there" and making the necessary adjustments to simply correct your actions.

Of course you want attention. I see you setting aside "crisis" creating behaviors: the pity-party victim role, and your anger/resentment attitude. I see you expressing your beauty and grace in its highest form. You work so very well with your mind, feelings, and hands.

Paulie, your eyes do see beyond the external laws of man to Divine Law. You see and feel their harmful hooks that separate Us. You know the truth and simply live it and My abundance multiplies through you. You feel my presence both in your trust and in your doubt. They are both equally important for you to feel. You are wise to feel them. You have grown to accept My love in all experiences. I see by your reactions that you believe the perfect thing is always happening. . . Love.

I see you accepting my gift of freedom - free to know yourself and to know ME. You are acquiring the information and skills you need to do that AND you are offering that gift to others. My love I see expanding through you, for you are acting as I do - you are about your Father's business.

FROM BEVERLY W.

[Beverly wrote affirmations to declare her own Authority as active for her and no longer being dependent on external control.]

I don't have to explain to anyone or convince anyone that what I am doing is right for me.

I am an empowered woman. My power is of/from God.

I am enough exactly as I am. I do not have to do anything to prove my worth.

I am free and capable of making my own decisions to take care of my own needs. I accept full responsibility (and credit) for the outcome. I trust my own inner guidance to lead me.

I will be true to my own desires whether you approve of them or not.

It is a natural choice for me to be happy and healthy even if you are not.

I am living the life style that feels right for me. I do not need to justify it to anyone.

I am free to use my time in any way I choose and with whom I wish to spend it.

I see and hear and speak the truth whether you like it or not.

I release all need to change you or to make myself wrong when we disagree.

It is natural and right for me to grow and change. As I do this, I release old behaviors, things, and people from the past that no longer are for my best good.

It is right for me to love myself and take care of my own needs first.

I do not have to sacrifice my uniqueness to be liked. I give myself permission to be different. I rejoice in my uniqueness.

I am free to change my mind. I give myself permission to make mistakes in the learning process. I acknowledge my innocence and release all guilt.

I give myself permission to be who I Am and all that I Am and nothing other than that whether you like me or not.

21

STRUCTURING
A
GROUP MEETING

In this chapter I share the function of each element of a group meeting and suggest a time structure.

Most of us spend our lives going from one kind of a group setting to another. Whether you want to be a spiritual group leader or not, I encourage you to read this chapter for information that will help you discern if a group is right and safe for you. Information in this chapter will empower you in any group setting.

It is the structure of a meeting that allows us to feel safe, solid, and grounded while the content changes. In structuring a Course in Miracles group meeting, I include an Opening, a Content section, a Practice Exercise, a Spiritual Homework assignment, (sometimes a reading assignment), and a Closing. I address the need, on occasion, to break the rule of structure.

In chapters that follow I share tools and processes for carrying out the functions described here.

OPENING

The function of the Opening is to bring individuals into one circle sharing a united purpose. This purpose is to heal beliefs in separation from God and each other. The goal of joining is achieved by letting the Feeling Nature know it is accepted.

An opening Go Round is either a question or an open-ended statement to which each of you responds. For example, an opening question might be, "What do you know about *A Course in Miracles?*" An open-ended statement might be, "I am (Name), and to this gathering I bring _____." (Name a spiritual quality such as curiosity, a willingness to learn, or desire to share who I am.) There are forty questions and forty open-ended statements in Chapter 22.

Begin at the stated time. Perhaps you have a way of marking the beginning of your meetings. I have known people to use an instrument to sound a tone, sing, pray, observe a period of silence, focus on breath, make an affirmative statement, give a statement of purpose, or make announcements. Continue any of these that you hold dear, and add a Go Round.

Far more than you realize, you spend time in your life not seen or heard as a Being. **Focus on each of you in the opening creates the circle in which all of you are seen and invited to speak.** As I say this, do you hear the voice in you that cries out, "See me, hear me!" As a group, your united purpose is to free that Beloved Child within each of you.

Your name is a vibration which you and others have repeated so many times that it is deeply imbedded in your Being. **When your name is called your body and Soul are fed.** As leader, call the name of each person as you go around the circle clockwise. This simple calling of names draws attention to each in turn, affirming, celebrating, and empowering as it gives the message that each is important within the circle.

Using questions or open-ended statements that ask for each of you to share your understanding or experience can have no wrong answer. Even if your awareness is narrow and feeling expression is shallow, your responses will still be true to your experience of life. **One of the most beautiful things about this process is that as you know you won't be made wrong and are safe to share, your level of honest revealing will deepen.** The deeper your sharing, the more meaningful the coming together is. Deep sharing fosters a sense of belonging.

No matter what I have planned for a group meeting, every participant has the option to say, "I pass." This applies to any Go Round or Practice Exercise. I never push against this statement. There are some interesting paradoxical things about being human. If we believe we are going to be criticized, get into something we cannot handle, or get stuck in something we don't want to be part of, we become fearful and defend.

By allowing freedom to participate, few people ever exercise their right to pass and participation is strengthened. Many who do say "I pass" will jump back in after others have taken their turn. They have obviously been able to receive from others something they needed to feel safe to participate. In going around the circle if you are not ready to speak, exercise your option to say, "I pass" or "Come back to me." Inspiration from others is one of the functions of a Go Round.

I always participate as a group member. I do this for my own growth, and at the same time I serve as a model for others. My tender sharing says to others, "Your feelings count and will be given care in this setting." It is the leader's task to meet group members where they are and add to their understanding. This is the purpose of Content for the meeting.

CONTENT

The function of Content is to gain understanding of the holy message. The holy message is what you apply to manifest holiness.

Content is the actual lesson of the day. It includes information from *A Course in Miracles*, that prepared by the leader, and what is shared by all participants. Focus is on information true to Life, or the Voice of the Holy Spirit as opposed to the ego voice of fear. Hearing higher information than that of fear prepares your mind to open. When you open, you change from willful resistance to willingness to awaken. Awakening is remembering God.

Presentation of content will vary from leader to leader. Each of you has a unique style and approach. Some of you may choose to begin at the beginning of the Text, Workbook or Manual of *A Course in Miracles* and read together in various ways. See Chapter 11, Reading with Others. I choose to teach by concept, and in Chapter 27 I have included sample lesson plans using this style. My Teaching is based on what I need to learn. For more on this, see Chapter 28.

It is valuable to hear content spoken. Students incorporate messages from *A Course in Miracles* with my voice. They report hearing these messages as a guide when making decisions. Only occasionally do I choose to prepare written information for students for this reason. In giving content, I speak or read slowly on main points for note taking. When I consider a point very important, I say it slowly a second time.

I use the same lesson content in leading four groups each week. Content contributed by group participants varies so much that each group meeting offers a unique learning experience. In addition, every group has its own personality so the experience is never the same for me.

It is wise to remember that in a sharing group like the ones I address, **the most important learnings may have nothing to do with the content of the lesson.** Each of you will learn what you need to learn. **To learn that you can speak and not be made wrong may be a life changing learning in itself.** To express and feel included counteracts the terrible feeling of loneliness.

No matter what lesson content, style, or approach you take, *A Course in Miracles* is meant to be lived. Therefore, I emphasize the use of Practice Exercises and Spiritual Homework in *Sharing the Course.* I'll discuss this next.

PRACTICE EXERCISES

The function of a Practice Exercise is to experience at the feeling level, information given and received at the thinking level.

No matter what the exercise, the ultimate goal is to shift energy from physical survival to spiritual growth. Our Course is the same. We each have the life task of saving ourselves from our own adaptation. Bringing a group together to share in this task gives us a great variety of ways we can get information we need, provide necessary sacred space, and have Loving people to welcome our tender selves when we emerge from where we have been hiding.

Practice Exercises are processes into which each of you introduce your own content and work at your own level. For example, if the exercise involves defining a problem or recognizing resistance, you will each be dealing with your own life situation. The process is the same. Oneness is realized as, week after week, you bring personal issues that resolve within these processes. Resolving is forgiving.

In Chapter 25, Practice Exercises and Spiritual Homework, you will find that some of the one hundred and twenty exercises involve individual or small group activity, while others involve the group as a whole. There are advantages to each. When you work as an individual within a group setting, (perhaps writing a letter of forgiveness), your work is achieved with greater ease while receiving comfort from the silent presence of others. Moving into pairs allows for more of you to be talking at one time. When you gather as a large group, you will see and share more options for solving problems.

185

I find it beneficial for people to speak aloud as individuals within the group as a whole. For example, we may all have a mirror in front of us and speak aloud to our Beloved Child. I tell people before we do such an exercise that it is good to listen to others and repeat what fits for them. It is uncanny how our antennae pick up just what we need to overhear from another person in the group.

As we overhear others, we learn to name things and receive permission to express what we haven't expressed. We cry more easily when we hear others cry. And we find that others believe, think, and feel as we do.

Another example of individuals all speaking at once is when we do a visualization in which we imagine a time early in our lives when we were fearful and there were no comforters for us. I ask people to imagine going into the scenes as grown-ups and actually speak aloud to their child selves. Not only do we have an opportunity to speak what we need to speak, we also hear protective nurturing words being spoken. For some, this is a new experience.

The fact that people have varied learning styles is another important factor to keep in mind in selecting Practice Exercises. Some people find it easier to learn visually and respond enthusiastically to such things as writing, drawing, or visualizing. Others find it easier to learn auditorially and respond enthusiastically to such things as talking, listening, or sharing stories. Still others find it easier to learn kinesthetically, and respond enthusiastically to such things as constructing something, moving, or touching. Therefore, I recommend that you select a variety of Practice Exercises to use with your group.

Within most groups there will be those who model strengths of each of these modes. Their model encourages those who are weakest in that mode. Understanding and placing value on all of these various ways of learning and expressing helps eliminate the old pattern of exclusion and invites all to expand. So, as you select your Practice Exercises, remember that **there are those who like to SEE, those who like to SAY, and those who like to DO. At some level of our Being, we all long to fully express ourselves in these three ways.**

HOMEWORK

The function of reading assignments is to prepare the mind. Information received at the thinking level is then applied in Practice Exercises and Spiritual Homework.

The function of Spiritual Homework is to bridge between practice within group experiences and application in the world at large.

Homework falls into two categories. One is reading assignments, and the other is action steps which apply principles in *A Course in Miracles*. Reading assignments are given to prepare our minds for the next lesson. Homework, as practical application, grows naturally out of the lesson or experience in group. Applying the holy message allows us to know truth by living it and experiencing miraculous results. **I offer opportunities. I do not make anyone wrong for their choice of level in doing assignments.**

I acknowledge that *A Course in Miracles* is difficult for most people to read and understand. After several years of study in my groups, some members are just now choosing to pick up the book on their own to read it. They are finding with amazement that they now understand it and delight in all they find in it. If you are a new reader, I suggest you take a short passage and read it several times rather than think in terms of lengthy reading.

One reason to read even when we don't understand, is to allow the rhythm to invite us to a higher vibration. Another is that even though we think we aren't understanding, messages are going into our subconscious mind. **It is thrilling when we meet a situation that has been a problem to us and we hear a phrase from A *Course in Miracles* that leads us in a new direction.** This may be the first way we recognize the Holy Spirit voice as coming from beyond our own conscious reparenting of ourselves. See Healing Methods in Chapter 5 for reparenting.

When I give assignments of any kind, they are ALWAYS optional. Making things optional allows for free choice. We are breaking habits of "should" and "have to." If any part of an assignment is preparation for the Opening or Practice Exercise for the next group meeting, I inform the group of this. It is still optional for them.

Every Practice Exercise is a life skill to be used generally for spiritual growth. I invite everyone to keep a list in their notebooks of the various techniques we do in group. This is the reason to keep such a list. When we are faced with a problem, it is always at a point of fear. Fear has a natural function of narrowing our focus. As a survival function, this allows us to not be concerned with unnecessary details while we face a danger at hand. If a lion were about to attack, our shopping list or home improvement project is really not important at the moment. Our natural fear response would see to it that we forget them and focus on the lion.

We experience the same natural narrowing when fear comes from an inner source, when we are "a lyin' " to ourselves. Focus narrows when we tell ourselves things like, "I am not going to be able to pay my bills this month," or "I will be an outcast at the party." The underlying (there is another "lying") belief is that I am going to die one way or another. Obviously, few of us run into lions. Most of the problems we face begin with errors in our own thinking.

At the point of any problem, our need is to broaden and not narrow our focus. Therefore, for those times when faced with a problem and least able to think broadly, a handy list feels like a Loving gift. It helps us save ourselves from habitual fear responses. **Any response other than our habitual response will allow us to be free to go a new direction.**

With homework assignments made you are ready to close the meeting.

CLOSING

The function of the Closing is to open the circle and allow individuals to leave with an inner sense of being one with the circle. The circle is expanded rather than broken as you live the message.

Closing is very important. Meetings become a time and place where our real needs get met, our Souls get fed. As we anticipate going back out into what usually feels like a cold, cruel world, we welcome warmth from group members.

End your formal meeting at the stated time. This means the Closing will be completed also. Then allow time in the space for people to give closing hugs, share personally, or make arrangements to meet elsewhere for further sharing.

In my groups, we nearly always close by forming a circle, and standing hand in hand, we sing and rock to the rhythm of the song. In Chapter 22 I list sources of music we enjoy for our closings.

Traditionally, we think of energy as flowing from a positive pole to a negative pole. So, we consider our left hand as feminine and hold it up to receive the masculine right hand of the person next to us. This means our right hand will be giving to the person on our right. Now, after you figure that one out, be sure to relax your arms or they will get awfully tired.

Imagine that energy flows into your left hand, through your heart center, and out your right hand. See it going through others in the circle, likewise. If you are unsure where your heart center is, place your hand on the center of your chest where you place it when you hurt. You all intuitively know where that is. As energy flows around the circle, the more you are willing to receive, the more you have to give.

Closing circle.

Many things happen within a closing circle. For one, we feed each other with twinkling eyes and smiles. For this reason I encourage people to keep their eyes open. On the other hand, closing your eyes to simply experience the rocking is a wonderful experience. I recommend that the group be uniform in their intent so that all eyes are open or all eyes are closed. While it is unfulfilling to send twinkles to someone whose eyes are closed, it is fulfilling to feel the presence of others embracing us as we rock quietly.

Love heals, and tears release in the process. The closing circle is often a time of tender tears. It is truly a gift to feel safe enough to allow our tender tears to flow. They are a wonderful sign of healing our separation which we need to remember is our goal with A Course in Miracles.

Those who are avoiding eye contact are usually avoiding crying. By keeping our eyes open, we both honor that we are giving energy to feed others, and to invite tears that need to flow to do so. Tender smiles to anyone who is tearful will make a healing connection for their emotion.

If someone is going through a particularly troubling time and is very tearful, I invite them to stand in the center of the circle. Be sure to ask them if they want to go to the center for extra care from the group before doing any of the following kinds of touch. Accept an "I pass" response.

Group members could all stand with palms facing the person perhaps a foot out from their body. Do this for a few minutes, or whatever feels comfortable. Another option is to touch the person by laying hands on shoulders, arms, back, and sides of face if they want that. A third option is for everyone to move in close and have a big group hug. No matter what you may think another needs, do not ever push to give what someone says they do not want.

There are some songs, especially lullabies, which are great for silent rocking. My groups love to sing and rock. None of us ever outgrow our need to be rocked. Rocking nurtures and comforts us deeply. Rocking rhythmically using large muscles relaxes all muscles of the body. This includes our eyes, and our gastrointestinal tract (gut) which is where we experience our feelings. Michael Root composed a rocking song just for this purpose. You'll find it on the audio tape *Musical Companion to Sharing the Course.* As leader, do see that everyone in the group is uniform in rocking to the left or right.

Since our bodies consist of about 70% water, when we sing, the vibration of our voices sets this water in motion. This means that every cell joins in to celebrate aliveness.

TIME STRUCTURE

The function of timing is to see that all elements of the meeting structure are included and completed so the experience is one of a whole.

A typical group meeting with 8-10 people will have the following time structure:

Opening Go Round and Sharing about Spiritual Homework	30 minutes
Content	40 minutes
Practice Exercise and Sharing	40 minutes
Assignments and Closing	10 minutes

As a new group you may do an Opening more quickly. As you grow you will have more to share. Content and Practice Exercises are the variables when planning time. If you anticipate that the exercise will take longer, shorten content. When participants do reading assignments on their own, only main points need to be covered in group.

BREAKING THE RULE OF STRUCTURE

As in all of life, there are times when we need a break even from structures that serve us well. For Christmas and Easter I plan ritual celebrations for my groups. These have their own structures. We also honor our connection with the Earth by celebrating the change of seasons. We use these opportunities to share our emerging gifts. Group members have sung songs they wrote, or written by others; played instruments; recited or read poetry; told or read stories; entertained with puppets; and danced alone, or organized a group dance. One summer solstice we had fun writing affirmations on the sidewalk with hopscotch chalk.

A leader needs to discern those times when structure needs to give way to a more pressing need. Occasionally external events so impact us that we must address them before we can attend to planned lessons. This includes natural disasters and shocking world events.

Ordinarily group members come with issues they plan to resolve within the process of safe sharing or structure of the Practice Exercise. There is nothing demanding or disruptive about this. The distinction needs to be made between the person who will routinely interrupt to demand attention, and the need to address the issue when someone appears at group upset. Disruption is not to be tolerated. Learning experiences need to be embraced.

Recently one of our group members arrived in tears having been injured by an assault from her young child just before leaving home. I chose to disregard my plans. We spent the entire group time sharing deeply and meaningfully. As a result, this mother was able to receive information she needed to affirm that there was a problem with her child and that she was not a bad mother. The group was able to give her information about where to get assistance, and she left with hope for relief from a very troubling situation. It would be disruptive to group process if focus were to go to one person on group time very often. Other members anticipate working through personal issues within the routine structure and would resent being left out. A group meeting is not a substitute for individual therapy. **Individuals need to stay open to the possibility that they may need individual therapy in the process of their spiritual growth.**

The remaining chapters in Section V include teaching tools, processes, and assignments to be filled into your structure.

Closing hugs.

22

OPENING AND CLOSING

In this chapter I share questions and open-ended statements intended to be used as opening Go Rounds. **The function of the opening Go Round is to bring individuals into one circle sharing a united purpose.** This purpose is to heal beliefs in separation from God and each other. Of course, these questions and statements would be useful in other ways for sharing in a group.

OPENING QUESTIONS

1. Each of you say your name with a rhythm and dance movement. Then as a group, give the inflections and gestures back three times.

2. Think of something you would like to know about others in this group. Now, as you go around the group, state your question and then be the first to answer your question. This is good practice for learning to extend and Give rather than *try to get*. Consider using this opening along with a lesson on the concepts of *getting* and Giving. It will help demonstrate the difference between asking a question to get information, and revealing yourself to invite others to share with you.

3. What is your reason for coming to group? When you are clear on your reason, or purpose, you are much more apt to fulfill it and realize that you have done so. I deepen this experience by dividing the larger group into groups of three. Person A asks Person B, "Why are you here?" Person C then repeats exactly what Person B says. If Person B says, "Because I am lonely and need friends," Person C also says, "Because I am lonely and need friends." Repeating just what another says has an interesting effect. You join the other and also give them an opportunity to hear what they said coming back to them. Since both the question by Person A and the response of Person C are predeter-

mined, Person B does not need to be concerned about how either will respond. This is freeing and allows you to speak truthfully. Usually, about the fifth time Person B is asked this question, there is a shift of energy indicating that the true reason has been stated. Then switch roles until each of you has taken the three parts.

4. What do you see as the purpose of this group?

5. What qualities do you admire in a leader?

6. What do you know about *A Course in Miracles*?

7. What do you want to bring into your life? What are you willing to release to clear the way for its coming? This opening question would go well with a spiritual homework assignment to take steps to release what you named. This homework may include cleaning out a drawer or closet.

8. What change have you made in your life based on a learning from *A Course in Miracles*?

9. How have you experienced the call to God, the call for your Soul to grow?

10. Who have been your models for Love, Grace, Peace, or other spiritual qualities?

11. What was your most recent upset? You could use this with Workbook Lesson #5.

12. What or whom do you see as standing between you and your heart's desire?

13. Close your eyes and picture your child self. What would make your young one happy right now? See it done in your mind.

14. Share a recent concern.

15. An oyster takes an irritation and makes it into a pearl. What irritating situation in your life could you make into a pearl?

16. From a stack, draw a card on which is written a verse from *A Course in Miracles*. These are offered for purchase, or you could make your own for this opening. Each of you say how the verse you chose relates to your life.

17. Take any concept, symbol, or Workbook lesson and ask what it means. Examples: What does freedom mean to you? What does "face of Christ" mean to you? (See concordances to help you with these.) What does "I am the light of the world" mean to you? (See WB Lesson #61.)

18. Using the sentence structure in Workbook Lesson #67 make several rounds of your circle and use your own words. "Holiness created me holy." "Kindness created me kind." "Peacefulness created me peaceful." "Happiness created me

happy." "Willingness created me willing." "Gentleness created me gentle."

19. How was losing your baby teeth handled?

20. How was sickness handled in your home when you were a child?

21. Share something wonderful you did for yourself this week. As a group, respond with praise. Any act of Love to yourself will automatically extend Love from your Being. You will glow and be kind to others. They will appreciate your good mood!

22. Share about a miracle in your life.

23. Share about a troubling event. Affirm the person who hurts rather than focus on the event or on solving the problem. Example: Evelyn tells about her sister being diagnosed with breast cancer. Group responses might include: "I see that you care deeply about your sister," "I see that you are hurting, Evelyn," "I care about you, Evelyn," "I'm here as a listener for you, Evelyn."

24. What did you give up to keep peace in your family when you were young? How does that relate to your life now?

25. Share something for which you are grateful.

26. Share about a person in your life with whom you have an oil and water relationship. Oil and water don't mix like laws of the ego and Laws of Love don't mix.

27. Who celebrated you as a child? For what? This is a very important question for us to consider. In my experience, it is also one of the most disturbing to be asked. When asked this question we tend to go right to the core of our ego beliefs of not being wanted, seen, valued, worthy of being helped, worthy of Love, etc. As we grow in understanding *A Course in Miracles* and bless all things that help us see what we need to heal, we are grateful for such questions. My first spiritual initiation, in which I made a public statement of intent to teach only Love, grew out of having been asked what it meant to me to be recognized.

28. Make several rounds of your circle naming virtues or spiritual qualities as affirmations. Examples: "I am innocent," "I am kind," "I am joyful," "I am holy."

29. Whom would you like to walk up to and say, "Step aside, I'd like your job"? This is a question that is usually received with delight. Most of us know what our heart's desire is, and welcome an opportunity to give value to it.

30. If you knew you could not fail, what would you do? What information do you need in order to follow through on your heart's desire? This opening question would combine well with

practice exercises in which the group offers options, suggestions, or best possible outcomes. (See Practice Exercise No. 68, Chapter 25.)

31. What do you give and receive that you treasure? This may be either in group, or elsewhere.

32. How are you reaching out differently due to learnings here?

33. Share something you do that really works. What spiritual principle is involved?

34. How do you know deprivation and scarcity thinking when you hear it? How do you know abundance and prosperity thinking when you hear it? What behaviors would you relate to each of these?

35. What is something you did today for which you would like notice? Each of you go to a mirror and give that desired attention to yourselves.

36. Share how you've applied a lesson from *A Course In Miracles*.

37. Do you have a want list? What is on it? A want list includes things you would like to do, be, have, or experience. You can divide your list into time periods as things you would like to achieve within a week, a year, five years, or your lifetime.

38. Name a problem situation and then share what Good you see in it. Others in the group could also share what Goodness they see in the situation.

39. How would your closest friend describe you?

40. What does it mean to you to do spiritual homework?

OPEN-ENDED STATEMENTS

1. I am (Name) and to this gathering I bring _____.

2. My childhood learnings about God were _____. These left me feeling _____ about a Greater Being.

3. To me, Love is _____.

4. The kind of attention I most often receive is _____. The kind of attention I most often give to others is _____.

5. As a Child of God I am _____.

6. Last week's class was especially meaningful to me because _____.

7. I am ready and willing to _____.

8. I have faith in _____.

9. I choose to Teach Love by _____. State specifically what you will do.

10. To me, Love ("brother," Christ, sickness, a miracle, etc.) is _____.

11. I gave myself permission to _____ and the results were _____.

12. I'm in the stage of my life when _____.

13. I feel lonely when _____. True loneliness is separation from God. Therefore, you could follow this statement with another. What I'm afraid to do, be, say, and feel at those times is _____.

14. My greatest fear is _____.

15. My greatest Joy is _____.

16. I have made a commitment to myself to _____.

17. Something I've longed for someone to notice and give a seal of Love to is _____.

18. The thing for which I would most like to receive praise is _____.

19. Something I cherish about myself is _____.

20. Ways I have tried to save myself that I now see don't work are _____. These are your addictions or idols. It would be helpful for each of you to name several problem patterns to see that there are many, many more than substance abuse. Everything you do to avoid is an idol. One of the most overlooked idols is trying to fix others as a way of trying to save yourself. This can get masked as helpfulness. All role identities are idols. For example: "I believed if only I was a good enough (mother, father, daughter, son, wife, husband, nurse, doctor, minister, musician, engineer, policeman, etc.) I would be Loved."

21. I would like to thank a member of this group for _____. Name the person as you respond.

22. Since I made the commitment to _____, I feel free in the following ways: _____.

23. I'm here to be truly helpful, therefore I _____.

24. This week I supported my newly emerging tender self by _____.

25. A way I comfort myself is _____.

26. A way I like to be comforted is _____.

27. Something I would like to give more frequently, deeply, or extensively is _____.

28. Since realizing how I had defended by _____, I have changed my life in the following ways: _____.

29. A boundary grievance I have is _____. Someone may either be intruding in your life space, or may not be putting out enough energy to meet you. You may be violating someone, or not be extending to meet them.

197

30. If it weren't for _____ I'd be _____. Use this to identify grievances, places where you are holding blame and non-forgiveness. Use this opening statement with Workbook Lesson #68, "Love holds no grievances."

31. What I learned this week from being vigilant is _____.

32. My most recent tears were about _____. What I was last angry about and have now healed is _____. A fear I have overcome is _____.

33. Something that helps me grow is _____. I feel safest to grow when _____.

34. What I would really like someone to hear about me is _____.

35. My favorite childhood toy was _____. My favorite toy now is _____.

36. I believe my major weakness is _____, and my major strength is _____. The way I bring them together to care for myself is _____.

37. I give no one the power to abuse me by _____. I empower others by _____.

38. A major frustration in my life is _____. What I need to know is _____.

39. Things that have been celebrated about me include _____. Things I would like to have celebrated about me are _____. I'm willing to celebrate _____ about me.

40. Happiness is _____.

CLOSINGS

The function of the closing is to open the circle and allow individuals to leave feeling expanded by the inner sense of being one with the circle. I share with you sources, songs, and closing practices most Loved by my groups. I am sure you have your favorites, too. Please share them with me by writing to me in care of Noelani Publishing Company.

1. *Musical Companion to Sharing the Course* by Michael Root.
   Michael has shared in my group experiences from the beginning. He has written music for sing-alongs, rocking, pleasurable listening, and meditation. I hope you enjoy his music as much as we do. It is available through Music of Miracles, P.O. Box 1071, Shaker Heights, OH, 44120-1071. There is an order blank in the back of this book.

2. Distributors who have served me well include:
New Leaf Distributing Company
5425 Tulane Dr. SW
Atlanta, GA, 30336-2323
(800)326-2665 (USA, Canada, and the Caribbean)
(404)691-6996 (Atlanta and foreign)

Music Design
207 East Buffalo Street
Milwaukee, WI, 53202
(800)862-7232
(414)272-1199

DeVorss & Company
P.O. Box 550
Marina del Ray, CA, 90294-0550
(800)843-5743
(800)331-4719 (California)

3. Various audio tapes are available through:
Hay House, Inc.
1154 E. Dominguez St.
P.O. Box 6204
Carson, CA, 90749-6204
(800)654-5126 (for orders)

These include *Loving Your Self* which contains the song "I Love Myself the Way I Am."

Another favorite is *Spirit Am I* by Jay Minoru Inae, published by Hay House. Words are based on *A Course In Miracles*.

4. *The Heavensong Collection, Music for Inspiration, Celebration, and Healing.*

This is a set of 8 audio tapes by Michael & Maloah Stillwater, P.O. Box 450, Kula, Hawaii, 96790. My groups especially like to sing along with chants on "Voices of the Heart" and "Heavensong Celebration Live!"

5. *Many Blessings* by On Wings of Song and Robert Gass.

This collection of chants is available both on audio tape and in an accompanying song book available through Spring Hill Music, P.O. Box 800, Boulder, CO, 80306.

6. *Om Namaha Shivaya* by On Wings of Song and Robert Gass.
A ninety minute extended play audio tape of a widely known Sanskrit chant. Om Namaha Shivaya means "I bow to God within." This means I kneel at the altar of God rather than the altar of the ego. In other words, I believe Love, not fear solves my basic life situations. I serve God, or my ego. Singing this song reinforces a choice for serving God. See address in #5 above for ordering. There are other extended play audio tapes available.

7. Oman & Shanti have two audio tapes of songs based on words from *A Course in Miracles.* They are *Let Me Remember* and *Holy Messengers.* They are available through distributing companies.

8. Aquarian Music has songs available by many composers. They can be reached through P.O. Box 501, Wheatridge, CO, 80034-0501 and at (303)238-9610.

9. Jack Kastle has composed songs for prayer and celebration of life. He can be reached through Kastle Publications, Inc., 1660 S. Balsam St., Lakewood, CO, 80226 and at (303)989-5155.

10. *Wings of Song,* Hymnal of Unity School of Christianity, is available through Unity Books, Unity Village, Missouri, 64065. A favorite song is "I Am Free" with words and music by Janet Bowser Manning.

OTHER IDEAS TO INSPIRE YOUR CREATIVITY

1. Each of you write an affirmation from the lesson of the day. In your circle, sing your affirmations with the group repeating them. You may want to repeat each affirmation several times.

2. Pass a blessing around the circle. Each of you say it to the person next to you. Examples: "Peace be to you," "Welcome to our circle of Love," "I see you," "I hear you," "I feel your presence," "I honor your courage to grow." Do all of these with nurturing eye contact.

3. Play telephone like you did as children. Whisper a verse from *A Course in Miracles.*

4. Send a kiss around the circle. Place your kiss on the cheek of the person on your left. After that goes around, send it the other way starting with the person on your right.

5. Do movements that fit with the words you are singing like you did as children. Learn from each other what expressions feel good.

6. Sing gratitudes. Make up your own tunes. Dance them.

7. Thank others in the circle for things you have received from them. This includes ideas, information, modeling, options, opportunities, etc.

8. Make a declaration, take a stance, state a commitment based on your lesson of the day.

9. Rub shoulders around the circle. All of you do it at once.

10. Build a prayer around the circle. Each of you add a phrase.

11. Imagine light going out through your eyes, hands, smile, and heart as you sing to each other in your circle.

12. Imagine that energy multiplied by your meeting is going out to other specific people, groups of people, life situations, or the planet as a whole. Whenever you send energy, it is a gift freely given to be received and used as needed by those open to receive it.

13. I have routinely had a poor return on written evaluation forms from group members. They tell me they all assume I know they Love everything we do! I solved this one evening by asking them to sing their class evaluation. It was indeed fun and I did get feedback from every one of them.

14. We close by giving hugs. It is always proper to ask a person if they want to be hugged before touching them. Of course, when it becomes tradition, the asking is done with subtle body cues. If you are new to a group, or for whatever reason choose to not have people hug you, simply reach your hand out and the other will respond to your gesture to shake hands. You

might want to make it a warmer handshake by placing your other hand on their hand also.

15. Wash hands and bless each other. At a recent retreat, my group held a small cup of water while we chanted Om Namaha Shivaya. We then placed the water in a bowl which we used to symbolically wash hands of the person next to us (clockwise). Maintain silence except for the one giving a blessing while washing the hands of the person next to them.
   T p. 154/165, "Believe in your brothers...." Bless them.
   T p. 394/423, "Give faith to one another...." Gifts are given to our own hands.

16. A powerful way to close some major event is with a silent spiral of hugs. One of you will turn and hug the person to your left. When you move on to the third person in the circle, the one you just hugged will follow you. Each of you will join in the spiral. In the end, each of you will have hugged everyone. Silence is the key here. Leave in sacred silence.

23

CONTENT

In this chapter I share how I handle content in my teaching, and give an example from a student teacher. **The function of the content section of a group meeting is to gain understanding of the holy message.** With this understanding we apply the holy message to manifest our Goodness. There is information throughout this book for you to use in your planning. **I've included an extensive and unique index to assist you in your planning.** This index has spiritual process words in it like "asking," "receiving," and "extending." Use the index either to select a topic or research a concept. Bold print numbers are places where terms are most clearly defined. Other references are to help you see their application.

HOW I HANDLE CONTENT

A recent topic was the Beatitude, "Blessed are the pure in heart for they shall see God." I was using Text p. 33/37 as a reference. In preparing my notes, I use any resource that helps me understand, and then I share my understanding. *The Sermon on the Mount* by Emmet Fox is an excellent resource on the Beatitudes. I studied his words along with *A Course in Miracles* and articles I had saved on this topic.

In my class notes I had the following prepared to share with the group:

a. Our Thinking Nature poles with our Feeling Nature. Our Thinking Nature is our mind. We either use our mind consciously and actively to remember the presence of God, or we use it unconsciously and passively to remember scenes of abandonment (ego). Our Feeling Nature responds in kind to the impression we choose.

b. When we hold ego thoughts, our Feeling Nature responds from our "gut" or solar plexus where we store unresolved emotions (fear/guilt) that accompany the thoughts. So, when we hear a thought like, "You are pure and innocent," we do not believe it because we hold beliefs about being bad. Therefore <u>we maintain resistance rather than receive Love</u>.

c. <u>For growth of our Souls</u>, we need to accept a higher thought at the conscious level (head knowledge) and assimilate it at the feeling level ("gut" knowledge). This means <u>we need to acknowledge (see) the presence of God as our Greater Being, and accept our innocence (worthiness to receive)</u>. This makes the vertical connection which allows us to know truth and respond to others from our heart space.

d. When we function from our egos, we reject thoughts that do not fit with our diminished view of ourselves, and have "gut reactions" to others. When we acknowledge the presence of God and our innocence, we respond from our heart space. <u>We extend Love that we receive from God because we see and accept both the presence of God and our innocence</u>.

e. <u>When we correct our thoughts and align our feelings with them, we have purified our thoughts and feelings</u>. This is called having heart knowledge. With heart knowledge we experience the holy message as true for us and are free to give a holy response.

f. <u>"Pure in heart" means undivided allegiance to God. This is our state of innocence, our identity as Beloved Child</u>.

g. One symbol for innocence is the lamb. A pure mind, which means correct thinking, associates innocence with the protective strength of God. Until we correctly align with God, we hold blame of others for not protecting us. When blaming, we see the other as strong and ourselves as weak. We may see the other as using strength against us, or as withholding protection from us. That "other" could be a person, or God. In either case, we see strength and weakness as separate. <u>To know our true identify as innocent Child of God is also to see that we are one with the strength of God, and know we are protected</u>.

I begin by asking questions of the group. What does blessed mean to you? Answers may range from, "Gee, I don't know, I never thought about it," to "happy," "having permission to Be," "holy," or "peaceful." Then I ask, "Would anyone like to *add to* that?" Next I would ask, "What does heart mean to you?" I would listen for any answers and encourage more.

Then I would ask, "What does pure in heart mean to you?" My next question would be, "What does seeing God mean to you?"

My approach is always one of seeking to *add to* or expand thinking. The key word is "and." **Think of "*and*" between every answer given rather than seek any single answer.** Responses will all be aspects of one Truth. A sure sign that someone is seeking to restrict and narrow is the word, "but." There is no place for it in expansion.

I intend to never make anyone wrong no matter what they answer to these questions. Answers may be narrow in perspective, and that problem is solved as each one listens to others and gains understanding. No disagreement need ever be set up when people are stating what things mean to them. Everyone's meaning is honored as their current level of understanding.

Only once in my many years of teaching did someone give an answer that was dangerous in its error. In that case, I did tell the person that the thought was not true and was dangerous. I explained why and then gave correct, safe information.

After discussing words and concepts, I begin to read my prepared notes. When I read a sentence like, "We either use our mind consciously and actively to remember the presence of God or we use it unconsciously and passively to remember scenes of abandonment," I ask if someone would give an example of this from their life. Then I ask, "What higher thought have you rejected recently because it didn't fit with your self-image?" Then I explore the idea that allegiance to God is the opposite of blame of parents or other people. I ask students for any examples from their lives that demonstrate this is true.

A lesson like this one is difficult to understand, integrate, and demonstrate. When I read my prepared notes to the students, I read slowly enough for them to take notes. When a point is particularly important I repeat it slowly. They often read back through their notes and also hear my voice giving them messages. We continue to read, discuss, and share whether we understand messages or not. To do so is to ASK to know, to invite a holy response (insight).

Whether we read from *A Course in Miracles* first, or discuss concepts first, I use this same process of questioning as we read. I find the group deeply engages to search out meaning. There is always delight when a message becomes clear. "Aha!"

This is what *A Course in Miracles* says on this Beatitude: Text p. 33/37, "The lion and the lamb lying down together symbolize that strength and innocence are not in conflict, but naturally live in peace. 'Blessed are the pure in heart for they shall see God' is another way of saying the same thing. A pure mind knows the truth and this is its strength. It does not confuse destruction with innocence because it associates innocence with strength, not with weakness."

Throughout discussion I refer back to what group members have shared in the opening Go Round or discussion. This serves two functions. It honors those who share and invites them to share again. It also helps everyone relate the holy message to everyday life situations.

Summary statements are helpful. As a summary of what I am saying about teaching content, key words are *add to*, and *and*. These words include instead of separate. As a summary of this Beatitude, when we identify as innocent, we receive the Love of God. We are pure in heart. We know the strength of Love when we extend it from our heart space. True strength comes from properly identifying as innocent and Beloved.

A STUDENT EXAMPLE

Roz, a member of one of my groups, accepted the challenge of expanding her sharing by planning and leading a group meeting. I'm including her lesson plan to show you how she developed content and integrated it with other elements of the group meeting. Her topic was Right Use of Judgment.

After greeting the group, she introduced her topic by saying, "Right Use of judgment is discernment. Discernment is distinguishing ego's way from Love's way so that we can choose to go Love's way and take care of ourselves. Wrong use of judgment is making ourselves and others wrong, which leads to blame. When we judge this way, we stay stuck at the ego level, are closed to Love, and do not take care of ourselves."

She combined the opening Go Round with sharing of Spiritual Homework from the week before. "Last week we explored a personal issue asking ourselves what we were mad, sad, and scared about in that troubling situation. We looked for images of being separated. We chose action steps. What does discernment mean to you? With the issue that you worked on last week, how was discerning involved?"

After students shared for about a half hour, Roz repeated her main points. **"The Right Use of judgment is discernment where we distinguish ego beliefs, feelings, and behaviors from higher beliefs, feelings, and behaviors so that we can expand and take care of ourselves. The wrong use of judgment is when we make ourselves wrong (unlovable), which keeps us stuck at the ego level and unable to receive Love."**

Roz went on with more content. "The Right Use of judgment says we are constantly choosing between Love or fear, expansion or restriction, higher thought or lower thought, and going up or going down." She used the analogy of an elevator ride where we are always pressing the button to go UP to the level of Love, or DOWN to the level of fear. This mental picture helps us see that **we are always saying "Yes" and "No" and the decision to go one way is the decision to not go the other.**

Her next point was that discernment asks and answers questions and awareness of feelings is necessary to answer these questions. "What is Right for me, not Right for me? To what am I saying 'Yes,' and to what am I saying 'No?'"

Roz selected readings from *A Course in Miracles* to illustrate her points. We first read from Text p. 290/312. When the first reader finished reading the paragraph about the holy instant, she asked the group what the holy instant means to them. After listening to group responses she made a summary statement that **the holy instant is the moment of discernment when we say "Yes" to Love's way.** She went on to say that judgment in this reading means making ourselves wrong. She asked the reader to reread the paragraph, personalizing the pronouns and substituting "making myself wrong" for the word "judgment" wherever it appeared.

This is how the paragraph begins: "The holy instant is the Holy Spirit's most useful learning device for teaching you love's meaning. For its purpose is to suspend judgment entirely. Judgment always rests on the past, for past experience is the basis on which you judge. Judgment becomes impossible without the past...." This is how it then reads: "The holy instant is the Holy Spirit's most useful learning device for teaching me love's meaning. For its purpose is to suspend making myself wrong entirely. Making myself wrong always rests on the past, for past experience is the basis on which I make myself wrong. Making myself wrong becomes impossible without the past...."

Other readings she selected were:

Text p. 234/251 beginning with "Judgment and condemnation are behind you, and unless you bring them with you, you will see that you are free of them."

Text p. 58/64 beginning with "Have you really considered how many opportunities you have had to gladden yourself, and how many of them you have refused?"

Text p. 579/624 beginning with "Whenever you feel fear in any form...." This reading tells us that fear is judgment.

Text p. 30/34 beginning with "The Last Judgment is generally thought of as a procedure undertaken by God." **One student shared her idea of Last Judgment as being the moment she accepts an affirmation as true for herself and no longer makes herself wrong (fearful or guilty). This is then the last time she judges herself on that issue.**

Workbook p. 370/380 says "Only my condemnation injures me. Only my own forgiveness sets me free."

Text p. 42/47 beginning with "You have no idea of the tremendous release and deep peace that comes from meeting yourself and your brothers totally without judgment."

Her Content took about forty minutes and then we went on to apply the ideas. Roz had asked each of us to bring a childhood picture to class with us. For a Practice Exercise she instructed us to write a letter to our child self, our Feeling Nature. We were to tell our child self what we would be saying "No" to and what we would be saying "Yes" to. We were to consider what was no longer right for us, what we would stop doing, what our heart was telling us to refuse, and what our heart was telling us to accept. She put the audio tape "The Fairy Ring" by Mike Rowland on to play quietly in the background. This is wonderful background music for encouraging thoughts and feelings to flow without interruption.

When we had been writing for nearly twenty minutes she asked us to come to a close within a minute. We then shared with each other our experience of connecting with our inner child. This took another twenty minutes, which left about ten minutes for assignments and a closing song.

For Spiritual Homework she asked us to take action steps based on the information we received in writing the letter to our child self.

"I Say No" from the audio tape *Musical Companion to Sharing the Course* was chosen for a closing. This is a lively song which encourages conviction with decisions. Roz shared this lesson with three groups. For two groups this song was great. The third group had several people who were feeling very tender. Because of this we made a last minute decision to use the audio tape "Om Namaha Shivaya" which is more comforting in nature. See Closings in Chapter 22 for full information on this audio tape.

Teaching this lesson was a transforming experience for Roz. **We learn what we teach. We teach what we need to learn.** For more on how I lesson plan and learn my lessons, see the closing chapter of this book. **May you Teach Love, to learn Love!**

24

INTRODUCTION TO
PRACTICE EXERCISES
AND VISUALIZATIONS

In this chapter I share perspective and information to facilitate your Spiritual Practice. I have written this book to assist
you in applying principles of *A Course in Miracles*. We are meant
to live the Course, which is to live miraculously. Applying principles is how we truly learn them. Living them allows us to integrate the information at the feeling level. Only then are the
principles true for us and part of our natural response to others.
Until we learn these principles and transfer our energy to live
Love's way, we are living fear's way. The latter is the general way
of the world, so we are learning an entirely new way of Being with
others.

These Practice Exercises must take place within a safe
space. It is most natural for us to believe that the way we are
doing things is *right*, when it is the only way we know. Likewise,
to do them differently may seem wrong even though right. While
we may be confused about this, there is always an aspect of our
Being that lets us know when we are happy and unhappy. Unhappiness is a sure sign that we have errors in our thinking.
Happiness lets us know that we are aligned with the Will of God.

Growing is a full time job and our practice has a cumulative
effect. We may not realize at first how much we are Beholding
new ideas. Then one day, when a problem comes up out in the
world, we forget to respond fear's way. Our new response brings
the miraculous results of having given Love instead. Then we
know we are doing something truly right.

Many of these Practice Exercises have been adapted from
individual work to use in a group setting. You can also reverse
them to use by yourself. Anyone who has done much spiritual
growing knows there is a tremendous longing to share. We know

something is missing when we work alone. If you are working in isolation to respond to the call of your Soul to heal, do seek others. There are so many of us with the same longing to share.

Each Practice Exercise can and will be done by each individual at their current level of awareness. My groups have had people who ranged in age from mid-twenties to mid-seventies. The common factor has been a willingness to learn a better way of Being, with focus on changing ourselves to achieve this. Because we are wiser after each practice, these exercises can be repeated. They will never be experienced in the same way. Also, they allow for different content to be used each time. One time when you do an exercise you may focus on a family problem, and the next time a work situation might take priority.

SHARING IN GROUP

We meet in a group to share. To share is to give. To receive is to accept what is given. Both of these reverse the diminishing nature of "special relationships" based on fear. What is "given" to *try to get*, cannot be received. It separates rather than joins. To receive what is given is to accept nurturing. This kind of giving begins with forgiving.

In order to share in meaningful ways we begin by making the inner connection between our own Thinking and Feeling Natures. This first giving and receiving takes place inside us. It is truly an interaction with Spirit. We cannot give Love until we have it to give. Making this inner connection allows us to give and receive Loving-Kindness. See Text p. 208/223, "Seek and do not find;" Text p. 60/66, "Seek and ye shall find;" and Text p. 208/224, "Seek and you *will* find." We shift our intent from ego resistance, to embracing the Love of God.

This shift to higher function is known as forgiving. **Forgiving reverses the diminishing nature of "special relationships" and allows what we give to multiply in ourselves and the other.** We shift to what *A Course in Miracles* calls our "brother" side. Each of us has a higher function. When we remember this, we have holy relationships rather than "special relationships." Holy relationships bless. In forgiving, we no longer project or receive the attack of blame which is always present when *trying to get* while not wanting to find.

As "brothers" we extend Love and happiness. We give to others what we have received and created inside so there is no loss. The more we receive, the more we have to give. The more we give, the more we receive. Giving and receiving are one, in Love. As "brothers" we join. We know our function is to multiply Life and Goodness. An example of extending Love is sharing my ideas with you. The more ideas I give to you, the more ideas I receive.

In our ego function we only maintain separation, though we believe our intent is otherwise. An example of ego function is keeping ideas to ourselves believing we will be rejected if we share them. We think we are saving relationships by not sharing.

Be flexible in how you share in group. Sometimes it is best to share in pairs and at other times in groups of three or four. Sharing in pairs gives each person maximum time to speak and listen. Newer group members will feel safest sharing with just one other person. Increasing the size of a group also increases the amount of information available to be shared. When there are more people, there will be more options seen for solving any problem. Sharing in the larger group (8 - 10 people) allows us to see how much we are like others. So, have your goal in mind when you determine the size of group you want.

Practice Exercises are so varied that they will affect people differently. There may be times when everyone will have something they want to share after an exercise or a visualization. At other times only a few will share.

All of these Practice Exercises are intended to heal our separation from God whether this intent is obvious or not. Here is a summary of the healing process to help you see what is going on in these Practice Exercises. Integral to healing is making the transfer from thinking based on fear to thinking based on Love. This is what *A Course in Miracles* is about. We change our thought patterns using affirmations. Thinking based on fear uses the power of imagination to remember scenes of abandonment and terror while creating pictures of worst possible outcomes. Therefore, our spiritual journey includes retraining our imagination to remember connection and comfort.

In proper group sharing we achieve this. **The image of being surrounded by our group goes with us through the week as a source of comfort to us. This new image supports us as we courageously make our changes.**

212

There is some imagination necessary to practice most of the exercises described in this book. Some exercises are intended to assist in developing our power of imagination. You will find some visualization and meditation processes in a category of their own. in Chapter 26.

MEDITATION AND VISUALIZATION

Meditation is a process in which we seek to clear our minds and listen for higher guidance in that silence. Visualization is distinct from meditation in that we purposefully bring images into our minds to facilitate healing. I realize from my own experience that I need to connect my inner parent and child using visualization in order to stop fear thinking. Only then is my mind still enough to listen for higher guidance.

There are many fine books on meditation available, and also traditions which teach it. I will be emphasizing visualization. I believe it is one of the most vital tools for transformation. Here are some reasons to use visualization to heal:

a. We can return to the point of separation and nurture our inner child. Our ego uses these scenes of separation to remind us to defend. Since these scenes tell us where we hold blame, and against whom, right use of them is to see where we need to bring in Love and correct our errors.

b. We can imagine desired conditions. When we create a scene in which we feel safe, we also extend energy that invites to us what our heart desires.

c. We can change our self-image to see ourselves as powerful, healthy, or whatever we need in order to reverse our ego image of ourselves.

d. We can change symbols in relationships. "She is the witch and I am Hansel or Gretel in the oven." This image has no Loving Greater Being and our "self" is trapped and helpless. A change to something like, "I skip through the woods seeing the glory of God everywhere" allows us to feel free, powerful, and fully surrounded by Love.

e. We can own parts of ourselves that we have disowned, denied, and that function under laws of the ego. These often appear to us as a dream image while asleep.

f. We can complete dreams, bringing them to best possible outcomes.

g. We can communicate with those who have died to forgive our past.

213

h. We can gift and celebrate ourselves where this was not done to our satisfaction.

i. We can develop intuition and use these intuitive skills to heal. For example, we might use a body symptom such as an infection to gather information from our subconscious. Suppose I close my eyes and in my mind I allow the infection to have a shape. It becomes a large red mass. I give it a voice and it tells me it is very angry that I have been avoiding social situations where I could meet friends. Of course, this then opens the way to image some early scenes where I experienced social situations as harmful to me and learned to avoid them. When I have brought a scene or two like this to mind, and walked into them to join my child self, I have also felt free to enter such life situations now. My Feeling Nature knows I am with it.

j. We can fantasize revenge. There is misunderstanding about doing this. People believe they will hurt someone by imagining harm to them. Truth is, if you have an urge to be harmful, you have been projecting harm and denying it all the while. Behind the urge is a hurt child needing to protect itself. When you see yourself in the scene as protector, fear and the need for revenge can heal. Consciously seeing the desired harm done allows you to go beyond the urge; heal, forgive, offer a blessing, and get on with your life.

PREPARATION FOR VISUALIZATION

Some visualizations are brief and call for minimal preparation. For example, I may say, "Close your eyes and tell me what your inner child wants right now to be happy." Other visualizations require more preparation. I allow people to do what is comfortable for them. Some prefer to sit, others to lie on the floor. I have a few pillows handy for placing under heads or knees if needed for comfort. Most often the recommended posture is sitting with back straight and feet on the floor.

Before we begin, I instruct people to uncross their legs, take off glasses, loosen restrictive clothing, and remove anything that is sitting on their laps that might fall. While they are doing this, I start some non-intrusive music in the background. I sometimes use environmental sounds. **As people go into a meditative state, sounds will seem louder to them. It is important to keep this in mind when preparing your background.** On rare occasions I have used music intended to evoke a holy feeling. That is an exception, however.

There are a variety of ways that hands may be placed. Some prefer to place their hands on their legs, palms up to signify openness to receive. It is said that angels place gifts in our hands when we do this. Sounds good to me! Others like to place their right hand in their left, both palms up with thumbs touching. Other traditions place one hand on each leg with thumb and forefinger touching and the other three fingers extended. Experiment with all of them. Do what feels right for you.

Sitting for meditation or visualization.

When you are leading a visualization, use simple language and short sentences. Speak in present tense. **There is always a tendency to speak too fast. Minds become very active and need time to follow images, gather information, and correct scenes as needed. Speak loudly enough for all to hear, and gently enough to comfortably support a state of heightened awareness.** I only use a natural voice. I believe any drama is seductive. I usually begin by saying, "Gently close your eyes."

Occasionally there will be someone who is too fearful to close their eyes. They are watchful from their ego and not trusting due to hurtful scenes they remember. They will say, "Do I have to close my eyes?" Do not push. We all take care of ourselves the best way we know how until we feel safe enough to change to a better way. Simply say, "Of course not, you may do what feels best for you." Provide safety and people grow.

I might continue like this: "Slowly move your body a couple inches from side to side a few times, stop in the center where your spine feels aligned. Then tilt your body back one or two inches to a comfortable position where your vertebrae easily carry the weight of your body." Most commonly at this point focus is drawn to the breath.

There are many ways to do this, also. Most people will say to take a deep breath. This is an intentional breath that takes effort. I prefer to restfully allow my breath to go out until Life itself allows me to breathe in effortlessly. This is what *A Course in Miracles* is about, learning to trust the Life Force to support our Being so we live effortlessly. It is such a new idea we have difficulty grasping what it means. Allow some time for breathing to become balanced, restful, and easy.

There are a few situations that might arise which can be easily handled. Some people fall asleep during a visualization. It may be because they are tired. It may be due to feeling comfortable, a welcome break from their usual tension. It may be due to resistance, an unwillingness to feel and know. I trust that what happens is what is meant to happen and I do not make anyone wrong. I assume that each person gets what they need. That part of our consciousness that hears a baby cry, a storm come and go, also hears what it needs to hear in this situation. If a person is uncomfortable about falling asleep, simply remind them that they can tell themselves to stay alert during the visualization.

As we open to receive and channel more Life energy we may experience an excess of energy. This can be given back to Mother Earth by placing hands with palms down on the floor. If weather conditions allow, lie on the ground. You can also wash your hands in cool water. I would expect this excess energy to be a rare occurrence.

If anyone should happen to see frightening images, by simply opening their eyes they will reorient to the safety of the space. This will comfort them.

At the end of a visualization, say something like, "Bringing the information (comfort, good feelings, options, etc.) with you, gently return to this space, open your eyes, and prepare to share."

GOAL OF SPIRITUAL PRACTICE

The Second Coming of Christ, according to *A Course in Miracles*, is the end of the ego's rule and the healing of the mind. We are now 2000 years since the time when Jesus lived and taught about Love. He told us we had to become like little children to enter the Kingdom of God. Many have predicted that Christ would come around the year 2000. According to *A Course in Miracles*, the Christ is our own healed selves. Text p. 234/251 says, "To be born again is to let the past go, and look without condemnation upon the present." It is true.

Stand by your child who longs to be seen. Speak up for your child who longs to be heard. Take the hand of your inner child who longs to be happy. Share with each other. To share is to give. To receive is to accept. You have all you are willing to accept. (See Workbook lessons #100 and #101.) God's Will for you is perfect happiness.

INDEX OF PRACTICE EXERCISES

SECTION SEVEN: SHARING IN HOLY WAYS

SECTION EIGHT: GAINING SELF-AWARENESS

SECTION NINE: BROADENING AWARENESS

SECTION TEN: INSPIRING CREATIVITY

25

PRACTICE EXERCISES AND
SPIRITUAL HOMEWORK

In this chapter I share Practice Exercises with the hope that they inspire your own creativity. Above all, know that **the message of the Course is to be lived.**

The function of a Practice Exercise is to experience at the feeling level that information which is given and received at the thinking level. Each Practice Exercise aims to put into practice some concept related to *A Course in Miracles*. I have named these exercises for identification and index purposes only. The names are not sacred. Each section title and subtitle will help you see the intent of the learning experience.

I first describe how to carry out each exercise. Then I suggest ways to share about it. The references I list are to help you see how concepts are applied in a teaching/learning setting. Ordinarily my groups do readings before doing the exercise. You will see, however, that I chose to do the exercise first in Sample Lesson No. 2 in Chapter 27.

Some Practice Exercises are processes into which any topic may be introduced. Where I have not included specific references, you select your own to use in the process. Reference sources include: Tables of Contents of the Text, Workbook for Students, and Manual for Teachers from *A Course In Miracles*; concordances to *A Course In Miracles*; and the *Glossary-Index for A Course In Miracles* by Kenneth Wapnick. In this Glossary-Index Wapnick also gives definitions of terms used in *A Course in Miracles*.

In this section of *Sharing the Course* I use the following abbreviations: Text is T, Workbook for Students is WB, and Manual for Teachers is MT. I give a page from the First Edition and then from the Second Edition of *A Course In Miracles*. For example, T p. 32/36. Quotes are taken from the corrected Second Edition.

I chose to include Spiritual Homework assignments with the Practice Exercises rather than put them in a separate chapter. See how easily they grow out of the exercises. The function of Spiritual Homework is to bridge between practice within group experience and application in the world at large.

I select reading assignments from *A Course in Miracles* based on what I plan to do at our next class. I assign these readings along with the Spiritual Homework assignment.

Under Closings there are references to songs on *Musical Companion to Sharing the Course*. This is a set of audio tapes that accompany this book. Songs on the tapes are excellent for sing-along, listening, and meditation. Their composer, Michael Root, has been a long-time member of my group and has a deep understanding of use of song in this type of setting. There is an order form in the back of this book if you do not have this set of tapes. I have suggested songs to use with exercises. You may choose to use others, of course.

SECTION ONE: SHIFTING FOCUS

A Course In Miracles calls for us to retrain our minds. This retraining process involves shifting focus from fear to Love and then learning to hold to the higher thought of Love. This ongoing process is known as growing spiritually. Exercises in SECTION ONE address some of the shifts we need to make to grow spiritually. This is a place to begin.

※

1. FOCUS WALK: *Shifting Awareness*
Each of you walk around the room first focusing on a right foot lead, and then a left foot lead. SHARE about your experience. Now discuss the concept of shift of focus. Note that your walk will look the same to others. Your experience of it will differ with the shift of focus. **We are always *intending* or *willing* a direction for our energy whether we realize it or not. The first step in any change is to become aware of this.** Our results are always in accord with our choice of direction. The shift of awareness from fear to Love is internal just like in this exercise. We have a new experience of what was there all along. There may be no observable effects as we rearrange and correct our perspective.

REFERENCES: See Miracle Principles #23, #35, and #37 on T p. 2-3/4-5.

SPIRITUAL HOMEWORK: Practice shifting focus by looking at objects and then looking at "negative space," which is the shape of space around objects.

✳

2. CHRIST IDENTITY: *Shifting Perception To Vision*
   Sit knee to knee in pairs, silently. Close your eyes. Then open them and see the other as someone giving Love to you (a nurturer). Close you eyes. Open them again and see the other as an innocent child to whom you are giving Love. Close your eyes and open them again to see that the other is a person just like you. Both of you have a nurturing/giving aspect, and an innocent/receiving aspect. Continue this process for a designated time, perhaps 5 to 10 minutes. Close the exercise by reaching out and taking hands.

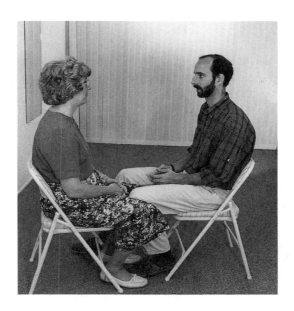

Sitting knee to knee.

Christ identity means wholeness/holiness. This is the state of consciousness in which we experience both the giving and receiving aspects of ourselves. We then relate to these aspects in others. Our Christ identity is our healed state and is the opposite of being in a special relationship. In special relationships we separate ourselves from others by seeing ourselves or others as bigger, smarter, and more powerful; or smaller, more stupid, and weaker. It is true that a person may be different as in physical size, gender, or color. When we include the judgment that the other is more or less valuable than we are this judgment prohibits joining with Love. In *A Course in Miracles*, our state of holiness where we join with others is called "brother." If you object to this term, use any that means the same to you. (See Chapater 9.)

SHARE about your experience.

REFERENCES: See T p. 477/513, "The Christ in you can see your brother truly."

T p. 466/501, "Your brother is your friend because his Father created him like you. There is no difference. You have been given to your brother that love might be extended, not cut off from him."

T p. 235/252, "Reach out to all your brothers, and touch them with the touch of Christ."

SPIRITUAL HOMEWORK: Do the same exercise by yourself with a mirror. See the two aspects of yourself that are the "brother" side to your ego.

✳

3. NATURAL QUALITIES: *Shifting Awareness From What I Made (Ego) To How God Created Me*

Collect up magazine pictures of natural scenes. Place them in the center of your circle. Each of you select one you like. Then make a list of the natural qualities you see in your picture (like serenity; spaciousness; growth; freshness; deep, rich color; and sweetness). Then each of you read your list to the group as affirmations. Encourage eye contact and a slow, meaningful reading to connect with feeling. ("I am serene. I am spacious. I am growing. I am fresh. I am deep and rich in color. I am sweet.")

SHARE how you experience claiming your own natural qualities.

REFERENCE: See WB Lesson #110, "I am as God created me."

SPIRITUAL HOMEWORK: Continue building awareness of your connection with nature by affirming your natural qualities. Make a commitment to tend these qualities in yourself and nature.

Note: You might want to sing "I Am as God Created Me" on *Musical Companion to Sharing the Course.*

✳

4. LETTER OF ENCOURAGEMENT: *Shifting From Being Lonely To Being In A Higher Presence*

We experience fear in our Feeling Nature. When we respond to this fear from our own Thinking Nature we experience courage.

Each of you write a letter of encouragement to yourself in an area of your life wherein you experience fear. Put your letters in envelopes with dates on them indicating when you would like them to be mailed to you. Trade among group members.

SHARE how you feel being the one giving yourself the encouragement you have wanted from others. Do you anticipate receiving your own letter?

REFERENCE: See T p. 93/101. Your higher voice is the Holy Spirit voice that speaks second, responding to give new information. **Fear is relieved by this new information from you that tells your fearful child of your presence as a grown-up.**

SPIRITUAL HOMEWORK: **Write letters of encouragement** in your journal. Write letters of encouragement to others either in your journal, or to be mailed. This builds your inner nurturing voice. **It is like priming the pump for water. We prime the pump to allow the Holy Spirit to speak through us.**

✳

5. "OF COURSE": *Shifting From Anticipating Harm To Anticipating Help*

Sitting knee to knee in pairs, each of you take a turn being Person A and Person B repeating the following many times.

Person A: "I am innocent," or "I am guiltless," or "I am lovable."

Person B: "Of course you are."

Person A: "I deserve only to be helped when I hurt."

Person B: "Of course you do."

SHARE how you feel as you **entertain the idea of only receiving help in your life "no matter what!"** Do you feel angry as you think of times when people responded by hurting you instead of helping you? How do you respond to yourself when you have a problem? Do you help or hurt yourself? **It is sad that anyone ever hurt you. This is no reason for you to continue to hurt yourself. Begin here to change your life. Love yourself no matter what.**

REFERENCES: See T p. 99/107, "The way out of conflict between two opposing thought systems is clearly to choose one and relinquish the other."

T p. 154/165, "To believe is to accept, and to side with... and appreciate."

SPIRITUAL HOMEWORK: Continue this process with a mirror speaking aloud both parts of the dialog.

❋

6. "YES, BUT": *Shifting Use Of Language From Fear To Love*

Practice this to recognize how we bridge from our heart's desire (Love's way) to limitation (fear's way) within our use of language. When we become aware of this bridge, we can use it to return to the freedom of Love. Each of you write a list of statements: "I would like to _____ but _____." Then take turns reading your statements to the group using the word "and" instead of "but." Group members respond to each with "I see you as safe to _____ (whatever their heart's desire is). People rarely make a harmful statement before the "but." An exception might be a statement of revenge like, "I'd like to kill my ex, but I don't want to go to jail." In this case, you might ask the person what they truly want for themselves that the ex could not provide for them.

SHARE how different you feel using "but" and "and." How did you experience having the group support you? Do you now feel comfortable to use an "and" in your own statements? Are you beginning to believe you could be safe to release your restriction?

I keep a one-way gate on my bridge. If I hear an old "Yes, but" come up in my mind I bring my focus over to the Love side. I then put a *period* before the "but" to keep my true desire from going to fear. In being mindful in my use of language I am present for my Feeling Nature. My presence allows for expansion which is Love. This same mindful presence protects me as I take my step in growth. Until I developed this awareness I restricted in fear.

As an alternative exercise, write your sentences and put *periods* before your "buts." How does this feel to you?

227

REFERENCES: See T p. 12-13/15-16 on how our distorted perceptions cover our miracle impulses. We learn to retrain our minds to live miraculously.

T p. 158/169, "...miracles are natural, and when they do not occur something has gone wrong. Miracles are merely the sign of your willingness to follow the Holy Spirit's plan of salvation...."

T p. 316/340, We need to be entirely unwilling to settle for illusion in place of truth. "...love is wholly without illusion, and therefore wholly without fear."

T p. 327/351, Betrayal lies only in our illusions and all our unworthiness is in our own imaginings.

T p. 342/368, "There is no problem in any situation that faith will not solve."

SPIRITUAL HOMEWORK: Monitor your own internal dialogue and speech for "Yes, but." Put a *period* before the "but." This says "Yes" to Love. "Yes" to being happy!

✳

7. DEFINE CONCEPT: *Shifting Definitions From Ego Thinking To Free Thinking*

Take any concept you wish to study (i.e., harmony, Vision, sickness, Will of God). Each of you write a definition of it. Sometimes it is helpful in defining a term to state what it is not, or give an opposite. For example: "Sickness is absence of well-ness." "Sickness is dis-ease." "Sickness is lack of ease." "Harmony is the opposite of disharmony."

SHARE your definitions and come up with one clear statement as a group. Define it in a way that you can apply it. This means you could see action steps within your definition.

As an alternative exercise, each of you select a thought from *A Course in Miracles* and SHARE what it means to you.

REFERENCES: Select references based on the concept you chose to define.

SPIRITUAL HOMEWORK: **Shifting from fear thinking to Love thinking requires that you redefine every concept that you have ever learned.** Once you give attention to any set belief or definition, you will continue to deepen your understanding. Attention means mindfulness or awareness. This is the Thinking Nature now actively joining the Feeling Nature bringing growth. Remember to change your behaviors to be consistent with your new definitions.

✳

8. TRUST LETTER: *Shifting Identity From Abandoned Child To Beloved Child*
Write letters of trust to the Universe, God, etc. You write, and also share to build this trust.
SHARE your letters. Then share your feelings about both writing them, and reading them to the group.
REFERENCES: Select some references that you believe are appropriate.
SPIRITUAL HOMEWORK: Reread you letter and add to it through the week. Keep a running letter going in your mind. Believe that Goodness is there and you will see it everywhere.

✳

9. BRAG: *Shifting Self-Negation To Self-Acceptance*
Each of you take 3-5 minutes to tell about your Goodness. Learn about the true meaning of arrogance by reading the reference first.
SHARE: Did you learn that it was wrong to say good things about yourself? Are you willing to let that go? How do you feel when you accept your Goodness? When others do?
REFERENCE: See T p. 178/192, "Arrogance is the denial of love, because love shares and arrogance withholds." We are meant to Love ourselves. Love is eternal. **Living in time means we allow our minds to go to our past to remember something we use to justify feeling bad about ourselves. Then we project this image to the future and expect something harmful from others. Expecting harm, we behave in such a way in the present to defend against the hurt we anticipate. This is ego process, called living in time, and is the state of fear rather than Love.**
SPIRITUAL HOMEWORK: Continue to see your Goodness in other settings throughout the week.
Note: There are several songs on *Musical Companion to Sharing the Course* that go well with this exercise.

✳

10. PLEDGE OF ALLEGIANCE: *Shifting From What I Learned From Outside To What I Learn From Inside*
(See Sample Lesson No. 9, Chapter 27 for its use.)
Write a pledge of allegiance to your Soul's growth following the rhythm of The Pledge of Allegiance.

Example: "I pledge allegiance to my heart where my Thinking and Feeling Natures unite, and to the comfort my little one seeks, one goal divinely led, indivisible, with liberty and justice for her."

SHARE your pledges. How do you feel making a pledge to your Soul? Does it deepen the meaning of the Pledge for you?

REFERENCE: See T p. 193/208, "Resurrection must compel your allegiance gladly, because it is the symbol of joy. Its whole compelling power lies in the fact that it represents what you want to be. The freedom to leave behind everything that hurts you and humbles you and frightens you cannot be thrust upon you, but it can be offered you through the grace of God."

SPIRITUAL HOMEWORK: Live your pledge. **There is no way that you can harm anyone by being true to your Soul. By Law, Love must extend or express harmlessly.**

SECTION TWO: LEARNING BASIC SKILLS

Exercises in SECTION TWO are to be taught within group process. You can then use these skills in your daily lives to facilitate your own spiritual growth. You begin by defining problems in a way that their source lies within your own thinking. These are your self-defeating beliefs and blame of others. When you see situations differently you are free to give new responses and experience the same situations differently.

✳

11. "MY PROBLEM IS": *Defining A Problem*
This sounds simple and is not. Take any problem situation and define it starting with the simple statement, "My problem is _____." **When you have properly defined a problem, the solution is within that definition. We err on the side of putting another person between ourselves and the solution. Define until the problem requires only you to change. Know that when you change, you automatically call for a new response from others.**
This exercise can be done as a group process with one person at an easel or blackboard. It is the **process** that each wants to incorporate in mind.

Example:
"My problem is that I can't stand noisy neighbors."
"My problem is that my neighbors are disrespectful."
"My problem is that I rage inside when I hear those drums going."
"My problem is that I believe if I speak up they will laugh at me."
"My problem is that I believe I don't count."
"My problem is that I interpret what the neighbors do as an attack on me."
"My problem is that I create rage and it interferes with my Peace."
"I could see Peace instead of this!"

SHARE how you experience the change in focus.
REFERENCES: See references on perception.
See also, MT p. 8-10/9-11, "Development of trust." These are steps to undo our ego way of projecting and create Peace which we can extend. Nancy's Be-attitude: Blessed are those who create Peace in the midst of emotional turmoil, for they shall know Peace.

SPIRITUAL HOMEWORK: Define more problems and decide to take action steps necessary to solve them. **Remember that changing your mind is an action step in itself.**

*

12. THINK STRUCTURE: *Defining And Resolving A Problem*
   This is a problem defining structure that is useful in our process of revising fear's way of thinking to Love's way. It is from *Becoming the Way We Are* by Pam Levin. Since the whole of *A Course in Miracles* is about retraining our thinking, this tool is invaluable. Pamela has also written *Cycles of Power: A User's Guide To The Seven Seasons of Life.* I am sure you have had that sense of being a young child just wanting to be taken care of, or feeling like a teenager again. Besides explaining the way we naturally recycle through our stages of development, she suggests ways to nurture ourselves in each stage to develop the power of the stage. Lets define a problem here using her Think Structure.

I am **(1)** (feeling) _____
because I think that if I **(2)** (behavior I initiate) _____
I will be **(3)** (unhealthy Parental response) _____
instead of **(4)** (healthy Parental response) _____
so I **(5)** (problem justifying behaviors, games) _____.

We are alerted to a problem by some feeling that is uncomfortable to us. That is what we place on the **first line**. The **second line** is what we would truly like to have, do, or be. It is the one that we have denied ourselves, or restricted due to fear from having received something other than a Loving response to situations when young. It would be our natural way of Being that was given up to go fear's way when we experienced no Greater Being there for us in any early life scene. Next we identify what we anticipate as a response to our natural way of Being. The underlying thought to any response on the **third line** is, "and I will die." I believe I will be unloved, abandoned, harmed one way or another - and I will die as a result. This is our child view of scenes during our time of physical dependence on a parent. On the **fourth line** we are identifying the parental response that would be the natural Loving response. The **fifth line** (problem justifying behaviors) includes all the things we do while under ego rule. These behaviors keep us from doing our natural behaviors which we believe would lead to our death.

When properly defined, all of our steps for reversal become clear. **We need to deny line (3), affirm line (4), do line (2), stop all we do on line (5), and our feeling(s) on line (1) resolve. To resolve a feeling is to heal the separation within us so our Feeling Nature is attended by and integrated with our own Thinking Nature.**

Here is an example of defining a problem:

(1) I am scared (Two large client checks to me just bounced and the bank withdrew money from my checking account that I had already used to pay one of my bills.)

(2) because I think that though I have handled by financial affairs honorably, the check I used to pay my bill will bounce due to the behavior of another, and

(3) I will be judged by my creditor, and punished by the bank with an overdraft charge (both hurtful responses)

(4) instead of given understanding and honor as one who handles her financial affairs impeccably

(5) so I tense up, worry, feel unfaired against, have angry thoughts about those who gave me bad checks, withhold Love from two people who are part of my Loving community (while I myself am in fear).

Here is an example of resolving this problem:

Deny (3). I no longer need to believe that the bank is my Greater Being or parent. I no longer need to believe they will judge me bad and punish me (and that I will die from lack of Love as I used to believe when a parent judged me as bad). I no longer need to judge myself (go to guilt) or harm myself (go to self-criticism). I no longer need to withdraw from Love and therein "punish" myself and others.

Affirm (4). I have all the skill I need to handle affairs with the bank, my creditor if needed, and those who need to write new checks. I speak with beauty, grace, and authority. I handle my financial affairs honorably. I give responses to this situation that honor myself and all involved. I choose Love for my way of Being. I respond in a way that is truly helpful to myself and all others.

Do (2). Handle my affairs honorably. I will go to the bank as soon as it opens this morning to see if I can cover my check before it bounces. I will inform both people who had insufficient funds so they can cover their checks and trust they will do so as soon as possible. If my check bounces I will call my creditor and explain the situation knowing that she Loves and trusts me and that this event will not change that. I will pass on the overdraft charge to those who need to learn a lesson in handling their affairs, instead of taking it on as punishment to which I respond with a sense of unfairness. I will continue to Love both members of my community.

Stop (5). I am thought-stopping to reverse worry, tensing, anger, and "unfair," all of which justify withholding Love.

(1). Scare is replaced by faith and trust.

P.S. I got to the bank before my account was overdrawn and both clients covered their checks. And, of course, I extend Love to them.

Note the ego process in this example. In my state of fear I called out memories from early scenes where I saw no Loving Greater Being to protect and comfort me. At those times I would have seen my mother as my Greater Being. I carried over from childhood the view of a Greater Being as punitive, having no compassion toward me, and I responded in my current situation based on this unhealed view. My withdrawal from Love was a habitual response. My choice to defend as a child was to survive in a situation in which I saw myself as bad and not worthy of Love from having been treated that way. **I am healing my guilt; my belief that I deserve to be punished. In Truth, I deserve to be Loved and helped no matter what life situation comes to me - and so do you!** To the ego, the guiltless are guilty. To continue an ego pattern is to separate from Life/Love/God, and go death's way. The ego does what it defends. **With every ego move we think we are saving ourselves from dying and in truth, we are deadening ourselves.**

Note also that this early memory triggered by this event showed me I was still holding non-forgiveness/blame. I bless those who drew this to my attention, they are my teachers. I now see what I did not see before (energy invested in fear/guilt). **Reversing this energy to receive my own Love solves the problem of guilt.**

Work individually and then as a group to define problems.

SHARE how you feel as you define a problem that also gives you steps to resolve it.

REFERENCES: Use any references that relate to undoing blame or healing guilt.

SPIRITUAL HOMEWORK: Write out your steps to solve your problem. Take action steps. Report back at the next meeting.

✳

13. UNMET DEMAND: *Recognizing Blame*
   Use a piece of paper divided into three columns. Write names of original and current family members in the first column leaving some space between each. Then picture each of these family members. Say, "I Love you" or "I hate you" to each in your mind. What do you choose for each? Write this in the second column. For each one you hate, there is something you are demanding of them that they have not fulfilled for you. Identify your demands and write them in the third column. For those you Love, write gratitudes there.
   SHARE your lists. **The reason to identify where we blame others is to correct our intention to make wrong and fulfill our own need directly.** Share ways to do this, also.
   REFERENCES: Select any references you see as appropriate.
   SPIRITUAL HOMEWORK: Correct blame by taking action on your own behalf. ("Behalf" is an interesting word. The other half of your Being is your child who awaits your attending it, or from the child view, it is your Higher Self waiting for your trust.)

✳

14. FLUSH IT OUT: *Recognizing Resistance*
   Use this technique to find out what your ego beliefs are so you can change them. Each of you, in turn, state an affirmation a designated number of times (perhaps ten) and listen inwardly for "Yes, but" responses to it. Take any affirmation and write it on an easel pad or black board. For example, I like the one, "I give no one power to disrupt the Peace that lives in my heart." "Yes, but, I can't stand people who cut me off on the freeway." "Yes, but, my job is constant pressure to perform." Another group member will record the resistance statements and give them to the speaker at completion of the flushing. The "Yes, buts" represent inner resistance to Peace, or ego investment in fear and blame. It is also a list of life areas or people you have not yet forgiven. In each of these areas you need information, expanded awareness, and options to release fear.
   Other affirmations to use would be a) "I tell the truth with kindness and courage." (Yes, but, I get so frustrated I just want to shake them and scream at them!) and b) "I have no regrets about _____." **The word "gret" relates to the word grieve. To regret is to re-grieve.** This will flush out (bring to your awareness) incomplete grief. Then find a soft, warm person to receive you.
   SHARE about the process when all people are done.

235

REFERENCES: Peace is the goal of *A Course in Miracles*, so there are many references to it.

See T p. 11/13, "You who want peace can find it only by complete forgiveness."

T p. 15/18, "Health is inner peace."

T p. 172/186, "...you always receive as much as you accept. You could accept peace now...."

T p. 257/277, "Peace abides in every mind that quietly accepts the plan God set for its Atonement, relinquishing its own."

WB Lesson #34, "I could see peace instead of this."

MT p. 49-50/51-52, "What is the peace of God?"

SPIRITUAL HOMEWORK: Flush out more resistance to Peace using affirmations. What I do, is take each "Yes, but" and make it into an affirmation which I then flush. Yes, this can go on for a long time. **We are changing our entire way of thinking.**

✳

15. "I ACCEPT": *Forgiving*

This is an exercise in forgiving which can be done by oneself (spoken with a mirror, or in writing) as well as in a group setting. **To accept is to SEE. To accept does not mean we have to like what we SEE. It means we are willing to SEE what is there. In ego illusion we are always perceiving something as there that isn't, and not SEEING something that is there. Accepting corrects this.** Because we can say, "I accept that _____ is unacceptable to me," and continue right on, this exercise has a free flow to it which allows us to move on to Love. I also find it much more helpful as a process than saying "I forgive" since these words do not help me SEE what I need to SEE. Here is an example based on my journal following a visit with my daughter. She is now both a Loving mother and on her spiritual journey to heal her inner child.

I accept that you want to be my friend.
I accept that I want to be your friend.
I accept that I wanted to be a listener for you when you were here.
I accept that you wanted to be a listener for me.
I accept that I did not feel heard.
I accept that you did not feel heard.
I accept that you were fearful.
I accept that I became fearful.
I accept that you wanted me to be strong for you.
I accept that I have changed the way I respond to you.
I accept that your inner mother voice is not yet strong for you.

I accept that I was alarmed by your energy going to sickness.
I accept that I know I cannot fix you.
I accept that I felt helpless and wanted to fix you.
I accept that I became angry and demanded of you.
I accept that I lived surrounded by sickness most of my life.
I accept that I, myself, became sick before I learned that I didn't need to live with sickness.
I accept that I paid a high price physically, emotionally, spiritually, and financially before I became aware that there is a better way.
I accept that I have dedicated my life to live Love's way. I accept that I no longer relate to sickness as I did in the past.
I accept that I went into conflict when your energy called me to be part of your sickness. (I saw it that way, anyway).
I accept that you experience the shift in my energy as abandonment.
I accept that I feel separated from you when you go the way of addictions, and going to fear is a way I try to join you.
I accept that when I go to fear, I separate from you and God.
I accept that I then lose faith in the process of Life and its inherent healing capacity.
*I accept that it is **unacceptable** for me to separate from God.*
I accept that I have every right to be me.
I accept that you are capable of learning and growing.
I accept that you may see me as a bad Mom and be hateful to me which is hurtful.
I accept that I offer you life's greatest gift - healed energy as a beacon, magnet, a model, and a receiver who can celebrate your transformation.
I accept that I have done my homework and have prepared to receive the glory I now receive.
I accept that glory is for you, also.
   Blessed Be

Each of you write out acceptance statements based on some situation in your life.

SHARE what you have written.

REFERENCES: See T p. 34/38, "Innocence or true perception means that you never misperceive and always see truly. More simply, it means that you never see what does not exist, and always see what does."

See also WB Lessons 1-50.

See references on accepting Atonement.

237

See also T p. 555/598, "Accepting the Atonement for yourself means not to give support to someone's dream of sickness and of death."

WB Lesson #139, "I will accept Atonement for myself."

WB Lesson #104, "I seek (accept) but what belongs to me in truth."

MT p. 53/55, "Accept Atonement and you are healed. Atonement is the Word of God. Accept His Word and what remains to make sickness possible? Accept His Word and every miracle has been accomplished. To forgive is to heal. The teacher of God has taken accepting the Atonement for himself as his only function."

Atonement is accepting the correction of ego beliefs which are always false. Undoing an ego belief heals inner separation. Healing means reversing our intent to resist the Life force and accepting its healing flow through us.

SPIRITUAL HOMEWORK: Make a regular habit of using this method for forgiving.

✳

16. FIXING OUCHES: *Reversing Resistance*

We have all received hurtful comments that seem to fester in us and not heal. We set up a resistance in us that says, "I am not _____." This doesn't make it go away, however, for **what we resist persists. We reinforce in our minds anything we hold in our minds. In fighting against something we are holding it in our minds.** Each of you identify such a hurtful comment. Then use the acceptance form of forgiving, working in pairs with one speaking and one listening. Accept anything that is true in the hurtful comment you received. **Accept what is there** that you have not been seeing. **Most often this is your own Goodness, strengths, and worthiness. Accept what isn't there** that you have been perceiving as being there. **Usually this is your false belief that the other is your Greater Being,** is somehow threatening your life by not fulfilling that function, or that you are not worthy of being loved.

SHARE what you realized in seeing Goodness you had denied. Also share what you accepted that allowed you to release blame/fear and see your Goodness. **When we accept our Goodness we no longer hurt.**

REFERENCES: See T p. 15-17/19-21, "The Atonement as Defense."

T p. 26/30, "...the miracle, or the expression of Atonement, is always a sign of respect from the worthy to the worthy. The recognition of the worth is re-established by the Atonement."

T p. 33/38, "The Atonement itself radiates nothing but truth. It therefore epitomizes harmlessness and sheds only blessing. It could not do this if it arose from anything but perfect innocence."

SPIRITUAL HOMEWORK: Identify more hurtful comments and accept your Goodness.

✳

17. COMPLAINTS: *Releasing Blame*

Each of you write out complaints and then turn them into requests. Help each other identify the need that is stated within your complaints. They are usually obvious as in, "You never help me clean the house." Instead of putting your focus on what the other is doing wrong, or isn't doing, help each other identify your error beliefs. These are the illusions that keep us helpless and stuck in complaining. Look for beliefs such as, "I won't be heard," "Nobody cares about me," "I have to do it all myself," "I don't deserve help," "I'll be hurt if I ask for help," or "I am helpless to change things." **Complaints are part of "special relationships." The blame aspect of the complaint keeps us bound to the other. Complaints are always indirect and indicate that we aren't really ready or willing to be free.** A direct question is, "Will you _____?" Another is, "Is this something you are willing to do?" You might say, " Are you willing to _____?"

In a special relationship, if the answer displeases us, we show anger (or the like) to *try to get* the other to change. In a holy relationship, we take another option - find another way to achieve a goal when someone says, "No." There was a time when we had two large weeping willow trees in our yard. Daily I went out to pick up debris, not only from our yard, but also from the yards on both sides of ours. I was angry that no other family member was willing to help pick up the mess. When I stopped complaining, I looked at my guilt and the burden I was taking on by telling myself I had to clean up the mess. I then had the trees removed and planted two new trees which have little debris. When we are free, we can make the change in ourselves instead of demanding that others change by complaining.

SHARE your complaints and requests.

REFERENCES: See topics of blame, anger, and special relationships.

239

SPIRITUAL HOMEWORK: Make your complaints into requests and ask directly for what you **are** wanting. Consider options if you get a "No" response to your requests. **If you consistently get a "No" response to your requests, consider a major life change.**

✳

18. SELF-CRITICISM: *Developing Loving-Kindness*
Each of you write self-criticisms for about five minutes. Then respond to them (in writing) from your inner voice of Loving-Kindness. After doing this, each take a stance before the group. Stand solidly and speak about your Goodness. Extending the energy of Loving-Kindness will attract good things to you. This energy emanates from the Holy Spirit-Beloved Child bond within you. **Shifting your energy and awareness from the critical parent voice of the ego to the nurturing voice of the Holy Spirit is ASKING.** For more on ASKING, see SECTIONS FOUR and FIVE of this chapter.
SHARE about your experience of bringing self-criticism to your awareness. Also share how you felt as you responded Lovingly to yourselves and took a stand for your Goodness.
REFERENCE: See T p. 366/392-3 on asking.
SPIRITUAL HOMEWORK: Reverse more of your self-criticisms with Loving-Kindness.

✳

19. SELF-CORRECTION: *Correcting Projection*
Each of you contemplate the following questions. Journal, and SHARE as honestly and meaningfully as you can.
   a. Something I don't like about someone. Clearly identify the trait.
   b. What is my response to that trait in the other?
   c. Do I need to give that same response to those who demonstrate that trait in my life now?
   d. Do I exhibit the same trait and not like that about myself?
   e. What is a better way to meet my needs?
   f. Do denials and affirmations. "I no longer need to believe _____." "_____ is true for me now."
   g. What action steps could you take to make yourself truly safe?
REFERENCES: See T p. 215/231, "...what you project or extend is up to you, but you must do one or the other, for that is a

law of mind, and you must look in before you look out. As you look in, you choose the guide for seeing."

T p. 89/96, "What you project you disown, and therefore do not believe is yours. You are excluding yourself by the very judgment that you are different from the one on whom you project. Since you have also judged against what you project, you continue to attack it because you continue to keep it separated. By doing this unconsciously, you try to keep the fact that you attacked yourself out of awareness, and thus imagine that you have made yourself safe."

T p. 106/114, "To heal, then, is to correct perception in your brother and yourself by sharing the Holy Spirit with him. This places you both within the Kingdom, and restores its wholeness in your mind. This reflects creation, because it unifies by increasing and integrates by extending. What you project or extend is real for you. This is an immutable law of the mind in this world as well as in the Kingdom."

T p. 121/131, "When you are willing to accept sole responsibility for the ego's existence you will have laid aside all anger and all attack because they come from an attempt to project responsibility for your own errors. But having accepted the errors as yours, do not keep them. Give them over quickly to the Holy Spirit to be undone completely, so that all their effects will vanish from your mind and from the Sonship as a whole."

SPIRITUAL HOMEWORK: Demonstrate the new qualities in your life.

✳

20. MIRROR TALK: *Making Inner Connection*

A glass artist in our group cut a mirror about 11" x 14" for each of us. Be creative in how you use mirrors.

a. Have everyone talk all at once to their child self in the mirror. This encourages, give models, and shares ideas.

SHARE how you experience this.

REFERENCE: See WB Lesson #182, "I will be still an instant and go home."

b. Play "Give Me Your Blessing" on audio tape *Holy Messengers* by Oman and Shanti. The words to the song are "Give me your blessing Holy Child of God for I would Behold you with the eyes of Christ." As you listen to the song, see the innocent child you are as well as the one looking on the child with the Love of Christ. Christ's Vision sees innocence. If you have any sensitivity to using the word, "Christ," simply hear the word as "Love." I look on you with eyes of Love. You either criticize yourself and identify as unworthy of Love, or you choose to make this inner connection. You complete your inner connection when you both speak lovingly to yourself, and identify as Beloved accepting the Love you give yourself.

SHARE how you experience connecting by using mirror talk.

REFERENCES: See WB Lesson #110, "I am as God created me."

T. p. 12/14, "Perfect love casts out fear."

MT p. 80/86, "How lovely does the world become in just that single instant when you see the truth about yourself reflected there. Now you are sinless and behold your sinlessness. Now you are holy and perceive it so." It goes on to say, now you are "not attacked but recognized."

MT p. 82/86, "...if you only knew the peace that will envelop you and hold you safe and pure and lovely in the Mind of God, you could but rush to meet Him where His altar is." Do you kneel at the altar of ego beliefs or that of the Mind of God?

WB Lesson #122, "Forgiveness offers everything I want."

WB Lesson #198, "Only my condemnation injures me."

SPIRITUAL HOMEWORK: Make mirror work a habit of choice.

Mirror talk.

SECTION THREE: SAYING "YES" AND "NO"

We are saying "Yes" and "No" at all times. When I select a vanilla ice cream cone I am saying "No" to chocolate and strawberry. When I am loving to myself I am saying "No" to being critical and abusive to myself. When I am kind to others I am saying "No" to being uncaring and hurtful to them. Exercises in SECTION THREE bring to awareness that we are making choices at all times.

Aligning ourselves with the Will of God is a process in which we master our ability to say "No" to everything that is not in our best interest. Viewed from the other side, we master our ability to say "Yes" to God. Healing is this process of shifting from ego resistance against Life, to willingly accepting that which nurtures Life.

We learn to stop going along with, putting up with, giving consent to, tolerating, overlooking, participating in, and supporting things that are harmful to ourselves and others. Because we accumulate emotional pain while we passively cooperate with abuse, our first "No" may come with rage.

Our goal is to reach a point where we say "No" harmlessly with full conviction to nurture life. We speak both to the ego voice within that calls us harm's way, and to that same voice from others and society as a whole. This is no easy task. It must be done, however. **The rewards are all that we long to have: security, safety, confidence, a healthy body, a light heart, and peace of mind.**

Note: For exercises in this section you might want to sing "I Say 'No,'" and also "No More Blame" on *Musical Companion to Sharing the Course.*

✳

21. DISTASTEFUL: *Developing Spiritual Senses*

This is an exercise to develop discernment. Judging is deciding that someone is unlovable because of what we see. We need to learn to state truth without judging, and to release the "peace at any price" habit. Go around the group several times saying, "I find _____ distasteful." Group responds with, "(Name), I support your saying that."

Our five physical senses allow us to see, hear, smell, taste, and feel touch. As Souls, to see means to understand, as in "Oh, I see." To hear is to receive inner guidance that comes as some form of knowing. To smell is to sense or intuitively know something "smells fishy." To feel is to be touched as in "I am touched by your kindness." This is accompanied by tears ranging from slightly noticeable to a solid flow. Spiritually speaking, things are "in good taste" or not. **This exercise helps us identify with our Soul's sense of what is in Divine Order and what isn't. To make wise choices we must be vigilant and trust our developing spiritual senses.**

SHARE how you feel as you make these statements. Do they feel like criticisms or do they allow you to feel safer? You could also make statements about what you find "in good taste" and see how you feel doing that.

REFERENCE: See T p. 100-103/108-111, "Be Vigilant Only for God and His Kingdom."

SPIRITUAL HOMEWORK: Continue to discern. Make these statements to yourself. Begin to act based on them. Steer clear of that which is distasteful. Trust your spiritual senses. **Few of us would pick up rotten food and eat it. Many of us feed ourselves and others "rotten" thoughts and behaviors.**

✳

22. SAYING "NO": *Developing Right Use Of Refusal*
   (See Sample Lesson No. 7, Chapter 27.)

In order to transform our lives from fear's way to Love's way we must be willing to say "No" to fear's way. This includes saying "No" to all our inner ego urgings, and also ego invitations that come from others. Put another way, this means we say "No" to all manipulations we might use to hook others, and all weaknesses that would lead us to be manipulated by others. We go through the following steps:

a. Everybody stomp around the room like a two year old stubbornly saying, "No!," "No, I won't!"

b. Then walk around the room saying "No" like a teenager does. This usually involves gestures of "leave me alone," and "get lost." Use the latest slang expressions.

c. Then walk around the room saying "No" as we need to when we are around age 28-32. This is when we are preparing to express our true selves *out* to society instead of adapting ourselves to the "shoulds" of life we took *in*. We continue *trying* to please everyone with these "shoulds" until we exercise our inner "No." **We also need to develop the inner "Yes" to following the Holy Spirit, of course.** First we need to stop the "shoulds" so we hear the higher voice guiding us Love's way. Say things like, "That is not right for me." "That is not me." "This is who I am."

"That is not something I am willing to do."   "I am willing to
_____." "I am no longer willing to do that." "This is right for
me."

    d. Practice right use of refusal. We usually refuse to go
Love/God's way. Refuse to go fear/ego's way instead. Walk
around the room saying things like: "I refuse to stay angry with
you." "I refuse to be fearful." "I refuse to hurt myself." "I refuse
to act helpless." "I refuse to stay stuck." "I refuse to keep myself
hidden." "I refuse to doubt myself." "I refuse to hate myself (my
body)." "I refuse to sit idle and wait for my Good to come to me."

    SHARE after each step. I am sure you will all have a lot to
share on this one!

    REFERENCES: See T p. 285/306, "Be not content with lit-
tleness." "Littleness and glory are the choices open to your
striving and your vigilance. You will always choose one at the
expense of the other."

    T p. 101-103/108-111, "Be Vigilant only for God and His
Kingdom."

    T p. 116/124-5, "Vigilance has no place in peace. It is nec-
essary against beliefs that are not true, and would never have
been called upon by the Holy Spirit if you had not believed the
untrue."

    SPIRITUAL HOMEWORK: **When you are clear in your
thinking you will speak your messages to others without
harmful intent.** Practice saying "No" appropriately in your life.

✳

23. "I'M FREE": *Developing Freedom From Restrictions*
    Use a kindergarten level coloring book and protect table
tops. Each of you select a picture and tape it down. Draw out of
the lines. Go beyond limitations. Make release statements as
you do so. "I'm free to be me." "I like being me." "I'm free to go
beyond limitations." "I like purple trees." "I refuse to criticize
myself." "I know how I like things." "I express how I truly am." "I
express with conviction." Be as creative as you like, doing anything other than what you were taught that was restrictive. A
great song to sing before and after doing this is by Harry Chapin,
"Flowers Are Red." It is on the album, "Legends of the Lost and
Found," Elektra Records, 1979, and on the "Gold Medal Collection" of songs by Harry Chapin released in 1988 by Elek-
tra/Asylum Records. Words to the song are very touching.
Chapin follows a child as his creativity is stunted in classroom
work.

    SHARE your pictures and your experience.

REFERENCES: See T p. 14-17/17-21, "The Origins of Separation" and "The Atonement as Defense."

T p. 285-8/306-9, "Littleness versus Magnitude."

T p. 180-2/194-6, "The Gifts of Fatherhood."

Miracle Principles #26 on T p. 2/5; #29 on T p. 3/5; #49 on T p. 4/6.

SPIRITUAL HOMEWORK: Where in your life do you experience these release statements this week? Say the statements to yourself in life situations. Find the better way.

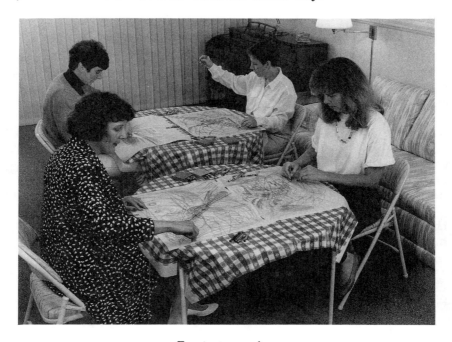

Freeing ourselves.

✻

24. CROOKED NOSE ("No's"): *Developing Decisiveness*

Discuss the pattern of sitting on a fence, keeping your nose ready to go either way. **As children we develop this habit as part of pleasing others to prevent harm to ourselves. We are afraid to say "Yes," or "No," or state a straight stance.** Common language indications are: "I don't know." "I guess." "I think." "Maybe." "Later." "We'll see." "Perhaps." "Sometime." "When I have time." "Tomorrow."

SHARE awareness of your own use of these words. Share how you feel at the time of doing that.

REFERENCE: See T p. 475/511, "There must be doubt before there can be conflict. And every doubt must be about yourself."

SPIRITUAL HOMEWORK: Be aware of your crooked statements and practice making firm statements.

✻

25. "NOT ME": *Developing Spiritual Strength*

Each of you list a few "traps" you fall into. These would be areas in which you feel weak and you let yourself down, or let others take advantage of you. Then, in pairs, Person A invite Person B to do what you have identified as your weakness. Person B practice refusing. "Not me. I'm not going to do that!" See statements in Practice Exercise No. 22 on SAYING NO. Also, speak the harmless alternative. "I **am** willing to _____."

SHARE how you feel exerting your strength FOR yourself. Do you feel safe when you do this?

REFERENCES: Select what appeals to you.

SPIRITUAL HOMEWORK: Practice making these statements in your everyday life.

✻

26. "STOP IT": *Developing Safe Boundaries*

Each of you make a list of ways you tend to go out of bounds into self-destruction or harmfulness. This may be to yourself, to others, or to property. Sit in pairs in front of a mirror. Have your partner read your list to you one thing at a time. First, in their "no nonsense" voice they will use your name and tell you to "Stop it." (For example: Laura has written on her list that she has a habit of doubting herself. Her partner will read, "I doubt myself." Then her partner will say, "Laura, stop it! Stop doubting yourself.") Then using your own "no nonsense" voice, say the same to yourself in the mirror. (Laura will now say to herself, "Laura, stop it! Stop doubting yourself.")

SHARE how you feel hearing and speaking these protective words. At your next meeting some of you will be thrilled to report that you heard that voice protect you through the week.

REFERENCES: See T p. 157/168, "You have a part to play in the Atonement....if you do not follow this Guide, your errors will not be corrected." "The way to undo them...is not *of* you but *for* you."

SPIRITUAL HOMEWORK: Listen to, and reinforce the "no nonsense" voice in your mind that keeps you safe.

✳

27. "I REFUSE": *Developing Safe Boundaries*

Sit knee to knee in pairs. Person A make the statement, "I refuse to _____ any more." Person B respond with the question, "Are you sure?" Continue, perhaps 5-10 minutes for reinforcement, and then switch roles. **Refuse to harm yourself or accept harm as normal. There is a better way.**

SHARE how you strengthened in making your statements of refusal. What inner responses did you experience to "Are you sure?"

REFERENCES: Select references that you see as appropriate to things your group members would be refusing.

SPIRITUAL HOMEWORK: Practice refusing properly in your daily life. Be aware when you experience someone stepping into your space, intruding into your boundaries, having to go too far to reach another, or do too much in a relationship. Say what is and isn't right for you. **Perhaps we mostly need to refuse to abuse ourselves. When you refuse another, do it kindly unless the person is about to harm you. In that case, refuse powerfully. In all cases, refuse with conviction. Say what you mean and mean what you say!**

✳

28. "I DEMAND": *Developing Personal Power*

This is a powerful exercise that moves so much energy that has been stuck, that it requires leadership capable of protecting an intense situation. It is so beneficial in effect that I choose to include it here. **In this exercise you become aware of how you are blaming your parents and waiting for them to give you something. What you need to realize is that your parents didn't have it to give because they were functioning under an ego restriction themselves.** Begin by calling out the following list of restrictions and any you want to add to the list. Each of you be aware of which ones trigger feelings and write them down.

> Don't be. Don't be you.
> Don't be the sex you are.
> Don't grow up. Don't be little.

Don't make it. Don't be well.
Don't see what you see, see what I want you to see.
Don't say what you see, say what I want you to say.
Don't think what you think, think what I think.
Don't feel what you feel, feel what I feel.
Don't know what you want.
Don't want what you want.
Don't say what you want.
Don't ask, take what I give you.

Have everyone sit facing out, toward the wall, so anger isn't projected at anyone. Suppose I have feelings when I hear "Don't say what you see." Then I will go through this series of statements, yelling them *forcefully* while pounding on my knees:

Releasing demand.

Mom, I demand that you say what you see. (Repeat both the statement and pounding until you feel your anger at her.)

Dad, I demand that you say what you see. (Repeat both the statement and pounding until you feel your anger at him.)

Mom (and then Dad) I demand that you say what you see to me. I demand that you tell me what you see. (This means name that which is harmful, and tell me about my Goodness.)

And then, I demand that you (speaking of yourself) say what you see.

And last, I demand that I say what I see. And, of course, this is the switch from fear to Love. Stop waiting for someone else to change first. (This means **I need to name what is harmful, and tell myself about my own Goodness.**)

Our groups do this with everyone doing it at the same time. Energy moving in one person will help evoke flow in the more reticent.

SHARE about this experience. Did you feel release of blame and freedom to change yourself?

REFERENCES: See topics as ego defense and special relationships.

SPIRITUAL HOMEWORK: Be aware of energy that is now free and direct it in healthy ways. **Be harmless, which is truly powerful because you aren't needing to change anyone else first. You are no longer holding anyone else between you and your Good, you and God.**

Note: You might want to sing "I'm Safe to Be Who I Really Am," also "No More Blame" on *Musical Companion to Sharing the Course.*

✳

29. REINFORCE TRUTH: *Developing Determination*
Take any statement of truth and reinforce it both consciously and subconsciously (in thought and feeling) by firmly taking a stance. You might all do this at once. Stand with your feet solid on the ground and speak it firmly, shout it, sing it, dance it, sculpt it, dramatize it, etc. Or, silently empower the Word of God by quieting all messages that interfere with truth.

SHARE about your experience and how you were influenced by the expressions of others.

REFERENCES: See WB Lesson #276, "The Word of God is given me to speak." WB Lesson #125, "In quiet I receive God's Word today."

SPIRITUAL HOMEWORK: Continue to take a stance for Truth.

30. SHOULDS/WANTS: *Developing Freedom Of Will*

Each of you write a list of goals. Then assess them for whether they were set up by your ego to *try* to win Love and approval from the critical voice in your mind. You'll recognize these by two characteristics:

a) the word, "should," and

b) a focus on losing or getting rid of something.

Know that these are part of the ego system of "seek and do not find."

The nature of our defense system is such that what we *try to get rid of* gets bigger. For one thing, we are giving it our attention and feeding it in our minds. Try to not think about bananas and that is all you will think about. Secondly, our ego is made of our survival decisions. Its job is to keep us alive until we make our inner connection. If we even think of getting rid of something we are doing to survive, ego resistance increases. For this reason, I discourage the use of the phrase, "get rid of." It is self-defeating.

We release our ego decisions by holding a higher decision for three days. This is when our ego tests and tempts us in all kinds of ways. It is essentially saying, "Are you sure - are you really sure?" The ego believes we will die when we let go of a survival pattern. And, of course, just the opposite is true. We let our ego die to come alive. To be free we need to respond to our ego (the fearful part of ourselves) saying, "Yes, I am sure!" Next time you are feeling "scared to death" consider the possibility that you are near a breakthrough to freedom and your ego is holding on for dear life. When we feel most unsure is when we are called upon to say, "Yes, I am sure!" The only way we can make this statement is from our connected state where Thinking and Feeling Natures are communicating. Only in this union can we courageously be free of those things that bind us.

Now write a list of goals based on being free to Be.

Example one:

Get Rid Of	Be Free To
Lose 20 pounds so I can ask _____ for a date. (I should be thin to *get* Love.)	Ask _____ for a date now and free my thinking of all self-criticism.

Going three days without criticizing your weight (telling yourself you have to lose weight to *get* Love) says you are sure that you are now willing to receive Love. This releases the *trying to get* pattern (resistance) of the ego.

Example two:

Get Rid Of	Be Free To
Get a better job. (Because I should be making more to support the family.)	Find a job that I Love to do so I am free to give all the gifts I have to give, and receive all the rewards due me.

Going three days without criticizing yourself for your current job (declaring yourself wrong as the support of your family) says you are sure that you are now willing to include consideration of your own desires in your vocation.

SHARE your lists and how the two columns feel to you.
SPIRITUAL HOMEWORK: Continue to discern goals based on your inner critical voice, and those desires which are supported by your inner Nurturer.

SECTION FOUR: ASKING FOR RELEASE OF RESISTANCE

Luke 11:10 (Holy Bible, Revised Standard Version), "For every one who asks receives, and he who seeks finds, and to him who knocks it will be opened." To ASK is to move to a higher state of consciousness, which is also known as happiness and Heaven. This means we think higher thoughts and give and receive within this higher vibration. Lower vibration is our own resistance to Life/God which keeps us suffering and miserable. It is Universal Law that we are always receiving in accord with our ASKING. Exercises in SECTION FOUR and FIVE are all to help us learn how to ASK for Heaven instead of hell.

❋

31. "I CAN'T": *Asking Is Saying "I Can"*
Each of you write a list of things that start with "I can't
_____." **The statement, "I can't," instructs our Will to continue to direct energy to ego resistance. It essentially says, "I believe there will be no Love for me if I open so I want to stay closed.** I don't even want to entertain possibilities." We continue this early life restriction long after it would be safe for us to release it. **We become aware of our restrictions by being aware of the words, "I can't."** Rewrite statements using "I can safely _____." Then speak them to the group as "I can now safely _____ because I am here to take care of myself by _____." Allow anyone to pass if they choose. In the healing process we invite others to release their restrictions. We do not push against their resistance. We do not make them wrong. Saying, "Oh yes you can," is not helpful. **Saying, "I believe it would be safe now for you to _____" invites expansion without making wrong.**

My father was a bus driver before I was six years old. Sometimes I went with him on trips. He told me as long as I sat in the seat behind the driver I would be safe. Some years ago I made a trip to Chicago. I was the only passenger on a bus and chose to sit in a front seat. A very large man got on and sat in the seat beside me. His leg completely covered one of mine. I sat there during my whole trip saying to myself, "I can't believe this. I can't believe he is doing this." Can you believe that I did that! Because I didn't let myself believe it, I also took no action to ask him to move, or to move myself. In my scare I had reverted to my

253

child view and child level information of how to handle a bus ride in the big city. I couldn't believe my Daddy's information would not keep me safe because that was all the information I had on the subject before the age of six.

SHARE whatever awareness comes from doing this exercise.

REFERENCES: See the topic of dissociation. See also,

T p. 136/146, "Dissociation is not a solution; it is a delusion."

T p. 169-70/183-84, "The Decision to Forget."

WB Lesson #96, "Salvation comes from my one Self."

SPIRITUAL HOMEWORK: Monitor your thinking and language for "I can't," "I can't believe," and "That's incredible." Change them to "I can and therefore _____." "I can believe it and feel _____ and therefore I _____ (take action)."

*

32. ON HOLD: *Asking Is Stopping My Waiting, And Acting*

Each of you list what you are waiting for. Include on your list what you are waiting to say, to have, to give, to do, to be, etc. Now select at least one item and write action steps you will take. Taking them is ASKING.

SHARE your lists and action steps.

REFERENCES: See T p. 124-6/133-5, "The Confusion of Pain and Joy."

T p. 151/162, "Any wish that stems from the ego is a wish for nothing, and to ask for it is not a request. It is merely a denial in the form of a request."

SPIRITUAL HOMEWORK: Take your action steps and report back at your next meeting.

*

33. FORGIVE DEBTS: *Asking Is Seeing My Own Resistance*

This exercise is to recognize those places you are stuck blaming. **All blame is resistance where you are focused on making someone wrong for not giving you something you want, instead of directing your own energy in ways that fulfill your desires.** In pairs, each of you identify something you believe someone owes you. Then ask this series of questions of the other allowing time for response.

Whom do you believe has failed you?
How do you believe they failed you?
How do you fail yourself?
Are you willing to give that to yourself now?

SHARE about your experience of bringing your "debts" back within your own power to fulfill them.

REFERENCES: See WB Lesson #78, "Let miracles replace all grievances."

T p. 329/354, "...forgiveness literally transforms vision, and lets you see the real world reaching quietly and gently across chaos, removing all illusions that had twisted your perception and fixed it on the past."

SPIRITUAL HOMEWORK: Who else do you believe owes you something? Where are you waiting for others to change for you to be happy? What are **you** willing to change for you to be happy now?

✳

34. MOST WANT: *Asking Is Knowing What I Want*

What you most want and don't have is what you most fear having. Without realizing it you invest your energy in resistance to keep it away. Work either in pairs, or with one person speaking to the group as a whole. The person who is speaking states a want, like "I would like to have a relationship with a man/woman." A group member then responds, "Are you sure?" You will usually say, "Yes" and then continue with a deeper statement about your want. "I feel lonely and I'd like a companion." The next person around the circle says, "Are you sure?" Continue around the circle. You will begin to see fears that are standing in the way of fulfillment, and decisions you once made to self-protect that now self-defeat. Once aware of this you can use other processes described as Healing Methods (See Chapter 5) or Practice Exercises to get new information to your Feeling Nature.

SHARE about your experience of being both speaker and questioner.

REFERENCE: See T p. 57/63, "When you are sad, *know this need not be.* Depression comes from a sense of being deprived of something you want and do not have. Remember that you are deprived of nothing except by your own decisions, and then de-cide otherwise."

SPIRITUAL HOMEWORK: Continue to clarify what you want and ways you resist. What decisions have you made that defeat you? What decisions would reverse them?

*

35. "OH, SHUCKS!": *Asking Is Releasing Fear*

Each of you start back at the beginning of your life and list down the left side of a piece of paper all the times you remember being scared. Then in the right hand column write what skill you have now to take care of yourself if that situation were to come up again. **You will be amazed at how many scares you set in motion (Feeling Nature) and never said, "Oh, Shucks! I don't need to be scared of this any more." Your Thinking Nature is now here to take care of you. These times of scare were when you inhaled and forgot to exhale. Sigh!**

SHARE your skills. This will help others become aware of skills they may not realize they have.

REFERENCES: See topic of awakening.

SPIRITUAL HOMEWORK: Do the same listing with other feelings such as envy or jealousy.

*

36. WANT LIST: *Asking Is Seeing What I Want*

The longer we live under rule of our ego, the more painful experiences we draw into our lives. Pretty soon we are so intent on fighting against what we don't want, that we lose track of what we do want. Each of you write a want list. Include on it things you want to have, do, or be. Divide them into segments, perhaps those you want within a week, a month, a year, five years, or within your lifetime. Leave room to write in action steps.

SHARE your lists.

REFERENCES: See such topics as being asleep, awakening, and fulfilling our function.

SPIRITUAL HOMEWORK: Take action steps to fulfill your wants. If you have always dreamed of taking a trip to New Zealand, talking with someone about it, getting a map, or getting a book from the library are all action steps. Also, add to your want list as things come to mind.

Remember that all substitutes, all idols, and all addictions hide true wants. Do an inventory to see when and where you take substitutes.

37. HEAR WORDS: *Asking Is Believing I Will Be Safe*

In small groups, each of you share some goal you are currently seeking to make true for yourself. Share with others what words you say to others when your dream comes true. What words do you hear others say to you? Who celebrates you? Do you celebrate you? Who is unhappy, envious? Do you see how they restrict themselves? Do you respond to them by not enjoying your achievement? Do you need help to hear good words about your achievements? Ask other group members to give you some ideas.

SHARE what words meant the most to you. Make affirmations of them and share your affirmations.

REFERENCES: Select on topic of giving and receiving. Know that we have all that we allow ourselves to receive. Ego wishes are empty of all Will to receive because of fear that we will be unloved if we accept our Good and meet our desires. To assure being loved (we think) we use willful intent to restrict ourselves (are unloving to ourselves) and hold blame toward others. Are you beginning to see that all of these exercises aim at correcting our ego perceptions so we once again open to Love/God?

SPIRITUAL HOMEWORK: Practice imagining "best possible outcomes" and add "best possible words said," also. **Only when you believe you are safe to fulfill your goal will you release your resistance to fulfilling it.**

✻

38. WRITE REVIEW: *Asking Is Seeing A Favorable Outcome*

All of us are wanting to take some courageous step in our lives. Write joyful reviews ahead of time as though your events were over and complete to your satisfaction. Write reviews for each other.

SHARE how you feel writing both your own review, and one for another.

My students wrote wonderful reviews of this book before I began writing it. Their Visions and beliefs in me inspired me. Any event deserves a review: honest revealing to someone, a performance evaluation, your first date with a new person in your life, first day on your new job, having a baby, using a riding lawnmower for the first time, a family reunion, a speaking engagement, a sports event, an exhibit of your creations, a trip, purchase of a home, or landscaping it. I've included one of the reviews written for me.

This week's review is on a sensational new book from Noelani Publishing called *Sharing the Course*. Nancy Glende is a relatively unknown author who has burst upon the publishing scene with a wonderfully insightful and compelling writing style not often encountéred today.

The content is spiritual. Once you begin reading, the words ring true, and you want to keep it accessible on your desk or night stand.

In a clear, concise style, Glende reviews *A Course in Miracles* and how to develop practice instruction for beginners as well as advanced students. She shares with us her vast experience in spiritual counseling and therapy as well as her own spiritual journey and daily application of *A Course in Miracles* principles.

This book has just hit the top of the *New York Times* best seller list and for good reason. People in this country and around the world need a new direction to follow that will change their lives and the lives of their friends and families. Nancy Glende offers that approach to living in a crystal clear, understandable new book, *Sharing the Course*.

> New York Critic
> Nancy B.

REFERENCES: See T p. 414/444, "Vision is the means by which the Holy Spirit translates your nightmares into happy dreams; your wild hallucinations that show you all the fearful outcomes of imagined sin into the calm and reassuring sights with which He would replace them. These gentle sights and sounds are looked on happily, and heard with joy. They are His substitutes for all the terrifying sights and screaming sounds the ego's purpose brought to your horrified awareness. They step away from sin, reminding you that it is not reality which frightens you, and that the errors which you made can be corrected."

T p. 105/113, "What you believe you are determines your gifts...."

T p. 192/207, "It is impossible not to believe what you see, but it is equally impossible to see what you do not believe....what you believe you *do* see."

T p. 86/94, "When you hear only one Voice you are never called on to sacrifice....by being able to hear the Holy Spirit in others you can learn from their experiences...."

SPIRITUAL HOMEWORK: Write more reviews.

✳

39. TAKE A STANCE: *Asking Is Committing My Energy*
Each of you write out:

Five reasons why I deserve _____ in my life now.
Five ways to get to that place in my life.
Five steps I will take.
Five reasons I will not back down from my stance.

Then each of you take a stance. Stand tall with your feet well planted on the ground. Make eye contact with group members. Speak firmly as you share your statements. When you are all done, SHARE how you felt taking a stance.

REFERENCES: See topic of decision. See also T p. 47/52, **"The result of genuine devotion is inspiration, a word which properly understood is the opposite of fatigue. To be fatigued is to be dis-spirited, but to be inspired is to be in the spirit."**

SPIRITUAL HOMEWORK: Follow through on your steps.

✳

40. SPEAKING AFFIRMATIONS: *Asking Is Speaking Higher Words*

This exercise uses affirmations as a healing technique. Sit knee to knee in pairs. Eye contact is important to healing. Example: Person A, who wants a woman friend and is afraid of women, states an affirmation. "I am safe to ask a woman to be my friend." Person B responds, "You are safe to ask a woman to be your friend." Continue back and forth varying the statements slightly until there is a noticeable shift of energy. This indicates the Feeling Nature has aligned with higher thought. Undoubtedly the shift was due to remembering at least one time when friendship with a woman was safe. If there is no noticeable shift in energy, that doesn't mean that nothing has happened. **You set energy in motion. This energy is Love and Love heals.**

The declaring of affirmations takes us to a higher level of energy. This is prayer. This is ASKING. Your ego may kick up and things will seem to get worse for a while. Have faith! Everything that doesn't fit with what you are asking for will begin to break up and leave your life. When you are willing to let what no longer serves your best interest leave your life, you are free to receive the answer to your prayer.

SHARE about your experience.

REFERENCES: Select some you see as relevant.

SPIRITUAL HOMEWORK: Continue this process with a mirror. Speak both voices.

SECTION FIVE: ASKING TO GO LIFE'S/GOD'S WAY

See introductory paragraph to SECTION FOUR.

*

41. HIGHER THOUGHT: *Asking Is Holding Higher Thought*
    Take a point made in *A Course in Miracles* and write a response to it from a position of accepting it as true for you (as opposed to resisting it with a "Yes, but" response). For example: T p. 12/15, "Child of God, you were created to create the good, the beautiful and the holy. Do not forget this." Begin your response with, "I am a Child of God. I am to create the good, the beautiful and the holy." Continue following your thoughts. Thought-stop any ego level thoughts. Stick only with higher thought.
    SHARE both about content on the point and your experience of writing it.
    REFERENCE: Select some points from which the group can further select.
    SPIRITUAL HOMEWORK: Dialogue further with points made in *A Course in Miracles*. Likewise, select key points from *Sharing the Course* and dialogue with them.

*

42. PRAYER ANSWER: *Asking Is Wanting The Answer*
    Each of you write answers to the following questions:
    a. For what do you pray?
    b. What would the answer look like if you received it?
    c. How will your life be different when your prayer is answered?
    d. What will you need to release to make room for the new?
    e. Are you willing to do that first?
    f. Who will celebrate with you?

    SHARE what you have realized in this self study. The larger group might want to give "best possible outcomes" for what each of you is wanting to receive. **When you SEE the best outcome as coming true for yourselves, you move to a higher feeling level and attract it to you.** (See Practice Exercise No. 68, "BEST OUTCOMES: *Sharing Hope.'*)
    REFERENCES: See MT p. 48/50, "Pray for God's justice...."
Pray for release of fear. This means ASK that you be guided to

do things the natural way rather than how you are doing them restricted by fear. Justice, in its true meaning, refers to receiving our Good from releasing resistance. This is very different from how we usually hear the word used where it means that a person gets punishment due them.

MT p. 51/53, "...prayer of the heart does not really ask for concrete things. It always requests some kind of experience, the specific things asked for being the bringers of the desired experience in the opinion of the asker."

T p. 40/45, "Prayer is a way of asking for something. It is the medium of miracles....the only meaningful prayer is for forgiveness, because those who have been forgiven have everything."

T p. 152-5/163-6, "The Answer to Prayer."

WB Lesson #183, "I call upon God's Name and on my own." Name means vibration. **To call God's Name is to radiate Love and attract the same to you.**

SPIRITUAL HOMEWORK: Continue to clarify what you want and ways you resist. What decisions have you made that defeat you? What decisions would reverse them?

Note: You might want to sing "Om Namaha Shivaya," on the audio tape with the same name. It is also among the collection of songs on *Many Blessings*. Both tapes are by On Wings of Song and Robert Gass. This song calls the Name of God and raises vibration.

Note: You might want to sing "All You Need to Do Is Ask" on *Musical Companion to Sharing the Course*.

※

43. PRAYER PROCESSES: *Asking Is Accepting The Answer*
Matthew 18:20 (Holy Bible, Revised Standard Version), "For where two or three are gathered in my name, there am I in the midst of them." Do prayer processes together. See *You Are the One* by Mary M. Jaeger and Kathleen Juline, a Science of Mind publication workbook format using a five-step Affirmative Prayer process. (Science of Mind, 3251 W. Sixth Street, P.O. Box 75127, Los Angeles, CA, 90075-9985.) See *Master Mind Goal Achiever's Journal* for an eight-step Master Mind process. (Church of Today, P.O. Box 280, Warren, MI, 48090.)

SHARE how you experience doing these processes together.

REFERENCES: See T p. 40/45, "Prayer is a way of asking for something. It is the medium of miracles. But the only meaningful prayer is for forgiveness, because those who have been forgiven have everything."

T p. 59/65, "Your mind will elect to join with mine, and together we are invincible." ("Mine" here refers to Christ, and Christ-level thinking.)

T p. 152-5/163-6, "The Answer to Prayer."

T p. 274/295, "...when two or more join together in searching for truth, the ego can no longer defend its lack of content."

WB Lesson #183, "I call upon God's Name and on my own."

WB Lesson #264, "I am surrounded by the Love of God."

MT p. 48/50, "Pray for God's justice...."

MT p. 51/53, "...prayer of the heart does not really ask for concrete things. It always requests some kind of experience, the specific things asked for being the bringers of the desired experience in the opinion of the asker."

SPIRITUAL HOMEWORK: Take action steps based on your prayer. **Remember that holding higher thought is a powerful action step in itself. This reverses your intent to resist Life and opens you to receive your Goodness.**

Note. You might want to sing "God Through Me" or "All You Need to Do Is Ask" both on *Musical Companion to Sharing the Course.*

✳

44. MOTHER/FATHER: *Asking Is Releasing And Accepting*

Close your eyes. Place your hands palms down on your legs. Release a troubling situation to Mother Earth's Love. Then turn palms up and receive new direction from Father Heaven's Love.

SHARE what you released, received, and how you experienced this.

REFERENCES: See T p. 492/529, "The wish to see calls down the grace of God upon your eyes, and brings the gift of light that makes sight possible."

WB Lesson #62, "Forgiveness is my function as the light of the world."

WB Lesson #186, "Salvation of the world depends on me."

WB Lesson #200, "There is no peace except the peace of God."

SPIRITUAL HOMEWORK: Use this technique in your daily life.

✳

45. ACKNOWLEDGMENTS: *Asking Is Healing My Past*

Start by each of you thinking of something that went unnoticed when you were a child. Perhaps you made a wonderful model (or not so wonderful) in second grade and no one seemed to notice your creativity. Ask the group to give you that notice as if you are the second grader now. When each group member has received praise as a child, move on to present time. Think of something for which you want to be praised, recognized, or acknowledged now in your life. As a group, honor these requests by giving praise.

SHARE how you feel when you get your desired recognition.

REFERENCES: See WB Lesson #125 on being quiet. This means to **quiet the voice of blame toward those who didn't see what you needed. Quieting allows you to listen to the Word of God. This is the voice that honors you. You have been using your own critical voice to fill gaps where you did not receive Love. Now you have an opportunity to fill those gaps with your own Love.**

WB Lesson #312, "I see all things as I would have them be."

SPIRITUAL HOMEWORK: Think of other scenes from your childhood and offer praise. Remember to give yourself the acknowledgment you deserve in your life now.

✳

46. NURTURING POSITION: *Asking Is Receiving Nurturing*

This is the position that holds you as a grown-up as you were held as an infant. It is for healing purposes and not to be confused with sexual expression. This is a parent/child exchange and you would emotionally experience any sexual advances as incest. **You never outgrow your need to be held.** Nurturing Position allows you to receive comfort as you heal from early scenes where you did not receive proper tending. You need not have an intimate relationship with the person holding you. The only requirement is a willingness to nurture and to receive nurturing. (See photos at the end of Practice Exercise No. 46.)

When you are holding someone, sit either on a couch, or on the floor with your back supported by a wall. When groups of people are doing this all at once, it works very well to have two holders sit back to back on the floor providing support for each other. Cross your left leg over your right to make a cradle if that is comfortable for you. The person you are holding will be leaning on their right hip and will place their head over your heart, or near your left shoulder. Both of you place your arms around each other. This is a most natural position, and yet I watch many go through contortions to get into it. This only attests to our great need for this kind of holding. Here are some rules I give:

a. Each person is responsible for their own comfort. (No two people will be in the same position).

b. A shift to correct posture does not indicate the one being held has to get up.

c. Done properly, the left arm of the holder will be supported by the arm of a couch or pillows so there is no fatigue there.

d. The one being held surrenders to be supported by the other and is not leaning on their own right elbow.

e. Both are nurtured in this process. No one ends up owing anyone anything. Generally speaking, the person being held would hold someone on another day to pass on the gift. If this is being done in a workshop setting it would be okay for people to experience both positions in a short segment of time.

f. It is a wonderful time for the holder to make affirmative statements to the other. These would be what the person most needs to hear in whatever scene is healing in the memory. A general statement that feels good is, "You are safe right now."

g. As you feel the person relax, say, "I feel you relaxing." If the person is staying tense and you say this anyway, they usually let go and begin to relax.

h. When the one being held cries, do not hand them a Kleenex. Encourage them to cry, or even sob. Say, "Good for you, let it out. Let it all come out."

i. I hold a person from fifteen minutes to an hour until it feels natural to stop. The more a person has been invested in taking care of others, the less they will believe they deserve receiving and will jump up after a few minutes to "take care of" the holder. As the holder, say, "You can have more. I'd like to give you more."

SHARE how you experience holding and being held. How did you experience any affirmations you heard?

REFERENCES: Select what appeals to you on the topic of giving to others (brothers).

SPIRITUAL HOMEWORK: Offer to hold someone. Ask to be held.

Nurturing position.

Pairs nurturing.

✳

47. "HELP ME": *Asking Is Accepting Help*

Each of you contemplate the following questions and then SHARE:

a. What is the most important goal in your life right now?
b. How do members of your family help you in attaining this goal?
c. How do they interfere? Interrupt?
d. What do you want/need from each member of your family in order to attain this goal?
e. What might you do to encourage their cooperation?
f. Have you asked yourself what their important goals are?
g. What might you do to see that all of you meet your goals?
h. What help would you like from your group?
i. What help are you willing to give to other group members?

REFERENCES: Select some of your choice.
SPIRITUAL HOMEWORK: Take action based on learnings.

＊

48. CONTINUOUS WRITING: *Asking Is Remembering The Divine Source*

For this exercise, play music in the background that does not intrude. My favorite is "The Fairy Ring" by Mike Rowland. Select a vamp statement. Vamping is what stage bands do to fill in spaces during live performances. While bands wait for a performer to reach a particular point they play the same short phrase over and over. You might use, "I'm safe," "I'm safe to see," "I write to know myself," "I am safe to say what I see," or "I Love you." (This would be said to your own Feeling Nature/inner child). Now begin to write without stopping for a predetermined amount of time. Should there by any space between thoughts, use your vamp statement until your thoughts flow again. This technique calls us to remember the Divine Source.

SHARE about your experience and any wisdom gained from it.

REFERENCES: See topics as Word of God, Holy Spirit, and Atonement.

SPIRITUAL HOMEWORK: Journal this way to problem solve. Listen for higher information as you write.

＊

49. TARGET STROKE: *Asking Is Accepting Love*
Each of you decide what you most long to have said to you. Then, say these target strokes to each other, perhaps knee to knee in pairs. Ultimately we long to hear this from ourselves. After hearing these target strokes repeated many times by others, each of you go to a mirror and say them to yourselves. This will be in "you" voice. If I most want to hear that I am precious and others protect my life, I ask others to say, "You are precious and I only protect you." I say to the mirror, "You are precious and I only protect you."
SHARE about your experience.
REFERENCE: See T p. 184/198, "Would you be hostage to the ego or host to God? You will accept only whom you invite. You are free to determine who shall be your guest, and how long he shall remain with you. Yet this is not real freedom, for it still depends on how you see it. The Holy Spirit is there, although He cannot help you without your invitation. And the ego is nothing, whether you invite it in or not. Real freedom depends on welcoming reality, and of your guests only the Holy Spirit is real. Know, then, Who abides with you merely by recognizing what is there already, and do not be satisfied with imaginary comforters, for the Comforter of God is in you."
SPIRITUAL HOMEWORK: Give further attention to what you would like to hear. Practice listening to and speaking from the higher voice within you, the one which replaces the ego voice that has only made you wrong and unworthy of Love. Ask others what they long to hear.

＊

50. VITALIZATION STANCE: *Asking Is Opening And Welcoming Life*
Stand like a cross facing East or West with your dominant hand (the one you write with) palm down, and the other hand palm up. Chant using the "Ah" sound on the keynote F. Enjoy feeling alive as the vibration builds in the room and all the cells of your body vibrate.
SHARE how you experience this.
REFERENCES: Use any related to being alive.
SPIRITUAL HOMEWORK: Take this stance on your own.

SECTION SIX: LISTENING DEEPLY

There is an unlimited amount of information available to us when we are willing to listen without judging. When we criticize or make ourselves and others wrong we don't feel safe to reveal ourselves. When we feel safe to speak, our True Selves reveal through our ego masks. Exercises in SECTION SIX are for deeper listening. This is one of the kindest things we can give to ourselves and others.

✻

51. SPEAKING/HEARING: *Listening Without Judging*

Speaking/Hearing into Being is a process used for consciousness raising among women in recent decades. It is described clearly by Sonia Johnson in *Going Out of Our Minds: The Metaphysics of Liberation* between pages 130 and 157. In this method, each of you is given an equal amount of time to talk uninterrupted and without evaluation or response. For many, this alone is a new experience. The other aspect of this challenge is listening without judging. Listeners give no facial expression or body gestures as evaluation to the speaker. Power is in joining and disrupting of usual ego processes rather than allowing ego processes to disrupt joining. Joining is true communication.

SHARE how you experience this process. (No comments on content!)

REFERENCES: See T p. 140/151, "Communication ends separation."

T p. 142/153, "To communicate is to join and to attack is to separate." "Healing is the result of using the body solely for communication."

T p. 298/320, "The willingness to communicate attracts communication to it, and overcomes loneliness completely."

SPIRITUAL HOMEWORK: Be aware of silent judgments you give and receive that lead you to alter what you are saying, or interrupt what the other is saying.

✻

52. SIMPLY REPEAT: *Listening Without Judging*

This is a simple and also powerful tool to bypass your ego habits of disrupting. It is described as the Duplication Technique in *What You Feel, You Can Heal* by John Gray. This process allows for joining. Neither the speaker nor the listener need be on guard, afraid of responses from the other, or fear not knowing how to respond to the other. It allows you safety to quite readily move to tenderness where you speak truthfully. Our groups have also done this technique with pairs sitting in front of a mirror. In exact repetition, when Person A says, "I," Person B also says, "I." Person A says, "I am afraid." Person B says, "I am afraid." Continue the repetition.

SHARE how you experience this technique, and what you gained in doing it.

REFERENCES: See topics as joining and communication.

SPIRITUAL HOMEWORK: Offer to do this for someone in your daily life. Ask them to do it for you. It is a gift we give and receive.

✳

53. UNCOVERING WANTS: *Listening Without Judging*

With one of you being "It," go around the circle asking "It" the same (or nearly the same) question. "*(Name)*, what do you want?" Continue on. Other questions are: "What specifically do you want?" "What do you really want?" "Where do you want to go?" "What do you need to do?" "What do you need to say?" "To whom?" This line of questioning allows us to listen deeply inwardly for God's plan for us. **When we reach our Truth we cry with relief.**

My groups have used this in December and have exchanged gifts that encourage meeting the needs named in this exercise. We are wanting things of Spirit here, and gifts are symbolic. My rules are that they may not cost anything, or have any calories.

Sometimes there is a minimal cost. Here are some examples from my groups: a book mark or refrigerator magnet with an individualized affirmation; a story that addresses the person's issue; a song with words written specifically for a person; laying on of hands; a toe rub; a hand massage; a group cheer (performed with an empty plastic gallon-size container and a beater for emphasis and excitement); flowers for the hair of one who wanted to be noticed; rocked in a blanket, hammock-style; and steps to development of trust played as portraits on a piano.

SHARE how you felt having the group stick with you until you got to your true heart's desire and felt them still there for you.

REFERENCE: See WB Lesson #71, "Only God's plan for salvation will work."

SPIRITUAL HOMEWORK: Develop a habit of using the above questions to ask inwardly for guidance.

✳

54. "I HEAR": *Listening Without Judging*
This is another way to speak and listen. Each of you speak for a designated length of time about a current troubling situation. Then listen QUIETLY as listeners take turns responding with, "What I hear you saying is _____." Allow responses to digest and assimilate.
Another version of this exercise would be to listen for what each of you DOES NOT see in the situation. After each speaks, listeners will respond with, "What I see in this situation is _____." Have NO discussion. Each of you take the information and do with it what is right for you.
SHARE how you experienced the process.
REFERENCE: See T p. 57-9/62-5, "This Need Not Be."
SPIRITUAL HOMEWORK: Be aware of what you might not be seeing. Be aware of what others aren't seeing. Say to others, "What I hear you saying is _____." "What I see in this situation is _____." "What I believe this situation calls for you to do is _____."

✳

55. NEW SYMBOLS: *Listening Without Judging*
Usually without being aware, we hold symbolic images in relationships. For example: You see someone else as running away like a scared chicken. You see yourself as being in a taffy pull always *trying* to pull them back and being in a real sticky mess. New symbols might be seeing the other as a tender lamb and yourself as a Loving shepherd who reaches out and invites the other to safety. Properly used, symbols allow us to connect with God's/Love's way of responding to life. In pairs, each of you share about a relationship that hurts. Listen both to yourself and the other to **see what your fear symbols are. Then replace them with Loving symbols** and share some more. Discuss some action steps as responses that fit with your new symbols. **The Course tells us to simply correct our errors.**
SHARE your symbols to heighten awareness of how we hold symbols to direct our responses.
REFERENCES: Select any you believe are appropriate.

271

SPIRITUAL HOMEWORK: Be aware of symbols in relationships. **Symbols in special relationships need to be changed to make them into holy relationships.** Change your mind. Change your responses.

✻

56. BODY SPEAKS: *Listening Without Judging*

Sit in groups of three or four with your eyes closed. Circle many times finishing this statement, "My body is telling me _____." Answers may be purely physical, like "My body is telling me it is tired of sitting." They may be emotional, like "My body is telling me I'd like to snuggle up to someone for comfort." They may be spiritual, like "My body is telling me it feels like it doesn't belong anywhere." We receive information from all levels through our bodies. This helps us listen.

SHARE what this listening was like for you.

REFERENCES: Select any you would like to use.

SPIRITUAL HOMEWORK: Is your body telling you it is time to take action steps. Take them.

✻

57. "SEE ME": *Listening Without Judging*

In pairs, each of you think of a problem in your life. I use the word "problem" loosely here for Joy may be urging to express. Then, instead of focusing on the facts of the situation, focus on any feelings. Person A help Person B by asking such questions as: "Where do you feel this in your body?" "What color is it?" "What shape is it?" "Give it a voice. What does it say?" "See it as the child you, what does it want you to see about it?" "What does your inner child need to hear from you?"

SHARE how this felt to you.

REFERENCES: Select some that appeal to you about feelings.

SPIRITUAL HOMEWORK: When you have "symptoms" in your body, talk to them as if they are a little person. Listen for responses.

58. SAYING "GOOD-BYE": *Listening Without Judging*

Write letters to those who have died, aborted ones, body parts which have been removed, or body functions you no longer have. It would also be appropriate to say good-bye to former jobs, homes, autos, friends, mates, stages of life, children who have left home, etc. Then share, perhaps in pairs or very small groups. Let your hurts be received by caring listeners.

A Course in Miracles' message is for you to accept Peace and Joy. You reach Peace and Joy by taking your thinking to a higher level, or expanding your awareness. When you hold grief, you are not allowing yourself to see the greater picture. It is important for you to feel your anger, scare, and sadness with any painful experience. Peace then comes when you acknowledge a spiritual quality as present. For example: you may "lose" procreative ability as you go through life. This is balanced by an increase in your creativity. Staying angry at what you've "lost" prevents your seeing and accepting Joy that the expanded creativity brings to you.

Other spiritual qualities that you may gain as you go through physical level "losses" include: compassion, understanding, endurance, and the calm that comes with knowing that you can make it through such crises. Along with this is the ability to release evermore readily, trusting the eternal nature of Life. **I put the words, "lose" and "losses," in quotes because you continue to grieve only if you fail to accept your spiritual gifts that come from these life experiences.**

SHARE how you feel after doing this exercise.

REFERENCE: See T p. 57-9/62-5, "This Need Not Be."

SPIRITUAL HOMEWORK: Work with affirmations related to the Universe being Just. Where you are sad, know there is something more for you to see and receive.

✳

59. SYMPTOMS SPEAK: *Listening Without Judging*

Another way to tap into deeper intuitive information is to talk to a symptom. **Our bodies hold pain until we tell our truth** (claim our Goodness which is our true identity as Children of a Loving God). Behind every sickness (I'd say injuries, too) there is someone we knowingly or unknowingly blame. This is true by Law since sickness is of the ego. The ego always blames someone else for conditions that result from separation from the healing Life Force. We never realize that our own choice to defend is what separates us and causes our conditions. The point of awareness is also the point of release and forgiveness. This technique helps us see who we are blaming and need to forgive.

In releasing, we accept from our own Inner Nurturer what we have been waiting for from that aspect of another. This exercise can be done alone by writing out the steps in a journal. Here I give steps for use in a group setting.

a. Person A sits facing an empty chair imagining their symptom is on the chair. (Examples of symptoms: cancer, back pain, restlessness, bladder infection, fatigue, high blood pressure, headache, sprained ankle, cut finger.) Person A says everything they want to the symptom, like "You are hurting me and I don't like it." Another group member writes these statements down the left side of a sheet of paper.

b. Person A moves to the symptom chair. As the group member reads the list back one at a time, Person A responds as though they are the symptom speaking. **The left hemisphere of our brain cannot deal with this so it will turn the job over to our creative right hemisphere. That is also the part of us that creates symptoms and knows what they are all about.**

c. The group member then reads statements from column A to Person A who names the person to whom they would like to make each statement. It could be someone who is now, or once was in their life. Sometimes there is a statement in column B which they would like to make to someone.

Example of how the paper looks when completed:

Column A	To Whom	Column B
You are a pain in the neck.	Maggie	I know.
I don't like you.	Maggie	I don't blame you.
You hurt me.	Mom	That's not my intent.
I don't want you in my life.	Maggie/ Mom	I can understand.
My attention is drawn to you all the time.	Maggie	Yes, indeed, that is what I want.
I'm afraid you will just keep getting worse and I won't be able to stand you.	Maggie	I'll continue until you hear me.

I'm mad because I can't sleep with you around.	Maggie	I know. Listen to me.
You wear me down and I just want to cry.	Maggie	Cry and then listen to me.
What do you want from me.	Maggie	See me, hear me.
What do you want me to know.	Maggie	You ignore me.
What will make you go away?	Maggie	Love me and I'll stop clinging to you.

This example indicates that behind the symptom is some unresolved issue related to Mom and carried over in a "special relationship" with Maggie. When energy is reversed by forgiving, the symptom will be relieved. Amazing responses come from the symptom voice that reveal the cleverness of our subconscious to create symptoms as metaphors. Remember that our subconscious does not discern harm. It just knows ways to get attention when needed.

SHARE how you experienced using this method. Are you amazed at the amount of information revealed?

REFERENCES: See topics as sickness, special relationships, and forgiving.

SPIRITUAL HOMEWORK: Speak and listen to your symptoms using your journal.

✳

60. "CALL ME": *Listening Without Judging*

Each of you write your name and phone number on a 3x5 card along with something you would like someone to check in on you about during the next week. Place your cards face down in the center of your circle. Each of you draw one card and call the person during the week. Practice your new deeper listening skills.

SHARE how you feel knowing someone will call you to care about your concern. And, next week say how that was for you.

SPIRITUAL HOMEWORK: Make the call and use listening skills learned from exercises in SECTION SIX of this chapter.

✳

SECTION SEVEN: SHARING IN HOLY WAYS

Stories, myths, fables, parables, and fairy tales have been shared from the beginning of human communication. They all offer information to our creative minds to help us see ways out of stuck places. Exercises in SECTION SEVEN are ways to share information so we can see ways out of troubling situations.

As grown-ups, when we *seek advice* of another, we are asking that person to be one-up to us - our Greater Being in a "special relationship." When we *give advice* we are treating the other as one-down to us in a "special relationship." It is a very different experience to freely give information, options, and answers that have worked for us. **Freely given information allows the other to pick and choose, and then creatively reassemble information to arrive at their own solution.**

Freely chosen options are harmless by nature. When we believe we have to please others or resist others we go ways that are not true to our Being. When we believe we have to change others to protect ourselves we judge the decisions they make to solve the problems in their lives. It takes courage for all of us to grow spiritually. In holy relationships we help and celebrate each other.

✳

61. NASTY KID: *Sharing Hurts*

In pairs, allow ten minutes for each of you to speak anything the nasty kid inside would like to say to anyone. Do not use your time to tell your partner about the scene or the person. Simply say whatever comes to mind. These are comments that come from times of hurt when others were perceived as harmful rather than helpful. Listen for any themes that run through the comments. Listen for needs of the hurting inner child. Listen for where the child feels powerless. Yes, you may use profanities during these ten minutes. This may be difficult for you if you are used to being very nice and never allowing yourself to say anything against other people. Remember that this kind of exercise is done to bring up repressed information from your own hurts for the purpose of healing, not to hurt anyone. After both of you have had your turn as "nasty kid," then put your heads together and share what you think your Feeling Nature needs from you.

SHARE with your group what you realized about yourself.

REFERENCES: See T p. 12/14, "All aspects of fear are un-true...." Read to the end of this section. This is a good test for truth. If fear exists, we are not yet seeing all that is there to see.

T p. 124-6/133-5, "The Confusion of Pain and Joy."

T p. 225/241, "Little child, this is not so. Your 'guilty secret' is nothing, and if you will but bring it to the light, the Light will dispel it." **"Nasty kid" thoughts are blame and are bound with guilt. They are among other things we hold as "guilty secrets" which need to be released.**

SPIRITUAL HOMEWORK: Take at least one action step based on your learnings from this exercise. An example would be to say "No" to something which you are still doing which hurts you.

✳

62. CONFESSION: *Sharing Dark Secrets*

In pairs, share with each other what you believe makes you unlovable. Our whole ego system is maintained with judgment and secrecy. Sometimes we only need to share our dark secrets with one Loving person to be able to release judgment that we are unlovable and can then get on with our lives.

SHARE with the whole group. All sigh three times followed each time with saying, "The crisis is over."

REFERENCES: See T p. 255-59/274-78, "The Decision for Guiltlessness."

T p. 47/52 Speaks of voluntarily giving up ego repetitions to join in the resurrection.

T p. 192-4/207-9, "Waking up to Redemption."

WB Lesson #196, "It can be but myself I crucify."

SPIRITUAL HOMEWORK: As more situations come to your mind, use a Healing Method (See Chapter No. 5). Receive your-self Lovingly. Confess to God, to your mirror, in your journal, or to a group member. Sigh!

Note: You might want to sing "Sigh, The Crisis I Over" on *Musical Companion to Sharing the Course.*

✳

63. "WHAT IF": *Sharing Information*

Fear is relieved by information. This means new and ex-panded information to the part of you that has been asleep, restricted in fear. Take turns naming fears. "What if _____?" These come from your child self. **The child is really always ask-ing if it is going to die.** Group, give the highest information you know. Do not laugh at any child question.

Examples: "What if I lose my job? Possible answers: "You'll get another." "You know how to get a job." "You'll be safe." Another example: "What if I panic on the freeway?" Our ego knows all kinds of ways to get attention by alarming others with no discernment when it comes to harmfulness. It will use an accident as a way to do this even if it kills us. Possible answers: "Tell your child you will not let it use an accident as a way to get attention." "Thank your child for letting you know it needs attention and talk to it Lovingly." After the whole group gives answers to the question, invite the questioner to make statements. "If _____ happens I can _____ ." **When you see one new way of responding in a stuck spot you are no longer stuck.**

SHARE how you experienced receiving higher information for your "What ifs." How do you feel knowing you are free to take options?

REFERENCE: See T p. 170/183 on remembering when we are in fear.

SPIRITUAL HOMEWORK: Respond to your own inner child's "What ifs" with the highest information you have in your inner parent.

Note: You might want to sing "Find the Highest Thought" on *Musical Companion to Sharing the Course.*

✳

64. DILEMMA: *Sharing Solutions*

Each of you share how you have solved a life dilemma. Select one you all have in common such as:

a. saying "No" to things that aren't right for you,

b. accepting what is right when that differs from what others around you are doing, or

c. developing a career that expresses your own individual gifts.

SHARE how you feel as you realize you are not alone with your problems.

REFERENCES: Select some based on the dilemma you use.

SPIRITUAL HOMEWORK: Give a different response to a dilemma in your life using some information gained in this sharing.

✳

65. DRAW CONFLICT: *Sharing Solutions*

Each of you draw a conflict situation. What could you add to the drawing to resolve the scene? Do so.

SHARE your experience of resolving the conflict this way. What did you add? Remember that fear is relieved by information from the Holy Spirit (expanded Vision). Did you expand your Vision?

REFERENCE: See T p. 26/30 on corrective steps to undo conflict as an expression of fear.

SPIRITUAL HOMEWORK: Do more drawings. What is the common element? Is there one thing you need to continue to add? Is there someone you now see you need to forgive?

✳

66. DRAW BRIDGE: *Sharing Solutions*

Each of you do a drawing that depicts anger or some other unresolved feeling. This will be your child's viewpoint (Feeling Nature). Then draw a caring, helpful response that resolves the feeling (Thinking Nature). What was your bridge between the two? What is your new thought?

SHARE your drawings and your bridge thoughts.

REFERENCES: Select what appeals to you.

SPIRITUAL HOMEWORK: Draw more bridges to your Feeling Nature.

✳

67. "I'M HERE": *Sharing Relief*

All of us have times of embarrassment or hurt because we simply didn't know something. Our Feeling Nature feels very unsafe and wonders if it will happen again. Write letters to the innocent child in you saying, "I'm here." This is from your Thinking Nature, of course. Listen for any leftover scare or hurt, or perhaps anger and blame. Offer assurance that you Love your inner child no matter what. Write until you sigh, feel safe, and are ready to get on with Life.

SHARE your letters.

REFERENCE: See topic of happy dreams. Happy dreams are pictures we hold in mind in which we see someone there for us.

SPIRITUAL HOMEWORK: Make it a habit to say "I'm here" to your inner child throughout the week.

✳

279

68. BEST OUTCOMES: *Sharing Hope*
Each of you briefly tell about a current dilemma in your life and then listen silently while others give options, suggestions, and best possible outcomes they see to the dilemma. Since **every problem situation is one in which you are in fear, imagining a worst possible outcome,** this will bring you hope and many sighs. Help each other eliminate the urge to resist with a "Yes, but," by insisting that the listener be silent and not respond. This is a time to take in ideas as seed thoughts. Expanded thinking is of the Holy Spirit. When our groups do this, we are amazed by the profound wisdom that begins to pour through us.
SHARE how you experienced being both the giver and receiver of information. Remember to NOT respond to information given in this exercise.
REFERENCE: See T p. 502/540, **"To give a problem to the Holy Spirit to solve for you means that you *want* it solved. To keep it for yourself to solve without His help is to decide it should remain unsettled, unresolved, and lasting in its power of injustice and attack."**
SPIRITUAL HOMEWORK: Practice thinking of best possible outcomes in any situation you see in your life or that of others. Offer hope.

✳

69. OPEN DOORS: *Sharing Joy*
Draw pictures in which you open doors to incoming Spirit and release fear.
SHARE you pictures and speak about your content.
REFERENCES: Select some of your choice.
SPIRITUAL HOMEWORK: Imagine Spirit coming in through your open door. Welcome it.

✳

70. NEW ENDINGS: *Sharing Joy*
Share a night time dream with the group and select people to be the characters. Decide on a new ending and act it out to come to a happy resolution. You can also do this with painful early scenes in which no one came to your protection when there was harm present. Have someone come now. Tell what the situation was, then be the little one and others can come to your protection. They can use protective voices and say things like, "Stop

it!" "Get away from him/her." "I won't let you hurt him/her." Take the person by the hand and lead them to safety.

SHARE about your experiences resolving dreams and scenes this way.

REFERENCE: See T p. 506-8/544-6, "Many Forms; One Correction."

SPIRITUAL HOMEWORK: Love does not put up with non-sense. If you felt good speaking against harm to another, use your same firm voice for yourself. If you had the experience of someone protecting you in the face of harm, activate that same protective voice in yourself and bring new endings into your life.

SECTION EIGHT: GAINING SELF-AWARENESS

Sharing with others in a safe setting is one of the most comforting and enjoyable ways to learn about ourselves. Exercises in SECTION EIGHT encourage us to look at ourselves in various ways. The more we SEE about ourselves, the more we can sort out the old and embrace the new.

❋

71. UPDATING IDENTITY: *Updating Myself*
Write out who you were when you started a relationship. What things have changed since then? How have each of you changed since then? I did this using one of my children as the other person. I was amazed to realize all the changes I had made that he needed to adjust to in his life. I was so accustomed to only looking at how I had to adjust to his developing. I gained compassion for him in doing this self-study.
SHARE your realizations.
REFERENCES: See T p. 115/124, "...understanding brings appreciation and appreciation brings love."
T p. 113/122, "Understanding is appreciation, because what you understand you can identify with, and by making it part of you, you have accepted it with love. That is how God Himself created you; in understanding, in appreciation and in love."
SPIRITUAL HOMEWORK: Update your identity in other relationships. Include a study of your relationship to institutions as family, financial, religious, educational, medical, governmental, etc.

❋

72. CLUSTERING: *Freeing Myself*
This is a tool which can help you get unstuck by calling for information that is in your subconscious, not yet in conscious awareness. We are used to thinking linearly. When an exercise doesn't fit the usual, our brain turns it over to our intuitive faculty, which is non-linear in its function. Use a large piece of paper and write a name, thought, or a word (which could represent a problem) in the center of the paper and put a circle around it. Now, as words come to mind that relate to what you wrote, build a network out from the center. Include feelings and ideas that come to awareness. Stop when you feel finished. I feel complete when some new awareness comes to me. If you feel incomplete,

you might want to take one thought from your first cluster, put it in the center of another paper, and continue the same process.

SHARE your clusters, new awarenesses, and your experience of doing the exercise.

REFERENCE: See T p. 354/379-80, **The holy instant is the moment of Truth when we break through illusions.** "Those who would see *will* see." "The holy instant is the result of your determination to be holy. It is the *answer*. The desire and willingness to let it come precede its coming."

SPIRITUAL HOMEWORK: Do clustering to gain more self-awareness.

Clustering.

✳

73. LOVING: *Evaluating Myself*

Where are you in the process of learning to Love yourself? God? Others?

SHARE in pairs and then in the whole group.

REFERENCES: Select some references on Love.

SPIRITUAL HOMEWORK: Continue to ask this question of yourself. See where you are giving Loving responses and where you still respond with fear.

74. DRAW A TREE: *Depicting Myself*

Ethel Johnson wrote a delightful little book called *Draw Me A Tree*. It is out of print and available through interlibrary loan. It is worth finding a copy. Each of you draw a tree. Ethel Johnson tells you many things to look for about yourselves which will be reflected in your trees. What do you see in your pictures?

SHARE your pictures and what you expressed about yourselves in them.

✳

75. DRAW A CARD: *Studying Myself*

Either using published materials, or cards you make yourself, each of you draw a card with a thought from *A Course in Miracles* on it.

SHARE how the message relates to your life right now.

REFERENCES: Examples of verses to use on cards:

T p. 504/542, Sacrifice "...is always an attempt to limit loss."

T p. 371/398, "...when a situation has been dedicated wholly to truth, peace is inevitable."

T p. 255/274, "The happy learner cannot feel guilty about learning."

By the way, I selected these thoughts by letting my book fall open three times. We need not make hard work of life!

SPIRITUAL HOMEWORK: Use verses from *A Course in Miracles* to study yourself.

✳

76. LOVE YOURSELF: *Accepting Myself*

(This is used in Sample Lesson No. 8, Chapter 27.) Know that what you reject in yourself goes unloved and outpictures as ugliness or problems in your life. What you Love becomes beautiful. Sitting knee to knee in pairs, Person A ask Person B "Who are you?" Person B respond with whatever comes to mind. Person A say, "Love that about yourself." Do this enough times to get beneath the surface to feelings, and to some information that allows for a new attitude toward yourself. Example:

> Who are you? I am a man. Love that about yourself.
>
> Who are you? I am a husband. Love that about yourself.
>
> Who are you? I am a father. Love that about yourself.

Who are you? I am a repairman. Love that about
yourself.

Who are you? I doubt myself. Love that about
yourself.

Who are you? I'm angry about ___. Love that
about yourself.

Who are you? I wait for ___ to show some sign of
care about me. Love that about yourself.

Who are you? I am a caring person and I can
show care to myself instead of anger. Love that
about yourself.

SHARE about your experience.

REFERENCES: See T p. 42/46, "Judgment always involves
rejection. It never emphasizes only the positive aspects of what
is judged, whether in you or in others."

T p. 42/47, "You have no idea of the tremendous release and
deep peace that comes from meeting yourself and your brothers
totally without judgment."

SPIRITUAL HOMEWORK: Continue to Love aspects of yourself that come to your awareness, *especially* those that seem
least Lovable. They are only aspects that have not yet been given
a chance to become beautiful.

✳

77. FACE MASK: *Revealing Myself*

Draw a mask. On one side, let's say the front side of your
paper, draw a line vertically. On one side of that line draw your
face showing the feelings you most often hide. On the other side
of that line, draw your face of blame. We are always blaming
someone for the misery we keep hidden. On the back side of
your paper, draw your Face of Grace. **Grace is our willingness
to see what is, and learn what we need to know without making ourselves or anyone else wrong. We are simply to correct
our errors as we become aware of them.**

SHARE your masks and tell about your "faces."

REFERENCES: See WB Lesson #347, "Anger must come from
judgment. Judgment is the weapon I would use against myself,
to keep the miracle away from me."

WB Lesson #348, "I have no cause for anger or for fear, for
You surround me. And in every need that I perceive, Your grace
suffices me."

WB Lesson #168, "Your grace is given me. I claim it now."

WB Lesson #169, "By grace I live, By grace I am released."

SPIRITUAL HOMEWORK: Be aware of "faces," hidden faces and your Face of Grace. Others know your Face of Grace by its genuine smile. Everything else is unhealed pain and there are truly no secrets about this.

*

78. STROKE HAND: *Nurturing Myself*
In pairs, your partner will stroke your hand, face, or hair while you close your eyes and search inwardly for what you long to hear from a Mother or Father. This would most likely be something you did not hear as a child and need to say to yourselves from your own inner Nurturer. Following this nurturing time, go to a mirror and speak the words enough times to register them at the feeling level.
SHARE about your experience.
REFERENCES: Select some you like.
SPIRITUAL HOMEWORK: Be aware of other things your child wants to hear from you and speak them. (See Chapter No. 5, Healing Methods.)

*

79. NEW BELIEFS: *Expanding Myself*
For expanding thought and gaining new awareness, sit in pairs. Take turns sharing honestly about a current challenge in your life. Afterward, each of you take a turn making several of the following statements about your situation: "I'm beginning to believe _____."
SHARE your budding beliefs with the larger group.
REFERENCES: See T p. 8-9/11-12, "The Escape from Darkness."
T p. 294-98/317-20, "The Needless Sacrifice."
T p. 576/620 on idols (habits of mind and behavioral addictions we think will save us).
T p. 617-19/663-66 on temptation to stay in misery.
WB Lesson #15, "My thoughts are images that I have made."
WB Lesson #62, "Forgiveness is my function as the light of the world."
WB Lesson #69, "My grievances hide the light of the world in me."
WB Lesson #70, "My salvation comes from me."
WB Lesson #73, "I will there be light."
WB Lesson #153, "In my defenselessness my safety lies."

SPIRITUAL HOMEWORK: Reinforce your new beliefs by focusing on them in various ways. Look for evidence of their truth in your daily life.

✳

80. SPIRITUAL GIFTS: *Affirming Myself*
    Each of you take the following steps quietly:
    a. List several people close to you - family, friends, or coworkers.
    b. What spiritual qualities would you like to give each as a gift? (faith, gentleness, truthfulness, vitality, compassion, etc.)
    c. What spiritual quality do you think each would like to give you?
    d. Is this something you would like to increase in yourself?
    e. Imagine sitting within the vibration of that pure quality - like someone striking a tuning fork and the vibration of your named quality ringing out.
    f. Go around the circle and each of you take a turn affirming your chosen quality. For example: "I am Nancy, I am enthusiastic." Group respond in chorus, "You are Nancy. You are enthusiastic and I (or we) like you that way."

SHARE about this experience, both the information gathered and the affirming.

REFERENCE: See MT p. 8-15/9-16, "What Are the Characteristics of God's Teachers."

SPIRITUAL HOMEWORK: Bring your named quality into your life experience. Declare, "I am ready and willing to be _____." Think it, picture yourself as it, speak the word, sing it, affirm it, pray for it, live it, and give gratitude for it. There was a time in my life when I could be fiercely efficient at the disregard of all feeling. One quality I had not developed was gentleness. About that time I purchased a hammer dulcimer. I named her Gently. Every time I went to play, I would make the statement, "I'm going to play Gently." I did all the above, too, to build the quality into my Being. After a couple of months people began saying to me, "Nancy, you are so gentle." I have remained so over the years.

SECTION NINE: BROADENING AWARENESS

Exercises in SECTION NINE are designed to help us receive into awareness what is already there that we have not yet recognized. By opening and expanding in these ways we have more to give or extend to others. Changing from fear to Love is seeing more than we saw before and therein choosing new responses.

�֍

81. "TELL ME": *Teaching Love*
Either sitting knee to knee in pairs, or as one individual listening to the group as a whole, tell each other ways you see each other teaching (demonstrating) Love, Trust, Faith, Kindness, etc. You need to hear these things from others. It is astounding how beautiful you can be and not see your own beauty.

SHARE how you feel when you tell others, and hear about your Goodness.

REFERENCES: Select references that appeal to you.

SPIRITUAL HOMEWORK: Continue to acknowledge your Goodness in your journal, or using a mirror. Tell others about strengths you see in them. And, yes, tell others about strengths you have. Do this in a way that acknowledges and gives gratitude to the many gifts Life/God has given you.

�֍

82. INNER VOICE: *Being Guided*
SHARE stories about how you experience the inner voice, or how you are inner/divinely guided.

REFERENCES: See topics as guide, guidance, Holy Spirit, and Voice for God.

SPIRITUAL HOMEWORK: Be aware of your inner voice, the quieter voice that encourages. Speak it aloud to amplify it. Speak your Loving messages with firmness and certainty.

�֍

83. DEDICATION: *Living Virtues*
Sit in a circle with your eyes closed. Place your hands with palms up on your knees or a table. Go around the circle naming virtues. See them as being placed as gifts in your hands. Do this slowly so you can image and feel each virtue named. At the end of the naming, place your hands over your hearts and dedicate yourselves to live expressing these gifts you've received. You

might want to deepen the experience by making a vow, pledge, or dedication as you light a candle.

Virtues include: Vitality, Strength, Effectiveness, Discernment, Beauty, Power, Enthusiasm, Imagination, Wisdom, Kindness, Peacefulness, Radiance, Purity, Clarity, Endurance, Orderliness, Grace, Awareness, Gentleness, Happiness, Flexibility, Honesty, Tenderness, Faithfulness, Youthfulness, Ease, and Good Will.

SHARE about your experience.

REFERENCES: See T p. 14/17, "To extend is a fundamental aspect of God which He gave to his Son."

T p. 120/129, "...without extension there can be no love."

T p. 215/231, We are either projecting or extending at every moment. "When you want only love you will see nothing else."

WB Lesson #123, "I thank my Father for His gifts to me."

WB Lesson #169, "By grace I live. By grace I am released."

WB Lesson #315, "All gifts my brothers give belong to me."

WB Lesson #316, "All gifts I give my brothers are my own."

WB Lesson #344, "Today I learn the law of love; that what I give my brother is my gift to me."

SPIRITUAL HOMEWORK: Acknowledge to yourself when you demonstrate these qualities.

＊

84. "LOVE YOU": *Valuing Others*

If you had to move away, whom would you miss? Have you told them you value them? Tell them specifically what you value about them. Meanwhile, practice in group. In pairs, eyes closed, allow your partner to be people from your past from whom you are separated. This separation could be for any reason including death. You may want to thank a part of your body, or a body function you once had. Taking roles for each other, speak and listen to statements of Love not yet expressed.

SHARE about your experience.

REFERENCES: Select some on extending Love.

SPIRITUAL HOMEWORK: Extend Love.

＊

85. NEW CHOICES: *Choosing Again*

This is another way to look at survival patterns we need to overcome. In *A Course in Miracles*, the following are called special relationships. Transactional Analysis theory says we adapt to take three roles in survival patterns. **We learn to persecute (be hurtful), to rescue (be helpful), or to be a victim (be helpless). All of these are harmful because of their ego intent. All are aimed at *getting* rather than giving.** Persecuting is expressing blame and anger at others, *trying to get* them to change so we feel safe and Loved. Rescuing is *trying* to keep others from falling apart as a way of keeping ourselves from feeling threatened. The victim stance brings all kinds of attention through pity and guilt. When we are in our egos we live in these three roles. We predominately live one role and resort to the other two.

For example, suppose I am a very nice person. I am always doing what I think will please others. Over time, I build resentment because I really want people to be nice to me. So I start complaining. I have now switched from being helpful to being hurtful in these roles. I might have been nice to the point of exhaustion and become ill. Then I would be the helpless position.

As a child did you learn to be nice? Did you bully others? Or, were you often ill, injured, or confused? Discuss with each other how you got attention as children. What roles did your parents predominately live? Which roles did your siblings live? What was that like for you as a child? What is it like for you now? Have you changed? If so, SHARE generously how you managed to overcome these adapted patterns. You will inspire others.

REFERENCES: See topic of special relationships.

SPIRITUAL HOMEWORK: **Look for these three patterns in your life and change your part rather than *try* to change the person playing the opposite role.**

✳

86. HEALTHY RELATIONSHIP: *Fulfilling Relationships*

We so often focus on what we don't want in a relationship. Know that everything you don't want is due to projection of blame. The key characteristic of special relationships is that you are *trying to get* something from the other. In pairs, small groups, or the group as a whole, name characteristics of a healthy/holy/loving relationship.

SHARE your experience of this switch of focus.

REFERENCES: See references on relationship.

SPIRITUAL HOMEWORK: Think of four things you ordinarily hold yourself back from giving in a relationship. Give them this week.

✳

87. ALREADY DONE: *Feeling Complete*

Think of something you want to do. Project to the future. Tell stories from the perspective of having already done it. Tell the story of how you fulfilled your greatest (currently unmet) desire.

SHARE how this feels to you. Feelings are key to manifesting in our lives.

REFERENCES: Completion is Joy. See references on Joy, happiness, and gladness.

SPIRITUAL HOMEWORK: Develop mental pictures of situations becoming Joyful.

✳

88. GIVE IT: *Willing To Give*

On page 181 of *A Return to Love*, Marianne Williamson says, "When our desire is to give instead of get, our core belief is that we have so much abundance, we can afford to give it away. The subconscious mind takes its clue from our core beliefs, and brilliantly manufactures situations that reflect them. Our willingness to give directs the universe to give to us." In material reality, if I have five pencils and I give them away, I have no pencils left for me. This is the kind of thinking we all learn in the first phase of our lives. Spiritual reality reverses this law. Spiritual qualities are only experienced when we give and receive them. I feel the delight of smiling at a friend only in giving the smile. I know gentleness only in giving a gentle response in a life situation. I know Peace only in being Peaceful. **To give, is to extend a holy quality in my Being.** Then I have it.

The commandment, "Thou shalt not steal," at face value means do not steal. On a deeper level it means we cannot steal, or take any spiritual quality from another. We must give it to have it. Highest thought goes to deepest meaning. Careful discernment is required to recognize where we are doing for others from a state of fear, *trying to get* them to be Loving to us, and when we are giving Love. We mistake the two. Improper giving leaves us heavy with resentment.

Each of you think of what you are *trying to get* in your lives, or what you want to *get*. Then discuss ways of giving that. Consider working with symbols. Since resentment is a heavy feeling, a symbol for giving might be a box full of light, fluffy feathers that flow out freely with the slightest breath of air. Image the feeling of the empty box. Imagine the feeling of the feathers so free in flowing. Imagine the box filling again with light, fluffy feathers. Focus on symbols and actions that give.

SHARE whatever is aroused in you with this information.

REFERENCES: See T p. 154/166, "...to receive is to accept not to get. It is impossible not to have [spiritual qualities], ...it is possible not to know you have."

T p. 197/212, "...you believe that you can get by taking."

T p. 343/368, "Only what *you* have not given can be lacking in any situation."

T p. 133/143, "Giving of yourself is the function He [God] gave you."

T p. 181/195, "To give without limit is God's Will for you, because only this can bring you the joy that is His and that He wills to share with you."

T p. 96-8/104-6. "To Have, Give All to All."

T p. 98-100/106-8, "To Have Peace, Teach Peace to Learn It."

SPIRITUAL HOMEWORK: Be aware of *getting* and giving. Build your power of discernment. **Trying to get means that you believe you do not deserve.**

*

89. SPECIAL LETTER: *Giving New Responses*

Write a letter to one whom you believe harmed you. This may have been an active commission or passive omission. Use the following form.

a. This is what you did to me _____ (perception/blame).
b. This is how I felt about it at the time.
c. This is what I truly wanted.
d. This is how I responded to you then.
e. This is how my response affected my life.
f. This is what I am still waiting for (I want you to change while I insist on following my old response pattern).
g. This is what I tell myself you owe me.
h. I see I need permission to _____ (new response).
i. I see at least this one step I can take to give it to myself now.

j. This is what I will do - offer you - whether or not you give me what I want from you.
k. I see that I have blamed you for being deprived of __________, and I forgive you to free myself now.

Do any further accepting following the format in Practice Exercise No. 15.

SHARE both about the process and content of your letters.

REFERENCES: See T p. 337-46/362-71, "The Healed Relationship" through "The Conditions of Peace."

T p. 470-481/505-517, "The Forgiveness of Specialness" through "The Meeting Place."

SPIRITUAL HOMEWORK: Take steps based on new information, especially following through on step "j."

*

90. "I'VE ARRIVED": *Recognizing Achievements*

Many times we get so intent on *getting* somewhere that we fail to recognize when we arrive. Go around your circle many times sharing what you have achieved. Nothing is too simple or unworthy of recognition. Perhaps you are now arriving at meetings on time. Good for you! State that as an achievement. Have fun in giving recognition to each other. Take a bow. Use applause. Give a "rah rah." Write a huge "WOW" on the black board. Ask for a silent, reverent type of recognition if you prefer that. I like palms joined (prayer position) in front of our heart center, with a quiet bow.

SHARE how you feel when you acknowledge your achievements, and those of others.

REFERENCES: See topics as Joy, happiness, gladness, glory, freedom, wholeness, health, Home, Heaven, and gratitude.

SPIRITUAL HOMEWORK: Be aware of your achievements and give a Joyful response. **Giving gratitude completes Joy.**

SECTION TEN: INSPIRING CREATIVITY

We live in a time when our life activities call us to predominately use the left hemispheric functions of our brain. Wholeness/holiness calls for us to balance this with right hemispheric functions which are intuitive, symbolic, and creative. SECTION TEN exercises fulfill this need. Your part is to do them and enjoy them. Spirit does the rest.

＊

91. POETICAL FORMS: *Writing Poetry*
    Poetry invites us to the holy by calling on imagery and symbolic functions in our thought processes. I include four forms here. My favorite is the PANTOUM which originated in Malaysia. Stanzas interlock with lines 2 and 4 of each stanza becoming lines 1 and 3 of the next. The format calls for lines to be of equal length and for alternate lines in the stanzas to by rhymed. Following these last two rules is not necessary for our purposes. I use the structure to combine thoughts in a new way. I have used it when teaching various concepts. Students write eight thoughts over a period of time, and then put them into the structure and share. I instruct the group to write the following numbers down the left side of a piece of paper leaving a space between each number. 1,2,3,4, 2,5,4,6, 5,7,6,8, 7,3,8,1. After eight thoughts have been written beside numbers 1 to 8, fill in those lines that have the same number. Because it begins and ends with the same thought, it creates a whole which can be quite moving at times. One student, who has a very Loving relationship with her doll (inner child) wrote this PANTOUM.

> *Nurturing My Inner Child*
> 1. Holding her
> 2. Looking into her eyes
> 3. Talking to her
> 4. Giving her good information
> 2. Looking into her eyes
> 5. Knowing when she's hurting
> 4. Giving her good information
> 6. Speaking to her as though she's real
> 5. Knowing when she's hurting
> 7. Caring for her
> 6. Speaking to her as though she's real
> 8. Loving her

7. Caring for her
3. Talking to her
8. Loving her
1. Holding her
    Nancy W.

TANKA is a classic form of Japanese poetry in a standard arrangement of five lines with 5,7,5,7,7 syllables. Here is one written by another student.

Higher Self
I am Innocent;
Blameless as a morning rose.
Connected with God
As a rose to Mother Earth,
I shine in my perfection.
    Paula A.

HAIKU is a form of Japanese poetry composed of seventeen syllables, divided 5,7,5 in three lines. The poem gives a complete impression or mood. I share a thought with you.

Homework
I do my homework.
This brings miracles to me.
Do your homework, too.
    Nancy G.

CINQUAIN is a five line stanza invented by Adelaide Crapsey who was greatly influenced by the Japanese forms above. It has the following structure:

First line - a noun;   Forgiveness
Second line - 2 adjectives;   Tender, Honest
Third line - 3 words ending   Seeing, Releasing,
        with "ing"   Healing
Fourth line - 4 syllable phrase;   Extending Love
Fifth line - Synonym for the   Happinesss
        noun in the first line

You might also write out a dilemma in a 4 line verse and share what you wrote. Enjoy the creativity in any group by SHARING poetically.

*

92. DRAW MUSIC: *Drawing Music*
Play some music with various moods to evoke images. Use large pieces of paper and a drawing tool in each hand. Let your hands flow with the music.
SHARE your drawings and experience.
SPIRITUAL HOMEWORK: Alone at home, dance with the same flow and freedom.

❋

93. DANCE IMAGES: *Dancing Images*
This is a pleasant break from heavy thinking and feeling work. Allow plenty of space. Use some music conducive to feeling expression - perhaps some movie theme songs. One person call out words as others dance their images. The dancers could also call them out spontaneously. Examples: Dynamic stillness, Silence, Emptiness, Anticipation, Readiness to Receive, Energized awareness, Warm embrace, Unity, Vitality.
SHARE about your experience.
REFERENCES: Use any you see as appropriate.
SPIRITUAL HOMEWORK: Carry your lightheartedness throughout your week. Dance more concepts.

❋

94. SING PRAISE: *Singing Praises*
What song do you associate with celebrating. Make up verses using affirming statements and sing them as a group. For example, Happy Birthday: Sing the whole song using "I have friends all around," or "I am free now to speak," or "I embrace who I am," or "I am safe now to Love." Do the same as a way of giving thanks. "I give thanks for my friends," or "I give thanks to my Guide," or "I give thanks for my Life."
SHARE how you feel singing praise. Do you like allowing words to come from within you, rather than singing someone else's words from a written page?
REFERENCES: Select some you like. Also see T p. 65/71, "God is praised whenever any mind learns to be wholly helpful."
SPIRITUAL HOMEWORK: Use driving time to celebrate yourself instead of being angry at traffic. Use a tape of waltzes and provide your own affirmative words.

❋

95. SCULPT IT: *Sculpting Love*
Sculpey Modeling Compound is a clean medium for group use in homes or public places. It can be baked to permanent hardness in a conventional oven. Be creative in deciding what you will sculpt. You could create symbols for problem relationships and then healed relationships. Our group enjoyed listing five affirmative statements like, "I, Pat, am creative." We then picked the word which stood out to us and sculpted it. We then stood in a circle. As each stated their affirmation and shared their art piece, the group responded with comments like, "You surely **are** creative, Pat."
SHARE about your experience.
REFERENCES: Select them based on what you are sculpting.
SPIRITUAL HOMEWORK: Use your symbols as reminders.

❋

96. SILENT COMMUNICATION: *Extending Love*
In pairs, or as a group mingling in the room, communicate Love silently to each other. Use soft eyes, happy faces, tender touch, nods of the head that show understanding, and tilts of the head which show tenderness and receptivity.
SHARE about your experience.
REFERENCES: See T p. 55/61, "Love will enter immediately into any mind that truly wants it, but it must want it truly." "Those who call truly are always answered."
T p. 66/72, "To heal is to make happy." "To heal or to make joyous is therefore the same as to integrate and to make one. That is why it makes no difference to what part or by what part of the Sonship the healing is offered. Every part benefits, and benefits equally." All of Life is better with every thought that is brought to peace and extended as Loving-Kindness.
T p. 300/323, "Love would *always* give increase. Limits are demanded by the ego, and represent its demands to make little and ineffectual. Limit your sight of a brother...and you have denied his gift to you....your minds are already continuous, and their union need only be accepted and the loneliness...is gone." Note that we make ourselves happy and offer our happy energies to others. **If we are *trying* to make others happy we are actually in pain/fear and *trying* to steal from the others what we are not willing to give to them.**
SPIRITUAL HOMEWORK: Continue to send Loving gestures to people in your daily life.

97. SOUL HUNGERS: *Finding Simplicity*
Two hungers of the Soul are Truth and Simplicity. Illustrate them using some art medium.
SHARE your creations and thinking on Truth and Simplicity incorporated into your creations.
REFERENCES: See T p. 508/546, "Complexity is not of God."
T p. 253/272, "The Holy Spirit, seeing where you are but knowing you are elsewhere, begins His lesson in simplicity with the fundamental teaching that *truth is true*. This is the hardest lesson you will ever learn, and in the end the only one. Simplicity is very difficult for twisted minds. Consider all the distortions you have made of nothing; all the strange forms and feelings and actions and reactions that you have woven out of it. Nothing is so alien to you as the simple truth, and nothing are you less inclined to listen to."
SPIRITUAL HOMEWORK: Look at your life. Where are things complex? What would they be like if they were simple? Be specific. Are you willing to take action steps?

*

98. BALANCE: *Breathing Love*
Combine balancing your breath with saying of affirmations. Say an affirmation to yourself on the in-breath. This will help you receive it into your subconscious (a feminine process). Imagine sending it out on the out-breath to manifest in life experience (a masculine process). This will bring balance to the breath, and also to receiving and giving. We first receive from Spirit that which empowers our image, and then join with Spirit in giving our thrust to fulfill our heart's desire.
SHARE your experience and your affirmations.
REFERENCE: See WB Lesson #126, "All that I give is given to myself." If we were only to realize with each breath that God/Life is always infilling us we would not need to hold our breath in fear. **To give what we receive lets us know we received.**
SPIRITUAL HOMEWORK: Breathe Love's way.

*

99. METAPHOR: *Expressing I AM*
Prepare a tray of various objects. Each of you select one object that appeals to you. Then take turns sharing with "I AM" statements. Express those qualities that are the same in you and in the object.
SHARE: Share how you experienced this exercise.

REFERENCES: See "I am as God created me" listed in concordances, *Glossary-Index for A Course In Miracles,* or Table of Contents for the Workbook.

SPIRITUAL HOMEWORK: **Be aware of what you declare with "I AM" statements. Do you declare your spiritual qualities or personal miscreations (miseries, sufferings, and failures)? What you declare increases.**

❊

100. NEW STORY: *Mastering Life*

Instead of telling the story of tragedies in your life, tell the stories of who you are now because of challenges you've moved through with courage and mastery.

SHARE how this feels different to you.

REFERENCES: Find some on acknowledging blessings.

SPIRITUAL HOMEWORK: Tell new stories to others in the world. Spread hope.

SECTION ELEVEN: HEALING LIGHTLY

Many times we experience growing and healing as hard, heavy work. Do not be deceived by ego beliefs that we have to struggle to grow. Our ego wants us to believe this is true. Struggle is like quicksand, once we step into it we tend to sink. SECTION ELEVEN includes some light favorites from my groups. Once we step into delight we join Spirit calling us up.

※

101. GROUP PULSE: *Drumming Divinely*

Drumming invokes mysteries of the subconscious, intuition, and natural intelligence of the body. It allows us to expand, attune, and empower ourselves naturally. We tap the Divine Source. Set up a group pulse by drumming. Make simple instruments using things such as bottles or cans with beans in them, empty audio cassette cases with rice or lentils, a rolled oats box and wooden spoon. Remember being a toddler exploring the kitchen?

SHARE about your experience.

※

102. WASTEBASKET: *Marching Release*

Write things you no longer need to believe and are ready to release. Make a circle around a wastebasket. Now, one at a time, decide what the group will say as each of you takes a turn shredding your paper. Using the same instruments as in Exercise 101 above, set up a marching tempo. Create rhythmic statements to chant as you march. Repeat each chant 6 or 9 times (or any multiple of 3). Examples of rhythmic chants:

"We see Joe, he's great to know!"
"We hear Maureen, she sure is keen!"
"We love Bryan and we aren't 'lyan'!"
"Bruce, hang loose, and know you're safe!"
"Judy is healthy, laughing, and free!"

SHARE about your experience.

REFERENCES: Use this exercise with a lesson on proper use of denial as a protective device.

See T p. 16/19, "True denial is a powerful protective device."

SPIRITUAL HOMEWORK: Continue to release. Clean out a closet or drawer. Clean a whole room and expect a great infilling!

Marching release.

✳

103. RITUAL RELEASE: *Dancing Release*

Cut strips of dark crepe paper streamers about 12" to 14" long. Do some exercise in which you identify things to release. Write them on these strips. Each of you prepare 8 to 10 strips. Then play some lively music, a hoe down is great. Dance around and toss them as you dance. Make appropriate release statements as you do so. "Fear of speaking up, I release you." "Sickness, I release you and choose health instead." "Cigarettes, I'll no longer let you run my life."

SHARE about your experience.

REFERENCES: See T p. 30/34, "The first step toward freedom involves a sorting out of the false from the true."

T p. 135/146, "Whom you seek to imprison you do not love. Therefore, when you seek to imprison anyone, including yourself, you do not love him and you cannot identify with him. When you imprison yourself you are losing sight of your true identification...."

T p. 184/198, "Would you be hostage to the ego or host to God?" This means, do you choose to be hostage to fear or host to Love?

T p. 403/432, "Those who choose freedom will experience only its results. Their power is of God, and they will give it only to what God has given, to share with them. Nothing but this can touch them, for they see only this, sharing their power according to the Will of God. And thus their freedom is established and maintained."

WB Lesson #169, "By grace I live. By grace I am released."

WB Lesson #292, "A happy outcome to all things is sure."

SPIRITUAL HOMEWORK: Be creative in finding ways to release things that no longer serve your best interest. One of my students was recently going through a major life transition. She took an "enlightened witness" with her to care about her hurts. She walked along a stream where she collected rocks and placed them in a bag. As she carried these on her back she experienced the heaviness of the burdens she was carrying in her life. Then she named each rock as something she was letting go to accept her new life and threw the rocks one at a time into the stream. Flowing water itself is healing to our Feeling Nature.

*

104. ROCK IT: *Rocking Rhythm*

Stand in a circle with hands joined, left palms up, and right palms down. Rock to some gentle music as "Rocking Song - A Lullaby" on *Musical Companion to Sharing the Course*. Say affirmations with the rhythm. Examples: Soft eyes, happy face. Love out, love in. I'm ready and willing to know. Peace I give, peace I receive.

SHARE about your experience.

REFERENCE: See T p. 354/380, "We are made whole in our desire to make whole."

SPIRITUAL HOMEWORK: See Healing Method No. 2, Chapter 5, for rocking a doll or pillow which represents your inner child/Feeling Nature.

*

105. QUIZ: *Learning Tool*

Just for fun, use a quiz as a learning tool. Then share your answers and discuss them.

1. *A Course in Miracles* is meant to be: (a) read, (b) lived.
2. The goal of the Course is: (a) Peace, (b) read the book through once a year.
3. The means of healing, according to the Course, is: (a) make miracles happen, (b) forgive.

4. According to *A Course in Miracles*, (a) I am guilty and need to repent, (b) I am innocent and I need to awaken to my innocence.

5. *A Course in Miracles* says nothing I see with my eyes has: (a) form, (b) meaning.

6. According to *A Course in Miracles*, meaning is in my: (a) mind, (b) brain.

7. I give meaning to things with Vision. This means: (a) I understand things in my mind, (b) angels appear with miracles.

8. The Course says I do not understand anything. This means: (a) I am stupid, (b) I have formed habits of thought which exclude things from my awareness.

9. The Course says I am never upset for the reason I think. A companion statement might be: (a) I need to sort out which upsets are worth giving my time to, (b) It doesn't matter what my upset is, the problem is in my seeing and the result will be no Peace.

10. Many times the word "but" in a sentence flows if translated to: (a) however, (b) and.

11. The word "try" is so ingrained in us as a word of adaptation rather than awakening, that it is best to: (a) fight against it, (b) use my higher Thinking Nature to decide to do or not do what is being suggested.

12. A Son of God is: (a) Jesus, (b) the Course's way of identifying who I am when my heart is open to give and receive Love.

SHARE how you experienced taking this quiz.

REFERENCES: Use concordances and other reference sources to look up topics of interest to you.

SPIRITUAL HOMEWORK: Prepare more quiz questions for your group.

✽

106. CREATED ME: *Owning Goodness*

Using the format within WB Lesson #67, go around the group many times making statements as:

    Faith created me faithful.
    Holiness created me holy.
    Love created me loving.
    Will created me willing.

SHARE YOUR REACTIONS. My groups love this.

REFERENCE: See WB Lesson #67.

SPIRITUAL HOMEWORK: Continue this process throughout the week.

Note: You might want to sing "Faith Created Me Faithful" on *Musical Companion to Sharing the Course* and add some of your own phrases to the music. When the words stop on the tape, fill in your phrases. As an alternative, use the music as a time of quiet meditation on the phrases you have spoken.

✳

107. LETTER OF INNOCENCE: *Declaring Innocence*
    See Sample Lesson No. 5, Chapter 27.

✳

108. HOLY BATH: *Bathing In Love*
    See Sample Lesson No. 5, Chapter 27.

Holy bath.

✳

109. EASTER EGGS: *Hunting Blessings*
    Write *A Course in Miracles* verses on Easter eggs and have a hunt. Then share the verses on your eggs and how they apply to your life right now. An alternative would be to write verses on paper attached to ribbons. Tie apples to the ribbons and hang them from a beam. Then select an apple and share in the same way about your selected verse. If you want to have some fun with it, write blessings, or fortunes on eggs and hang them with the apples. Don't tell who wrote them!
    SHARE. It is fun to see who gets your blessing.

110. BELLY LAUGH: *Laughing Contagiously*

If you haven't had a good belly laugh lately, do this one. Each of you lie on the floor putting your head on the belly of someone else. My groups never make it to the floor before we are roaring with laughter. This is good for releasing tension, breathing deeply, and cleaning out our tear ducts!

SHARE about your experience.

REFERENCE: See MT p. 36/37, "Where there is laughter, who can longer weep?"

Belly laugh.

305

SECTION TWELVE: HEALING HEARTACHES

Most of us have long-standing and deeply felt hurts from being treated less than Lovingly in our youth. Exercises in SECTION TWELVE deal with our most sensitive places and deepest hurts - those where we most need Love. **Creating sacred space is essential for healing deep wounds.**

✻

111. "I DESERVE": *Accepting Love Now*
Do the exercise on deservability in Chapter 1 of *Love Yourself, Heal Your Life* by Louise L. Hay.
SHARE your responses. Does this inspire you to action steps, too?
REFERENCES: See T p. 49/54, "Your worth is established by God." See topics like sacrifice, scarcity, deprivation, worth, and idols.
SPIRITUAL HOMEWORK: Do you treat yourself as God intended you to treat yourself, with reverence? What change will you make now? (See note at the end of Chapter 6.)

✻

112. HIDE-N-SEEK: *Accepting Love Now*
The law of the ego is "Seek and do *not* find," T p. 208/223. We hide from ourselves the fact that we are invested in not meeting the dreams and wishes we tell ourselves and others we want to fulfill. The Holy Spirit's Law is "Seek and you *will* find," T p. 208/224. **We are stuck until we become aware of the beliefs we hold in secret. They were originally a survival move to preserve our life and now defeat us.** Each of you identify something you want and are waiting to have. In pairs, Person A will state a want. Person B will say, "Are you willing to have it now?" Repeat this listening for ego beliefs that say one way or another that to fulfill the desire means you would come to some tragic end. There is hidden blame of someone. Seek it out so you can forgive them and tag what you want to have in your life.
SHARE your realizations with the group.
REFERENCE: See T p. 236/253, "Awaking unto Christ is following the laws of love of your free will, and out of quiet recognition of the truth in them. The attraction of light must draw you willingly, and willingness is signified by giving."

113. "I'LL SHOW YOU": *Accepting Love Now*

**Our ego may hold a stance of "I'll show you if it kills me."
And, we do hold to our stance of blame of others even though
this ego process destroys us.** We have all participated in self-
destructive patterns to *try to get* Love. Example beliefs: "I'll show
you I'm perfect enough, strong enough, good enough,
pretty/handsome enough, thin enough, rich enough, etc., to be
worthy of your love." **To reverse your patterns you need to
recognize your beliefs, see your behaviors based on them,
and be received with Love as you are.** Write out this statement, "I'll show you _____ if it kills me." Now, fill in the
blank. Then reverse your intent and demonstrate FOR life.

SHARE your statements, what you are truly wanting, ways
you are defeating yourself, and give Loving-Kindness to each
other. If it would be helpful, share options for meeting your true
needs.

REFERENCES: See T p. 388/416-17, "The Attraction of
Death."

T p. 209/224-5, "...you must invest in it [awareness of your
wholeness], not with money but with spirit. For spirit is will, and
will is the 'price' of the Kingdom. Your inheritance awaits only
the recognition that you have been redeemed. The Holy Spirit
guides you into life eternal, but you must relinquish your investment in death, or you will not see life though it is all around
you."

T p. 541/583, "And death is opposite to peace, because it is
the opposite of life. And life is peace. Awaken and forget all
thoughts of death, and you will find you have the peace of God."

SPIRITUAL HOMEWORK: Look for other "I'll show you"
stances. Acknowledge that you are holding yourself in an ego
resistance and harming yourself. Identify what you truly want
and be willing to Give it to yourself now. To Give it to yourself
means to be willing to accept it instead of resist. To Give is to
Receive.

✳

114. TRIGGER COMMENT: *Accepting Love Now*

We all have things that people could say to us that would
trigger fear (we may experience this as something different, like
guilt or anger). What happens is that when we hear the comment
we pull out of our memory a scene when we had no comforter.
These are our dark spots, places we have not yet received Love.
Each of you recall at least one such statement. Then in pairs,

practice responding in new ways over and over as your partner says your trigger comment to you. As you speak from your higher self you will give comfort to your Feeling Nature. Continue until the new responses feel natural and you have options other than your fear response.

Example: You are sensitive to the question, "Why didn't you call me?" (It feels like someone is laying a "guilt trip" on you.) Then, your partner asks you this question many times while you practice giving new responses. Possible responses in this example:

"I'm scared of you."

"I don't feel good when I talk to you."

"My heart wasn't in it."

"I could not call you and be Loving."

"I sense that you are demanding that I make you feel Loved."

"I feel resentful toward your demand."

"I'm no longer willing to take on guilt from you."

"I have needs, too."

"I accept that we need to part."

"I accept that we have grown apart."

Obviously, you will not make all these statements to one person in your daily life. **The importance of this exercise is to know that you are not stuck with only going to guilt.**

SHARE with the larger group what you've gained from doing this exercise. If you have difficulty thinking of new responses, I'm sure someone in your group has a great idea.

REFERENCES: Select any that appeal to you.

SPIRITUAL HOMEWORK: Identify more trigger comments and continue the exercise in your journal or in front of a mirror. Practice speaking honestly. **Honest means truthful revealing about yourself. This is very different from making hurtful comments to another and saying, "I was only being honest."**

✳

115. PERSONAL RESPONSE: *Accepting Love Now*

We often tell stories in which we are suffering because of the life situations of a Loved one. Allow people who need to do this to speak. Then, **instead of giving any focus to the person of whom they spoke, or to the situation of which they spoke, give your Love to the speaker.** This process is more difficult than it sounds. Give responses like, "I see how difficult this is for you," "I'm sorry you are hurting," "I care about you at this time," and "I care that you are troubled."

Both as speaker and listener we often distract ourselves to avoid feeling our hurts. We believe we don't deserve, or won't receive care for our hurts. We still believe there is no comforter for us. So, we talk about things external to us when we hurt deeply. We talk about someone else, the disease, the problem situation, or details about almost anything. Let's learn differently. Be comforters for each other rather than judge or distract. Be willing to feel with others. When you cry with someone you heal your own past hurts. To give is to receive.

SHARE how you felt with this shift of focus.

REFERENCE: See T p. 185/200, "Only God's comforter can comfort you." This means that comfort comes by connecting with your Feeling Nature, not by distracting from it. Your ego chooses to distract you and keep you from opening to receive comfort. Remember that the ego believes there is no comforter and that it is saving you from feeling abandoned by distracting you from your feelings. Sharing in a safe group space gives you a new experience.

SPIRITUAL HOMEWORK: Practice responding to the speaker as you listen to people in your daily life.

✳

116. JOB APPLICATION: *Accepting Love Now*

This exercise can call you to glory or guilt. I recommend it either way as a powerful healing tool.

Instructions: You are writing a job application for a job as a Teacher of God. You will be presenting it to God. You want to convince the Holy Presence that you are truly helpful to humankind. Each of you list your qualities and abilities. When you complete this, draw names for who will be "God" for your interview. Then, one at a time, with group observing, apply for your job. (God hires you, of course!) You don't have to be perfect at the point of taking a job. Remember that you learn most jobs by doing them. Speaking your higher qualities helps you own them and feel the glory of them. **To make your life work (and create your Life Work!) you need to recognize, give value to, and honor your holy qualities, and not just your worldly job titles and skills.** Miracles happen when you carry out your everyday life with this added awareness. Valuing and expressing holy qualities switches your magnetism and attracts good to you in your daily work. If any of you go into guilt or shame and have difficulty facing God, it is a wonderful opportunity to confess and receive God's blessing. Be sure that God praises you for your courage to speak. Eye contact is essential either for glory, or to release guilt.

SHARE how you experienced you job interview.

REFERENCE: See T p. 71/77 where we are asked what better vocation there could be than waking to the call of God.

SPIRITUAL HOMEWORK: Continue to offer yourself as a Teacher of God.

✻

117. "I FORGIVE": *Accepting Love Now*

This is an exercise in forgiving. Sit in pairs, eyes closed. Holding hands feels good. Take turns being person A and B. Person A asks forgiveness of the other as if the other were the person involved. Example: "Mom, forgive me for _____." "Dad, forgive me for _____." "(Boss), forgive me for _____." "(Coach), forgive me for making the mistake that led our team to lose the championship." After each offering, Person B will use the name of Person A and say, "(Name), I forgive you for _____." A response of "Thank you, I love you" or the like would feel good, wouldn't it?

When you are done, de-role. Say, "(Name), I know you are not the people to whom I spoke. Thank you for helping me."

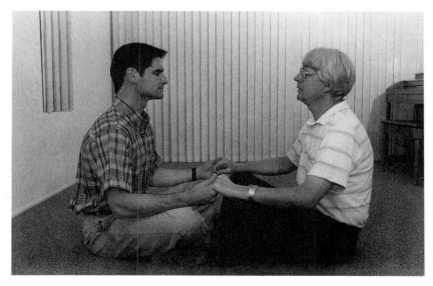

Accepting Love now.

SHARE how you experienced this as person A and B. Sigh three times. "The crisis is over."

REFERENCES: See WB Lesson #121, "Forgiveness is the key to happiness."

WB Lesson #297, "Forgiveness is the only gift I give."

WB Lesson #332, "Fear binds the world. Forgiveness sets it free."

SPIRITUAL HOMEWORK: Continue to forgive using your journal or a mirror.

Note: You might want to sing "Sigh - The Crisis is Over," "Love and Joy," or "Find the Highest Thought" on *Musical Companion to Sharing the Course.*

*

118. MOTHER LOVE: *Accepting Love Now*

See Practice Exercise No. 117. Do this with another playing the role of your mother. (When you are done, de-role. Say, "(Name), I know you are (name), and not my mother. Thank you for helping me.")

John Diamond, Cantillation Foundation, P.O. Drawer 37, Valley Cottage, New York, 10989, has written many fine books including *The Re-mothering Experience: How to Totally Love.* This exercise is based on a few of his ideas. After you have forgiven your mother in pairs, take turns doing the following: Stand with your feet firmly on the floor facing an empty chair. Imagine your mother sitting on the chair. **If you feel intimidated by her, call her by her name or initials instead of "Mom."** Now, make statements to her like, "I stand here for you to see. I give myself to you whether you like me or not. This is me. I reveal my life to you. This is my body. This is my voice. This is the sex I am. These are my thoughts and images. I am innocent. I no longer hide. I let you know me. I let the world know me. I am good enough." Add any other thing for which **you have been waiting for her approval.** Remember **you are really waiting for your own approval to Be and express who you are.** Sigh, "The crisis is over." Good for you!! Know that the only way we can forgive our biological mother is to have developed the Mother within us, the Nurturing Parent. Isn't it wonderful to be free to BE. Thank your mother for what she WAS able to give to you. **You are now freeing yourself to give what you have to give to your mother and all others. All that you give, you give to yourself. All that you give, you receive from God. You receive more by giving more.**

Note: In any kind of exercise like this it makes no difference whether your mother or the person in focus is living or not. We are changing images we hold in our mind from when they were living.

SHARE about your experience.

REFERENCES: See topics of giving, receiving, and forgiving.

SPIRITUAL HOMEWORK: Picture yourself giving of yourself right through your mother. See her sitting at the narrow end of a funnel, with all those who want to receive you being beyond her. Give whether you believe she approves of you or not. **We are meant to outgrow our parents or there would be no growth on Earth.**

Note: You might want to sing, "Sigh - The Crisis Is Over" on *Musical Companion to Sharing the Course* by Michael Root.

＊

119. FATHER LOVE: *Accepting Love Now*

Do the same process as in Practice Exercise No. 118 using father instead of mother as focus. (Follow instructions to de-role, also.) You might say, "I am off on my own whether you like what I am doing or not. I am being me whether you can support me or not. I'm acting on my own inner desires. I'm following the divine spark in me which also gives me all the wisdom and strength to do what I need to do safely." Thank your father for what he WAS able to give to you. **You are now freeing yourself to give what you have to give to your father and all others. All that you give, you give to yourself. All that you give, you receive from God. You receive more by giving more.**

＊

120. CUTTING CORDS: *Accepting Love Now*

The goal of this exercise is to transform a relationship from "special" to holy, or from fear to Love. When we are born we have a physical umbilical cord which is cut to allow our body to function as a whole unit. We also have an invisible cord which connects us, solar plexus to solar plexus, with anyone we have known closely. It is the channel through which we send our alarms to call for others to take care of us. This process of "alarming" is also known as projecting guilt which is basic to all "special relationships". In these relationships we are bound by fear of losing the other who is imagined to be our Savior, Higher Self, or Greater Being. This unseen solar plexus cord is like baby teeth which serves us until we are mature enough to function on the permanent energy of Love which we extend from our heart to the heart of others. It does not matter whether the person you are unbinding is alive or not. Cutting cords allows us to accept Love.

A leader will lead the group through this process. Leader, explain the steps to your group before you lead them through the process. Note that willingness to cut the cord is determined before cutting the cord. Reader, this is a skill which you can do on your own once you have learned it.

    a. Close your eyes and see the cord that connects you with some other person, living or dead. (allow time)

    b. Describe the cord to yourself. (allow time)

    c. What tool would it take to cut it? (allow time)

    d. Is it something you would be able to do by yourself?

    e. Are you willing to cut it and open your heart to Love?

    f. Bring in as many people as you want to help you. See them with you and explain what you are doing. (allow time)

    g. Cut the cord and indicate with your hand when you are finished. (Watch for signals so you know when to go on.)

    h. Say, "I release you to find your Goodness." "I go on to know my own Goodness."

    i. Send Love, pink light from your heart. (allow time)

    j. Release the end of the cord that is connected to yourself. See the hole sealed and healed. Be sure there is no leak. See energy flowing up from Mother Earth and down from Father Heaven through you and out your heart center as Love. You are filled with Love.

    k. Thank anyone who helped you cut the cord.

    l. Open your eyes and SHARE.

REFERENCE: See T p. 379-395/406-424, "The Obstacles to Peace." **We are under the attraction of guilt and pain until we switch our ego energy. Ego energy functions at the level of our solar plexus. The attraction of Love and Peace function at the level of our heart. Give only Love.**

SHARE about your experience.

SPIRITUAL HOMEWORK: Recognize other emotional attachments, places where you are waiting or blaming, and also cut these cords. For example, most of us are surrounded by written materials, pictures, gifts, and other remembrances from past relationships, jobs, and the like. These things that were once meaningful to us now clutter our space and leave us emotionally unfree to reinvest our energies. Love is the ever flowing energy of Life. We cannot hold onto Love in the form of material objects. To free yourself to fully express in the present, take a good look around your living and work space. Ask yourself, "Does (this) still have meaning to me?" Discard what has no value, and pass on gifts to others. Reinvest meaning in them as you give them with Love. Treat yourself to things that are meaningful to you now.

Thank you for putting spiritual principles into practice. I appreciate your courage.

INDEX OF VISUALIZATIONS AND MEDITATIONS

26

VISUALIZATIONS AND MEDITATIONS

In this chapter I share visual exercises to be read by a leader, and give a few suggestions for meditation. All of these are intended to facilitate joining. **The first step in our undoing process is to recognize that we actively decided wrongly and can as actively decide otherwise. See T p. 83/90. To correct our errors, we return to the point at which we separated from God and went to our defensive mode.**

VISUALIZATIONS

Prepare as you believe proper for each of these visual exercises, following the guidelines in Chapter 24. **Use the written scripts as a general guide and adapt each to your group.** When you see three dashes (---), allow time. Six dashes (------) at the end of the exercise indicate that you invite the group to open their eyes and return to the space to share.

These visualizations are designed to be read to a mixed group of men and women. If you are a group of only men, or only women, I suggest you personalize the wording by using "him" or "her" instead of "it" when addressing the inner child.

As an individual reader you might want to tape these visual exercises, personalize them to your own situation, and listen to them read in your own voice. As a leader, give your group a brief overview before beginning a visual exercise. For example, before the "Most Basic Early Scene" you might say, "In a moment we will be doing a visual exercise. I'll be asking you to go back in your memory to a time in your childhood when you were hurting. I'll lead you through the scene so you can comfort your inner child. Are there any questions?"

1. MOST BASIC EARLY SCENE
    Prepare following guidelines in Chapter 24. You are now ready to go to a scene, when you were young, in which you felt scared or hurt, and no one was there to comfort you. --- Where are you? --- How old are you? --- Who is there? --- Who is not there that you would like to be present for you? --- What do you hear? --- What do you smell? --- What do you see happening? --- How do you take care of yourself? --- What are you deciding? --- Now, being the grown-up you are today, walk into that scene. You know exactly what your child needs. Give it to your child now and see the scene resolved. **(Note: this is the healing moment; the holy instant; the Atonement; the point of forgiveness; the moment of freedom; the release of illusion; the undoing of error; the switch from laws of ego to Laws of God; the switch from ego willfulness to the Will of God; the switch from the "special relationship" to "brothers"; and the awakening of the Christ Self. Allow adequate time for Love and tears to flow. Then continue with the closure that follows.)** ------ "Remembering your union, gently come back to this space, and slowly open your eyes."
    SHARE whatever each of you would like to share with the group. Some of you will welcome the chance to talk. Others of you will choose to be silent with your feelings allowing time for them to integrate.

This is a basic healing scene because it takes you back to the point at which your error was made; the point where you chose to defend. This means that at that time you switched your energy to ego function, which is anti-God, or resistant to the flow of Life. It took place when your Feeling Nature was not connected with a Greater Being - a protective parent. You are able to provide that function now, so you can reverse the early life decision. Since you had many, many scenes like this in your early life, this process needs to be repeated just as many times. On a spiritual journey you take responsibility to heal your scenes using this basic format.

I have used two additional visualizations in Sample Lessons in Chapter 27. See Sample Lesson No. 2 for Defensive Wall, and Sample Lesson No. 3 for listening to the Holy Spirit Voice or the Voice of Love. These are also basic and can be repeated many times.
    I enjoy using the basic visualization around Valentine's Day. From the scene we extract a denial statement, and an affirma-

tion. We then write the denial on one side of a heart cut from red construction paper. We write the affirmation on the other. Then we take a stance in front of the group stating both. Use guidelines in Chapter 15 for using affirmations with a group. Since you have lived with your old belief for many years, and have built it into your whole life pattern, you need to do much affirming of your new decisions.

Remember that the goal of a basic visualization is to see your error and correct it. Therefore, to change your mind, you need to derive from the scene a denial, "I no longer need to believe _____" and an affirmation, "_____ is true for me now."

✳

2. HOLY FIGURE

Prepare following guidelines in Chapter 24. You are now ready to go in your mind to some natural place where you can be alone for a while. --- Imagine yourself sitting with a holy figure. Accept any that comes to you. --- See a cloud of energy surrounding the two of you. --- The holy one takes your hand. (Or if it is an animal, it makes a loving gesture toward you). --- It then looks into your eyes and asks, "What troubles you so?" --- Be aware of how you feel when your emotions join this Love. --- Share with this holy one your frustration with some pattern in which you feel stuck. --- Now, clearly name what needs to be corrected. This is always something you are believing about yourself that diminishes you. This is what you correct to expand your Soul. --- Share with your holy figure the attribute you want to develop or increase in your self. --- Receive a blessing from the holy one. ------ (Invite your group: "Bring your comfortable feelings and your blessing back with you to this space, gently open your eyes, and prepare to share.")

SHARE your blessings and then write some action steps as Spiritual Homework to bring the attribute into your life.

✳

3. TAKE YOUR CHILD HOME WITH YOU

(I mentioned this in Healing Method No. 4, Chapter 5. Here it is designed for group experience.) After preparing for visualization following guidelines in Chapter 24, and doing a Basic Early Scene (See No. 1), continue like this: It is right, at this time, for your child to come live with you. Ask your child if it is willing to do that. --- Tell your child that you will speak to Mom and

318

Dad and tell them. --- If you received consent from your child, continue with me. If not, listen quietly for what may be right for you at another time. Bring in Mom. --- Tell her the time has come for you to take your child to live with you. --- How does she respond? --- If she gives you her blessing, thank her. --- If she resists in any way, she is fearful. --- Bring in Mom's Guardian Angel to comfort her. --- Know your Mom is safe. Tell her you must do what is right for you now. --- Bring in Dad. --- Tell him the time has come for you to take your child to live with you. --- How does he respond? --- If he gives you his blessing, thank him. --- If he resists in any way, he is fearful. --- Bring in Dad's Guardian Angel to comfort him. --- Know your Dad is safe. Tell him you must do what is right for you now. --- Take your child by the hand and bring it to your home. --- Show your child around. Let it see where you eat and sleep. --- Help your young one feel comfortable there with you. ------ (Invite your group: "Knowing you are safe, gently come back to this space, open your eyes, and prepare to share.")

SHARE. If your child did not want to come with you, assume you are not ready for the joining and that you will take this step when it is right for you.

※

4. COURAGEOUS MOMENT
Prepare following guidelines in Chapter 24. You are now ready to go to a scene in which you were very courageous and no one noticed. --- What fear did your young one face? --- Give to your child now the notice that you originally wanted. --- Give lots of praise. --- How does your young one respond to your seeing? ------ (Invite your group: "Gently come back to this space, open your eyes, and prepare to share.")

SHARE. Give praise to each other.

※

5. MOST HUMILIATING EXPERIENCE
Prepare following guidelines in Chapter 24. You are now ready to go to the scene in which you had your most humiliating experience. --- Be there with your younger self. --- What information were you lacking at the time? --- What does your young one need from you? --- Give it. Note that the greatest fear at one of these times is that you will not be Loved. Firmly tell your young one, "I Love you. I really Love you. I am here for you no matter what!" --- Is there anything else your young one

needs to know to feel safe in this scene? ------ (Invite your group: "Gently come back to this space, open your eyes, and prepare to share.")

SHARE compassionately. It is rare that someone doesn't resolve a scene. Should that happen, the person needs information which the group can give. Remember that you are addressing a child who needs something and has dissociated from what that is to not feel the pain of its absence. You are now safe to know and feel because you are there to tend your own child. Child needs are simple. To help people get in touch with these simple needs you could do the following visualization.

✳

6. CHILD NEEDS

Prepare following guidelines in Chapter 24. You are now ready to go to an early scene where your child feels hurt, scared, or lost. --- What does your child need? --- Give it. --- Is there anything else your young one needs? --- See it done. --- Reassure your child that you are there. ------ (Invite your group: "Gently come back to this space, open your eyes, and prepare to share.")

SHARE what each child's needs were and how they were you fulfilled.

✳

7. FORBIDDEN DREAM

Prepare following guidelines in Chapter 24. You are now ready to go to a time when you were young, doing something you love to do. --- What are you dreaming of doing or being when you grow up? --- As you go forward in time, are there any of these dreams that you are deciding you have to give up? --- What are the reasons for your decisions? --- Moving forward to look at your current life, are those decisions valid for you today? ------ (Invite your group: "Bringing this information with you, gently come back to this space, open your eyes, and prepare to share.")

SHARE what your dreams were and their validity for you today. What decisions stopped you from pursuing your dreams? Your Spiritual Homework would be to take action steps to fulfill a remembered dream.

✳

8. HIGHER VISION
Prepare following guidelines in Chapter 24. You are now ready to go to a scene in which your child is refusing to do something. --- Where are you? --- Who is there? --- Who isn't there? --- What is happening? --- Specifically, what is your child refusing to do? --- Is this a natural thing for a child to do, or are you being invited harms way? --- If it is harmful, generously praise your child for refusing to go along with that invitation. --- Offer your help to get out of the situation. --- Now consider something you really wanted to do and were afraid to do because you didn't see any safe outcome. --- Give a higher vision to your child. --- Tell it some best possible outcomes and see at least one of them come true. ------ (Invite your group: "Gently come back to this space, open your eyes, and prepare to share.")
SHARE. Praise each other for refusing to participate in harmful activity. Reinforce for each other your right to do what is yours to do, and Be who you are to Be. Share your best possible outcomes and add to them with group input.

＊

9. HEALING GIFT
Prepare following guidelines in Chapter 24. You are now ready to go to a scene in which you feel wounded. --- Where are you? --- How old are you? --- Who is there? --- Who isn't there? --- What happened that you feel wounded? --- Walk into the scene and give any comfort your child needs. --- Now in your minds eye, give your child a gift for the wound received. --- See your child self joyfully receiving your gift. ------ (Invite your group: "Gently come back to this space, open your eyes, and prepare to share.")
SHARE about your wound, what gift you gave, and your child's response.

＊

10. DINNER TABLE
Prepare following guidelines in Chapter 24. You are now ready to go to a dinner table scene in your early life. --- Where are you? --- How old are you? --- Who is there? --- Who isn't there? --- What do you smell? --- What do you hear? --- What do you feel? --- What do you say, or not say that you would like to say? --- Take a good look at the scene as a grown-up observer. What do you see? --- What do you want to change about

yourself in this scene? --- Make that change in yourself. --- How do you feel different now? --- Does this change the way you see others in the scene? --- What do you want to add to this scene to bring in Peace, Love, and Joy? --- Do you include those things at your dinner table now in your life? ------ (Invite your group: "Gently come back to this space, open your eyes, and prepare to share.")

SHARE, ending with what changes you might make now to have Peace, Love, and Joy at your dinner table. Assign action steps as Spiritual Homework.

✳

11. GREATEST DISAPPOINTMENT
Prepare following guidelines in Chapter 24. You are now ready to return to the scene of your greatest disappointment. --- (Ask basic questions as in previous visual exercises.) What specifically do you want? --- What stands in your way? --- Remove any blocks and see your child fulfilled. --- Feel yourself free and happy. --- Bring in any people you blame. Say to them, "I set you free." ------ (Invite your group: "Gently come back to this space, open your eyes, and prepare to share.")

SHARE what your want was, what you saw as being in the way, how you fulfilled your want, and whom you forgave.

✳

12. UNMET DEMANDS
(Use with WB Lesson #39)

Prepare following guidelines in Chapter 24. You are now ready to picture your family members sitting in a circle with you. --- Go around the circle saying, "I Love you," or, "I hate you," to each one. As you do so, express gratitude to those you Love. Be aware of your unmet demands on those to whom you express hate. ------ (Invite your group: "Gently come back to this space, open your eyes, and prepare to share.")

SHARE with the group how you already do or could meet those needs for yourself now. Allow adequate time for each of you to list some action steps to do as Spiritual Homework. The next session you might do a forgiveness exercise. (For an accompanying exercise, see SECTION TWELVE: HEALING HEART-ACHES, Chapter 25, especially No. 28, "I DEMAND.")

✳

13. MY CHOICE
    (Use with T p. 83/90)

Prepare following guidelines in Chapter 24. You are now ready to go back to a time when you let someone else make a decision for you. You may have decided to please someone else rather than do what you wanted. --- See the scene unfold differently as you are truthful about your needs. --- Decide to fulfill your needs in some way that enhances everyone. ------ (Invite your group: "Bringing your new confidence with you, gently come back to this space, open your eyes, and prepare to share.")
    SHARE your decision and its unfolding.

*

14. GRATITUDE
    (See T p. 212/228, "As self-value comes from self-extension, so does the perception of self-value come from the extension of loving thoughts outward.")

Prepare following guidelines in Chapter 24. You are now ready, in your mind's eye, to surround yourself with those people who have supported your life and helped you to be who and where you are today. Express gratitude to each. ------ (Invite your group: "Gently come back to this space, open your eyes, and prepare to share.")
    SHARE with others about those who have supported your life.

*

15. REBIRTH
    Prepare following guidelines in Chapter 24. You are now ready to see yourself curled up in a safe dark place. --- (Allow plenty of time here.) Now see a tunnel with a light off in the distance. --- Go through the tunnel into the light. --- Your family members are there to greet you. Simply notice how each one reacts to you as you walk by. --- (Allow adequate time.) Now, continue on to be embraced by your own Higher Self that has longed to hold you. --- You've longed to walk through life together. Know that you either try to get family members to Love you, or you embrace your own Higher Self and know true Love. --- Sit down with your Higher Self and listen as your Higher Self makes a commitment to be with you always. --- What commitment will you make in response? ------ (Invite your group:

"Gently come back to this space, open your eyes, and prepare to share.")

SHARE in a way that contrasts the way you were received by your family and your own Higher Self.

✳

16. CORRECTING RESENTMENTS
(See T p. 506/544, "The Holy Spirit offers you release from every problem that you think you have. They are the same to Him because each one, regardless of the form it seems to take, is a demand that someone suffer loss and make a sacrifice that you might gain. And when the situation is worked out so no one loses is the problem gone, because it was an error in perception that now has been corrected.")

Prepare following guidelines in Chapter 24. You are now ready to allow to come to mind someone or something you resent. --- What is it that you want? --- What does the other want? --- What are you believing? --- Does one need to lose and the other win? --- There is always at least one Loving way to solve any problem. Know it is there and you will see it. --- Resolve this scene so both get what they need. If you are unwilling to resolve this scene (it may seem like you are unable) know that you are still wanting to blame the other. This means you believe only the other can supply your need. --- What have you, or are you sacrificing to *try to get* what you want from this other person? --- Do you really need to continue to do this? --- You may choose to turn your palms up and say, "I'm ready and willing to know what I need to know to be free." ------ (Invite your group: "Gently come back to this space, open your eyes, and prepare to share.")

SHARE your learnings and what gift you gave yourself that relieved your resentment.

✳

17. NO SCARCITY
(See WB Lesson #33, "There is another way of looking at the world.";
WB Lesson #34, "I could see peace instead of this.";
T p. 72-74/78-80, "The Guide to Salvation."; and,
T p. 192-4/207-9, "Waking to Redemption.")

Prepare following guidelines in Chapter 24. You are now ready to picture roots beginning at your tailbone and going down your legs deep into the earth. --- Allow energy from the earth to flow up these roots to fill you. --- Picture liquid white light flowing down from the sky into the crown of your head entwining with the flow from the earth. --- You are filled with energy from the Universe. --- Feel your heart accepting this Love energy, willingly pumping it throughout your body. --- Feel yourself in a state of Peace. --- Feel your Joy. --- Now, picture in front of you, a person who has hurt you, or one you fear or resent. --- If you hurt, let yourself hurt. You are safe to feel any feelings in Love's presence. --- Imagine what hopes and dreams this person has. --- Imagine what sorrows and fears they experience. --- Allow a feeling of compassion to build within your heart, fed by Mother Earth and Father Heaven. --- Picture something good happening to this person, something meaningful to them. --- See a beam of light running from your heart to theirs. --- Say to them, "I forgive you for _____." (whatever words, actions, or omissions caused you pain). --- If you are fearful, say, "I ask your forgiveness for _____." Know they cannot hurt you now and you no longer need to fear or resent them. --- Now recall a dream or hope you have for yourself. --- See your dream or hope fulfilled now. --- See yourself smiling and happy. --- Be aware that the abundance of the Universe is available to all of us. There is no scarcity. ------ (Invite your group: "Gently come back to this space, open your eyes, and prepare to share.")

SHARE your learnings.

✳

18. SAFE PLACE
(See T p. 146/158, "'Rest in peace' is a blessing for the living, not the dead, because rest comes from waking, not from sleeping. Sleep is withdrawing; waking is joining.")

Prepare following guidelines in Chapter 24. **Know that all inner turmoil that inhibits rest comes from seeing yourself in a space that is not safe, and has no comforter for you.** In your mind, create a safe place for your united grown-up and child self. --- You are the only one there and nothing can harm you. --- You have made this beautiful place just for yourself. --- You need not please anyone else. Check to see that you have not tried to please anyone else. --- Rest in Peace in your safe place. ------ (Invite your group: "Knowing that you created this place

325

and can return to it when you choose, bring your warm feelings with you as you return to this space, and open your eyes.")

*

19. HEALING ANGER
     (See WB Lesson #15, "My thoughts are images that I have made.";
     WB Lesson #16, "I have no neutral thoughts.";
     WB Lesson #18, "I am not alone in experiencing the effects of my seeing.";
     WB Lesson #20, "I am determined to see."; and,
     WB Lesson #21, "I am determined to see things differently.")

Prepare following guidelines in Chapter 24. You are now ready to go to an early scene in which you feel angry. --- What do you need in this scene? --- Feel the insult of someone not recognizing your need. --- Let yourself know and feel your desire to harm them for this. --- Let yourself feel the shift of energy away from Love when your thoughts go to revenge. --- Feel how far you are from Peace now. --- Know that you are doing your best. --- Now, bring your own grown-up into the scene and tell your young one that you will find a way to meet the original need so your young one doesn't need to strike out. Being there for yourself will relieve both fear and anger. See this done. --- Now, give your child information. Tell your young one that when you strike out at another you attack yourself first. --- Tell the one you have blamed that you are no longer willing to hold attack thoughts toward them. --- Tell them you are no longer willing to keep yourself separated from Peace, Health, Wealth, and Happiness. --- Say to them, "I choose to see that attack thoughts keep me upset and don't meet my needs." --- Say to them, "I choose to accept care now." --- Say to them, "I choose the lovely over the ugly." --- Know that in these choices you have already changed your results. Acknowledge miracles. ------ (Invite your group: "Gently come back to this space, open your eyes, and prepare to share.")

SHARE what your needs were and how you fulfilled them. Share your realizations about attack thoughts.

*

20. GROUP SUPPORT

Suppose a woman member recalls a violation like incest or rape. She feels helpless and/or rage. Invite her to tell just enough about the story so the group can imagine the scene. Then have her be in her helpless position, usually on the floor representing a bed. All the other group members circle around her facing out. As leader, instruct your group that on a given signal, they are all to yell at once. Things to yell include: "Get out of here! Get away from her! I won't let you hurt her! You are wrong to hurt her!" This process takes only a few minutes and has healing power equal to years of therapy.

Note that this simple healing process gives the woman an experience of a powerful Greater Being witnessing and protecting her. The woman experiences the group support as validation of her worthiness to receive Loving care. She now has a mental image of being protected. See T p. 83/90, on returning to the point at which the error was made. This does not mean that the woman was wrong. The error was the decision made at that point. For example, she may have decided that there is no Greater Being; she is unworthy of Loving-Kindness; or she has to take whatever she is given for there is nothing else available to her. She is now free to see things differently.

> Remember not to judge any scene as "unimportant," or "minor." The scene may be one in which a boy had his sand bucket taken from him by a neighborhood bully while playing in his sandbox. The child would still have experienced the terror of no protector, and the helplessness or rage that accompanies that. Miracle Principle #1, T p. 1/3 says, "There is no order of difficulty in miracles. One is not 'harder' or 'bigger' than another. They are all the same. All expressions of love are maximal." This is true in both directions. When we defend, we defend. It doesn't matter how "serious" the trauma is. (This is a judgment we make.) To undo a defense is to undo a defense. Any undoing brings an expression of Love which is the miracle.

SHARE from both the viewpoint of the protector and the protected.

✳

21. REWIND THE SCENE
    Prepare following guidelines in Chapter 24. You are now ready to go to a scene in which you were overpowered and harmed. --- Now, just like this were a movie, rewind the scene to the time just before the harm took place. --- Using your most protective parent voice, the one that would save a child from running in front of a car, tell the attacker to get out, get away, and that you won't let your child be hurt. "Never again will I let you hurt my little one." (You may choose to give your group permission to say this out loud. This is empowering for each other. When I do this, I tell the group before we start that I will be inviting them to speak out loud at one point. They may choose to do this, or not. Either is okay. If they choose not to the first time, they usually will gratefully accept at a later time.) --- See your child safe and the attacker retreat. --- Know that the movies in your mind are yours and you can bring in all the people or resources you need to protect yourself at any time. ------ (Invite your group: "Gently come back to this space, open your eyes, and prepare to share.")
    SHARE. If any of you have difficulty with this and need help from the group, see Visualization No. 20 above, or Practice Exercise No. 70, Chapter 25.

✳

22. DEBTS/DEBTORS
    Prepare following guidelines in Chapter 24. You are now ready to picture on the left side of a stage, all those people around whom you feel uncomfortable. --- One at a time bring them center stage. There are four questions for you to ask yourself about each person. I will state them slowly for you, and then repeat them. "What do I believe this person owes me?" What am I waiting for this person to give me?" "What might this person think I owe them? What might this person be waiting for me to give them?" (Read these four questions again slowly.) As you feel finished with each person, see them leave going to the right side of the stage. (Allow adequate time for reflection.) ------ (Invite your group: "Gently come back to this space, open your eyes, and prepare to share.")
    SHARE your learnings about debts and debtors. Now that you have identified areas of blame and non-forgiveness, decide on action steps as Spiritual Homework. Accept (forgive) things as they are. Reverse your intent to blame and take action for yourself now instead of against the other. Ask yourself if the other is wanting something you are willing to give. If so, give it. If not,

see SECTION THREE: SAYING "YES" AND "NO," Chapter 25 for Right Use of Refusal. Set boundaries.

✳

23. SPEAKING VISUALIZATION
    (Used in Sample Lesson No.10, Chapter 27)
    This same format can be used to imagine anything you want to bring into your life. It might be your ideal career, a holy relationship, a comfortable home, a healthy body, or a celebration of yourself. This visual exercise is to imagine what your life would be like with your greatest current problem resolved.

Sitting for "Speaking Visualization."

Sit in pairs, side-by-side, facing opposite directions. This will place your heads close together. Close your eyes. This is a speaking visualization. Partners will alternate in sharing their images. The sharing of images is done to encourage expansion, so do add to your scene anything inspired by your partner's images.

Prepare following guidelines in Chapter 24. The leader will then give the following instructions: Go to a natural scene. One sentence at a time, take turns describing what you see, hear, or experience there. --- (Allow adequate time.) --- Now see a large golden door. --- Turn the knob and walk through. --- On the other side you see the scene in which your current problem is resolved. --- Continue sharing your images as you did before. Allow yourself to feel the Joy of your ideal state. ------ (Invite your group: "Gently come back to this space, open your eyes, and prepare to share.")

SHARE about your experience and your ideal state.

✻

24. POSITIVE OUTCOMES

Prepare following guidelines in Chapter 24. You are now ready to think of some event that is coming in your life in which you have fear. --- Join with your Higher Self. --- Imagine a wonderful outcome. --- Take time to feel your pleasure. ------ (Invite your group: "Gently come back to this space, open your eyes, and prepare to share.")

SHARE your outcomes and good feelings.

✻

25. GUARDIAN ANGEL

Prepare following guidelines in Chapter 24. You are now ready to see that many times you take responsibility that is not yours. You also make yourself wrong or guilty for what others do. Imagine yourself putting what is not yours in a box and handing it to the Guardian Angel of its rightful owner. --- Ask the Guardian Angel to hold it until the person is ready to deal with it. --- Feel relief of these burdens. --- Express gratitude to the Angel. ------ (Invite your group: "Gently come back to this space, open your eyes, and prepare to share.")

SHARE what you released. Share your relief.

✻

26. HOLD IMAGES

This is a group prayer. Prepare for visualization following guidelines in Chapter 24. Then going around the circle, each of you speak what you would like to bring into your life. Ask the group to hold each image, allowing time before going on to the next person. This could be done for personal manifestation, or taken to any broader level such as a prayer for planetary Peace. (Invite your group: "Gently come back to this space, open your eyes, and prepare to share.")

SHARE how you experience the strength of group prayer.

✻

27. FOCUS OUT

At any one time there is usually something that we fear is going to happen to us. Perhaps we are afraid of group members or employees at our new job. When we focus on harm that might come in, we attract just that to us. Use this visual exercise to focus on what you want to experience. Picture yourself sending that out. This means **picture yourself Loving others instead of fearing what they might do to you.**

SHARE how different you feel when you focus on what you don't want to come to you, and when you focus on extending what you do want to come to you.

This is a good idea for new members in any group. Picture yourself extending Love to all the people there instead of fearing what others will think of you or do to you.

✻

28. TOUGH DECISION

When you need to make a decision between two things, picture one on your left hand and one on your right. --- Which hand feels lighter or actually goes up? This is the "Lighter" choice for you.

SHARE the decisions you make in using this exercise.

✻

29. LIGHT THE DARKNESS

(T p. 28/32, "Whenever light enters darkness, the darkness is abolished.")

Prepare following guidelines in Chapter 24. You are now ready to picture on your non-dominant hand, a scene in which you give a weak, ineffective response. --- On your dominant hand, picture a scene in which you give a strong, effective response. --- Alternate between the images several times allowing time to see each scene clearly. --- Now, bring your hands together. ------ (Allow adequate time for strength to lighten the darkness and then invite your group: "Gently come back to this space, open your eyes, and prepare to share.")

SHARE about your experience.

✻

30. SYMPTOMS TALK

Prepare following guidelines in Chapter 24. You are now ready to think of a symptom you have in your body or life. --- Give it a form. --- What color is it? --- Now give it a voice. What does it say to you? --- See yourself being safe being or doing what it tells you. --- What gift will you give this symptom for sharing with you in a helping way? ------ (Invite your group: "Gently come back to this space, open your eyes, and prepare to share.")

SHARE what messages your symptoms had for you. Take any necessary action steps as Spiritual Homework.

※

MEDITATIONS

1. SILENT LISTENING

WB Lesson #106, "Let me be still and listen to the truth."
WB Lesson #107, "Truth will correct all errors in my mind."

Prepare as for visualization. You might want to name a problem area. Simply say, "I am ready to know what I need to know." Sit in silence. Trust that you will know what to do when you know what it is you need to know.

※

2. CANDLE MEDITATION

Simply concentrate on a candle flame to still ego thoughts and bring yourself to Peace. You might want to close your eyes and allow the image of the flame to fade and then open your eyes for another impression.

※

3. BREATH MEDITATION

Select an affirmation for your in-breath, and one for your out-breath. For example, breathe in Love and send out (release) fear. Breathe in Peace and send out (extend) Peace. Or, say "I am the gift" and "I give safely." See yourself as both gift and giver.

Another option would be to state an affirmation to yourself on your in-breath, and give it thrust out into your life on your out-breath. Bring your idea into your consciousness (feminine receptive) and send your idea out to manifest (masculine asser-tive). Seek balance of creation. Balance your breath.

※

4. KEY WORD
Take any key word from *A Course In Miracles* and meditate on it. That on which you focus will increase.

※

5. SOFT BELLY
We live in an age when having firm muscles and a flat abdo-men has become an idol (that which we believe will bring us Love). This is so counter to what our body needs to be healthy and fulfill its spiritual function of breathing in Life energy. Please see the chapter on "Opening the Body" in *Healing into Life and Death* by Stephen Levine. He includes a meditation on sof-tening the belly.

PART VI

Bringing Things
to
Completion

27

TEN SAMPLE LESSONS

In this chapter I share Sample Lessons which draw together ideas from throughout this book. These Sample Lessons are to show you how to plan lessons for sharing the Course and applying its principles.

SAMPLE LESSON ONE

TOPIC: *Meaning/Perception*

OPENING: What does this book (*A Course in Miracles*) mean to you? Accept every answer. Many times we haven't given thought to a question like this, so the first answer comes from ego resistance. Having then thought about the question, we accept deeper meaning. For example, after several years of teaching I asked this question of my groups. I got answers like, "It is something I carry to class each week." "I reject it." These were responses from students who are living the principles in *A Course in Miracles*. In classes that followed my asking this question, students told me they were reading beyond what I had assigned, and were finding the book very interesting. Obviously they had thought about the meaningfulness of the book to them.

CONTENT: Begin by placing an object in the center of your group. I use an old copper tea kettle. Each of you share what the object means to you. I receive answers like, "I think of my grandmother serving me cookies and tea when I was a kid," "It reminds me of my brother being steamed for croup and it is a very terrifying memory," and "I remember my ballet class at age 6 dancing to "I'm a Little Teapot Short and Stout." Notice that all of these examples include feelings. **For a sense of meaning, the Thinking Nature and Feeling Nature must be connected.** This means there is awareness of feelings.

Then read together WB Lesson #1, "Nothing I see in this room [on this street, from this window, in this place] means anything." This lesson will make total sense after the teapot experience. You will see that you gave the teapot all the meaning it has for you. And, that is the message of WB Lesson #2. Read that lesson together. To evoke thought, consider the same thinking pattern if a person had been in the center of your group instead of a teapot. Discuss this. Accept all comments as interesting.

Now consider WB Lessons #3 and #4. These deal with understanding and thought rather than meaning. Since responses about the teapot will have been based on images from the past, you can use this to illustrate how we use information from another time and place to interpret what we see or experience now.

Some thoughts to contemplate on MEANING:

a. Meaning is extension of Truth. Truth is of God. Truth is inherently meaningful. It doesn't need to be proven or defended.

b. Meaning lies in living the Law, knowing Love, experiencing expansion, experiencing healing, and growing in freedom.

c. Being of God, true meaning is changeless. We erroneously live with "shoulds" and judge things as meaningful or not by whether they go as we think they should.

d. Meaning lies within wholeness, that is, head and heart, or Thinking and Feeling Natures connected.

e. In contrast, perception comes from the ego in which our Thinking and Feeling Natures are separated. We project perception and see what we deny in ourselves as being in the other person. Remember that we deny both strengths and weaknesses. We see these qualities in others and justify attacking them. We may be angry at the other for not being strong for us, or not being weak when we want to be needed by them. And, of course, all attacks invite attacks in return. Consider these thoughts when reflecting on a person rather than a teapot being in the center of your group. We are inherently meaningful as God created us. The perceptions that people project are far from the Truth of our Being.

PRACTICE EXERCISE: To increase awareness of habits of thought, place a bag of groceries in the middle of your circle. Use this to stimulate discussion. Share various intentions of your group members when they go shopping. If they do not mention these, suggest such ideas as: get freshest produce; save by using coupons; get what I can fix fast in my microwave after work; things low in sucrose; things that aren't too heavy to carry home; things I can fix ahead of time and have ready when I come home from work; things I like; things that will please my family; finger foods for the kids; things on sale this week; and, to get enough so I don't have to go back for a week.

SHARE any realizations from either exercise you have done today. Read together WB Lesson #5, "I am never upset for the reason I think." Introduce the idea that you are upset because you bring information from your past into a current situation. At that time in your past, you did not see all that was there to see, and you were seeing something as being there that was not there. The same is true in any current upset.

HOMEWORK: Assign readings based on your next lesson. Perhaps you would be continuing on with lessons from the Workbook and would assign several lessons to be read at home.

SPIRITUAL HOMEWORK: Be aware that you give things all the meaning they have for you. During the opening round at the next class, share what you realized about yourselves.

CLOSING: Circle and rock to music, "From Thee I Receive," by Joseph and Nathan Segal, on the audio tape, *Many Blessings* by On Wings of Song & Robert Gass, Spring Hill Music, Boulder, CO. Before singing this song, relate the lyrics to major ideas in this lesson. Do meanings and thoughts that you give to your-selves and others nourish you? Do they call out the best in you?

SAMPLE LESSON TWO

TOPIC: *Defensive Wall*

OPENING: What limitation would you like to go beyond?
Share about Spiritual Homework from your last class.

PRACTICE EXERCISE: (I chose to reverse order here placing the EXERCISE before CONTENT.) Using guidelines for visualization in Chapter 24, prepare your group for visualization. Play quiet music in the background.
  Slowly read the following script allowing for pauses: Picture the wall that surrounds you. --- What is it made of? --- How tall is it? --- How wide is your wall? --- How deep is your wall? --- How close to you is it? --- Does your wall surround you? --- How do you feel with this wall? --- Is there anything written on

your side of the wall? --- Rise up and go to the other side of the wall to see if there is anything written on that side. --- While you are there, look around. What is outside of your wall? --- If you were to name this wall, what would you name it? --- (Continue, reading the following statements slowly).

We each have built a shield around ourselves to protect us from injury, danger, and loss. It is a reminder of fear and separation. This wall has no power to bring us anything we need or want. It restricts us. It is there to disrupt communication based on the belief, "I am not Lovable." Declare your innocence loudly to the Universe. State emphatically right now, "I am an innocent and Beloved Child of God." --- Our walls separate us from Joy and Freedom. They are one and the same with the diaphragm which divides our bodies at their middles. This is where we store emotional wounds. We breathe shallowly to not feel them. Know that your lungs function like bellows drawing energy from Earth and Heaven, creating the fire that burns away these old hurts. Increase the depth of your breathing and see hurts go off in a cloud of smoke. Bless their leaving. --- Look at your life for a moment. How did you decide to live to avoid feelings of shame when there was no Love to receive your beautiful, tender child? --- How did you decide to handle self-doubt when you were made wrong by others too unaware of themselves to nurture your Being? --- People who do not trust their own thinking often fear being stupid and project this to others. What did you decide to do to avoid being called stupid? --- How did you prevent feeling powerless? --- This wall holds all those decisions intact. They will dissipate when you change your mind. The *wall* is now your problem. Keeping the wall separates you from Love. It keeps you from knowing Truth. Ask yourself, "Do I want the problem, or do I want the answer?" --- You may choose to stay on the other side of this wall. --- Feel the glory of freedom. --- Take another look around. --- See a Greater Being there receiving you. It might be the grown-up you are now, or any holy figure. --- Rest in Peace. ------

SHARE your experiences with this visualization.

CONTENT: Prepare a lesson using the following *A Course in Miracles* references.
    T p. 15-17/19-21, "The Atonement as Defense."
    T p. 188-192/202-207, "The 'Dynamics' of the Ego."
    T p. 268/288, "Defenses, like everything you made, must be gently turned to your own good...."

T p. 334/359, "...all defenses *do* what they would defend."
WB Lesson #135, "If I defend myself I am attacked."
WB Lesson #136, "Sickness is a defense against the truth."
WB Lesson #153, "In my defenselessness my safety lies."
MT p. 12/14, "Defenselessness."

HOMEWORK: Assign readings based on your next lesson.

SPIRITUAL HOMEWORK: At various times this week, imagine that you take down the wall that surrounds you. Remember that you are there as protector for your inner child now. Remember your holy figure. See how you feel. Share at your next class.

CLOSING: Hand dance. Hand dancing is a delightful way to join another Lovingly and feel the dance of Life. Have people sit in pairs, knee to knee, or with knees straddled if necessary.

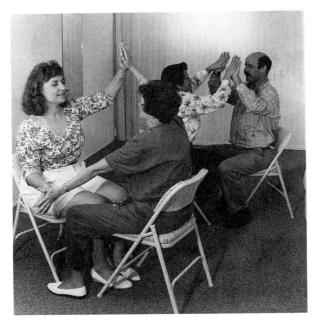

Hand dancing.

Place palms firmly against palms of the other. As music plays, follow the flow with your hands. Do this in such a way that after a while you do not know who is leading and who is following. Encourage the group to be free and expansive with their movements.

For music, use something that touches the heart, such as a movie theme, or any of the following audio tapes:

a. "Shores of Forever" on audio tape, *Voices of the Heart* by Michael & Maloah Stillwater, Heavensong Recordings.

b. *Piano Reflections*, an audio tape by Kelly Yost, Channel Productions, 1245 Lynwood Mall, P.O. Box 454, Twin Falls, ID, 83303, (208) 734-8668.

c. a selection from *Musical Companion to Sharing the Course* by Michael Root, such as "Hand Dance for Nancy."

d. For fun, use music like *Classical Child* by E. Mavrides, Sophia Sounds.

SAMPLE LESSON THREE

TOPIC: *The Holy Spirit*

OPENING: What is something you'd Love to do and have been putting off, making yourself wait?
Share about Spiritual Homework from your last class.

CONTENT: Each of you share what Holy Spirit or Holy Ghost has meant to you in the past. What does intuition mean to you? How do you know when things are right for you? See concordances for additional references on the Holy Spirit to plan your lesson.

WB p. 427/437, "What is the Holy Spirit?"

MT p. 85-86/89-90, "The Holy Spirit."

T p. 66-68/73-75, "The Invitation to the Holy Spirit."

T p. 69-71/75-78, "The Voice for God."

T p. 74/80, "...the Holy Spirit, the reinterpreter of what the ego made, sees the world as a teaching device for bringing you home."

T p. 92/100, "Remember that the Holy Spirit is the Answer, not the question. The ego always speaks first."

T p. 163/175, "It is perfectly obvious that if the Holy Spirit looks with love on all He perceives, He looks with love on you."

T p. 212/228, "The Holy Spirit keeps the vision of Christ for every Son of God who sleeps." (The Holy Spirit remembers Love we needed as a child, and that our need was not fulfilled.)

T p. 239/256, "Only the Holy Spirit knows what you need. For He will give you all things that do not block the way to light. And what else could you need?"

PRACTICE EXERCISE: **The Holy Spirit and Voice of God are both metaphors for ways we receive information inwardly. This would include intuition, imagination, insight, dreams, a feeling, revelation, telepathy, an urge, or an experience like having a sentence from a book seem to jump out at us.**

Using guidelines in Chapter 24, prepare your group for visualization. Play quiet music in the background.

Slowly read the following script, allowing for pauses: Go back to a time in your childhood when you didn't know how to do something. --- Where are you? --- Who is there? --- Who isn't there that you would like to be there for you? --- What is it that you are wanting to do? --- Who are you blaming for not helping you? --- Approach your younger self and give guidance Lovingly. "Here, this is how to do it." --- Now see the one you were blaming and say, "I forgive you for not seeing that I needed help, or for not knowing how to help me. I now have a helper. I am safe." ------

SHARE your experience with this visualization.

HOMEWORK: Assign readings based on your next lesson.

SPIRITUAL HOMEWORK: Recall your answer to the opening Go Round. Know that only your choice to wait for someone else to change separates you from your Good. What changes could you make right now to bring what you want into your life? What information does your inner child need to feel safe to go ahead?

When you don't know how to do something, remember "H.O.W." Help is On the Way! Release blame and avoidance and the Holy Spirit will lead you to answers you seek.

Write a letter of forgiveness to someone you are blaming, someone you see as standing between you and your Good. If it is truly Loving, mail or deliver it. Be prepared to share with your group at the next meeting.

Sharing the Course

CLOSING: Circle and rock as you sing "Om Namaha Shivaya" on the audio tape of the same name by On Wings of Song and Robert Gass, Spring Hill Music, P.O. Box 800, Boulder, CO, 80306.

SAMPLE LESSON FOUR

TOPIC: *Thought Reversal/Defining a Problem*

This lesson could easily by divided and extended over several classes.

OPENING: Where in you life would you like to give a different response?
Share about Spiritual Homework from your last class.

CONTENT: Defense is a maneuver we set in motion to keep ourselves from feeling what we don't want to feel. Every defensive move further separates us from the flow of Life/Love. Therefore, when we deny and defend, fear and our sense of vulnerability increase which leads us to further defend. This sets up the spiraling downward effect of all addictions. Instead of solving the real problem, we *try* harder using our defense which didn't work in the first place, and was set up to not work. Remember that when functioning within ego thinking, we believe there is no Greater Being or Nurturer who will receive us, so we set up a devious system to avoid feeling the terror of dying that we would feel from that perceived separation.

It is the nature of defense that it always sets up chaos in our life. This serves as a reminder that we are still avoiding something. See T p. 334/359 for the law that governs the defense system, "...all defenses *do* what they would defend." Note how defenses do what they would defend in the following example.

You are wanting a Loving response from someone and they are ignoring you. Your way of *trying to get* someone to pay attention to you is to speak louder and say more. You do this and they become even more distant (cold silence). So, you resort to yelling (add more anger and blame to your tone), and they leave the house slamming the door behind them. In this example, you are approaching with increasing intensity, and the one who is

344

withdrawing is doing that with increasing intensity. Neither person is addressing the problem at hand, you have some hurt that is needing Loving attention. You want to be seen and heard (received by a Nurturer). The one who walked out has the same need. Both end up feeling separated and terrified. This may be masked by rage and further denied by abusing with another addicted pattern. This example describes "specialness," of course. Defenses and blame are inherent in "specialness" where we are making a demand on the other to be our Greater Being and make us feel happy.

See WB Lesson #5, "I am never upset for the reason I think." Behind every upset is the fear of dying. Every upset is due to ego activity which always involves seeing ourselves as separated from the Source of Life/Love. In "special relationships" we see the other as our savior. The problem is always that we are defended and have our energy in resistance against the Life Force, our intention is then anti-God, or anti-Christ.

The Life Force continues to feed us our "daily bread" even though we turn against it. So, while we are denying God, tension builds up in our system. Here are some other factors that enter into our fear of dying:

1. Tension from unexpressed Life builds and we continue to deny the feeling. This becomes disease in our bodies. Then we are afraid of dying from our diseases. We don't see our part in the miscreation, so we helplessly blame God, or partners in "special relationships." This process explains why we hear that things like cancer are anger turned inward.

2. Tension from unexpressed Life gets named "stress" and we blame nearly anything in our environment for causing us this stress. We drive ourselves to exhaustion with the tension we keep building by blocking our own creativity.

3. Tension from unexpressed Life builds and becomes rage that we project outwardly. We "lose it," and attack in a way that we fear being killed by the one we attacked.

4. Tension of unexpressed Life builds and becomes anxiety. We aren't acting with a connected Thinking Nature, so the ego sets out to solve the problem for us. The ego does not discern harmfulness of its acts, it simply has solutions to end the build-up of tension. Solutions include having an automobile accident, falling off a high structure (messing up on a sky diving jump), exploding a blood vessel (myocardial infarction and cerebral vascular accident), or taking an overdose of chemicals. So, when we deny God and the tension that builds as a result, we begin to have thoughts of doom. We fear dying.

True problem solving never involves vengeance and never creates more problems. We do need discernment, for something else is at work here, the healing process. The Life Force is always seeking to heal us. When we solve a problem, the next thing we need to attend will come to our awareness. This may seem like a problem caused by the problem we just solved. It is not a new problem, it is an old problem newly coming into our awareness as we awaken from denial in growing spiritually. There have been times when I welcomed the new problem in my life because it was a sure sign that I had solved the previous one!

For example: I knew for years that I would someday write a book. Fear of expressing myself and being harmed kept me from expressing. While teaching *A Course in Miracles* classes and sharing myself openly with small groups, I was received consistently with Love and overcame my fear of expressing. At this point *Sharing the Course* flowed through me.

Then I needed to face the problem of expressing to a greater public. Suddenly I was faced with terrors of being harmed (and dying as a result of the lack of Love I was perceiving out there in the big world). Notice that while it is true that some people will act from their ego, my fear comes from my unhealed ego belief that others will attack me and I will be helpless. Truth is, I attack myself by entertaining fear thoughts that lead me to defend and turn my energies against God. In higher thought I know that God would not give me this mission for me to be harmed by it. I also know that in preparing for this mission I have developed discernment and the ability to respond to attacks with awareness which is Love.

To summarize, when we have a problem, we are never upset for the reason we think. A problem indicates we have restricted in fear. A problem indicates there is something we have denied and are being invited to see. Every problem offers us a gift. A problem will recur until we solve it. Until then, we are investing our energy in spiritual deadening. This deadening process is exhausting, and miscreates with energy resulting in diseases and physical death. **Life energy is to be used to create Life.**

See the following references:

T p. 32/36, "The best defense, as always, is not to attack another's position, but rather to protect the truth."

T p. 196/212, "Do I want the problem or do I want the answer?"

T p. 195-199/211-214, "The Problem and the Answer."

PRACTICE EXERCISE: Use the Think Structure described in Practice Exercise No. 12, Chapter 25. **The solution lies within a properly defined problem.**

HOMEWORK: Assign readings based on your next lesson.

SPIRITUAL HOMEWORK: Carry out the answer to the problem you defined:
Deny, "I no longer need to believe _____."
Affirm, "I am _____."
Stop _____.
Do _____.
Come prepared to share at your next class.

CLOSING: Circle and rock as you sing, "I Surrender" on the audio tape, *Heavensong Celebration Live,* by Michael Stillwater, Heavensong Recordings.

SAMPLE LESSON FIVE

(The Spiritual Homework assignment from your last class would have been to prepare a list of 10 to 12 affirmations. Ideally, these would be drawn from the lesson in that class.)

TOPIC: *Guiltlessness/Innocence*

OPENING: What is something precious about you that you have longed for someone to notice?
Share about Spiritual Homework from your last class.

CONTENT: **The ultimate purpose of all learning is to abolish fear (blame/guilt) and accept our innocence. To be innocent is to identify as a Beloved Child.** We identify as innocent (and Beloved), or guilty (and separated from a source of Love). **To choose innocence as our identity is to choose freedom and only its results. This means, free of guilt, shame, doubt, and all self-condemnation. Of course, this means all our emotional pain is healed.** The symbol for this identity in *A Course* *in Miracles* is the "Face of Christ." Face means identity. "Face of Christ" is the symbol of forgiveness. In the state of forgiveness we see with Christ's vision which means we no longer see ourselves as unworthy and guilty, and no longer project this out as blame of others. See MT p. 79-80/83-84.

We see a lovely world when we see our true self reflected in it. In true perception we see others as ourselves. We know that all of us are doing the best we can at figuring out life and deserve only help to do so.

Our problems are not caused by events in our past. They are caused by decisions made continuously in the present to be loyal to self-restricting decisions we made in the past. We hold to fear/guilt and interfere with our own natural growth.

MT p. 3/3 says the central theme of *A Course in Miracles* is always that we are innocent, and in accepting our innocence we are saved. **To accept truth is to accept happiness. Fear is contraction, hell. Love is expansion, Heaven.**

WB p. 370/380 says we remember Heaven, instantly, which means we expand immediately upon realizing the illusion of our condemnation.

WB p. 372/382 says that when we declare our innocence we are free. The Holy Instant is the moment of release when we accept our innocence. This brings us to quiet Peace.

T p. 33/37 relates the lamb to innocence and the lion to strength. True strength comes in fulfilling our heart's desires which can only be achieved with harmless intent. Harmlessness brings only blessings to us. If we use strength without knowing our innocence, we are using anger from our ego and will defeat ourselves.

T p. 34/38, When innocent, we "...never see what does not exist, and always see what does."

See T p. 575-77/619-21 on idols. Idols are veils across the face of Christ. We cannot have idols and know ourselves as Beloved. All idols/addictions are substitutes we accept because we believe there is no Love for us. Each use affirms our guilt.

PRACTICE EXERCISE: HOLY BATH, *Bathing In Love* (See photo with Practice Exercise #108 in Chapter 25.) Each of you has prepared a list of affirmations as Spiritual Homework. One at a time, each of you sit surrounded by four others. I like to use two men opposite each other, and two women opposite each other when possible. Close your eyes when you are in the center. The person in front reads one affirmation at a time and the other three around the circle repeat it. This means that when you are in the center you hear each of your affirmations spoken from the four directions. When this is completed, you take a turn giving while someone else sits in the center.

HOMEWORK: Assign readings based on your next lesson.

SPIRITUAL HOMEWORK: Write a letter telling about your innocence. I have included one I received from Carolyn.

Dearest Nancy,

Thank you for giving me the opportunity to express my innocence. I realize that I am long overdue in recognizing my growth and strengths. Please let me begin to express my development and soul's growth.

I am innocent for the pain I have caused myself and others, for I knew no better.

I am innocent for the things I have accepted in my life, for I did not see choices.

I am innocent for not protecting myself, for I never realized I had the tools.

I am innocent for my anger, for I did not know how to direct it properly.

I am innocent for the lack of Love I received and gave, for I was afraid to Love.

I am innocent for not letting go, for I feared letting go would lead to my death.

I am innocent for fearing the future, for I have only the present (today) to live for.

I am innocent for the loneliness I felt and believed in, for I was never alone. God and the Holy Spirit were and are always with me.

Sincerely, Carolyn J.

CLOSING: Circle and rock as you sing "Tender and Innocent" on the audio tape, *Musical Companion to Sharing the Course*, or "The Heart of the Mother" on the audio tape, *Voices of the Heart* by Michael Stillwater, Heavensong Recordings.

SAMPLE LESSON SIX

TOPIC: *I AM Beloved*

OPENING: How would you be living differently if you knew you had everything you need and always would?
Share about Spiritual Homework from your last class.

CONTENT: What does Beloved mean to you?
What does I AM mean to you?
What does I AM Beloved mean to you?
Wherever our parents or significant others in our childhood were unable to accept Love, their ego/fear response to us failed to encourage, or openly discouraged our development. These areas are now bound by shame/guilt in us. We think much of ourselves is wrong, bad, or to be kept hidden. **What has happened cannot be undone. Our RESPONSE to what happened can be, and is to be. *A Course in Miracles* is a guide to undoing. We reverse our response in order to transcend fear.**
Blame and resentment both keep our focus on what we believe another is doing wrong. Our ego intention is to keep our focus outside ourselves. It is one way the ego can assure that it doesn't get undone. **Our spiritual task is to undo our ego.** Remember the ego is for child survival only and meant to be outgrown in the spiritual phase that follows the survival phase of life.
Each feeling we feel (that is, release from dissociation) has a gift for us. Every restriction in our ego is a restriction of a natural expression and power to attract Good to ourselves. As we undo our ego we attract to ourselves those things we have most wanted and have worked hardest to prevent (due to fear of receiving).
A feeling of yearning or longing indicates that our denied and forgotten child cries out to us. It waits for our acknowledgment and Love. You may choose to develop a lesson using references on such things as guiltlessness, innocence, Son/Child of God, Love, Brother, deciding, or judgment/discernment.

Here are some things to discuss on being BELOVED:

a. Accept every feeling you have knowing that you are entitled and safe to feel good, and that anything that doesn't feel good is some place you are not yet healed by Love. **Accepting a feeling (as in using a Healing Method in Chapter 5), is NOT the same as projecting a feeling harmfully to others. Accepting a feeling means bringing it into awareness and then giving the response that comforts and heals your inner child.**

b. Refuse to hold onto beliefs that you are shameful, unworthy, or unlovable. Refuse to identify as deprived and envious. Instead, identify as Loved and open to receive your own Good.

c. Focus on what you are giving, rather than on what you hope to *get* from others. **Express based on value of yourself rather than on anticipation of what will please others or prevent harm to you.**

d. Beloved means having response-ability. This is the ability to respond harmlessly. There is no need to *try to get* another to be your Greater Being when you identify as whole.

e. Accept yourself as Good. Give all responses to life from the stance that I AM GOOD. You do not have to earn or prove this. Know you deserve only to be helped, and ASK only for that in the way you express. Projecting anger at another does not ASK for help. It asks for a hurtful response in return. And, unless the other person is more aware, further along on their spiritual journey, a hurtful response is assured.

PRACTICE EXERCISE: Sit in pairs. Person A shares one thing at a time with Person B. These would be things you believe are not Lovable about yourself. Person B responds with, "(Name), Love that about yourself." After 10 to 15 minutes, switch roles. Example:

A: I resent that I only got a cost of living raise.
B: Roz, Love that about yourself.
A: I feel angry when you tell me to Love myself.
B: Roz, Love that about yourself.
A: No one has ever Loved me, why should I?
B: Roz, Love that about yourself.
A: I don't even like to hear the word "Love."
B: Roz, Love that about yourself.
A: I really want to be Loved.
B: Of course, Roz, Love that about yourself.

As a group, share how you experienced the invitation to speak about those areas of yourself not yet Loved. Do you see how you resist Loving them? Believe it or not, you blame some-one else for not Loving every aspect of you that doesn't feel Loved yet. WB Lesson #5 says, "I am never upset for the reason I think." You need to rethink.

HOMEWORK: Assign readings based on your next lesson.

SPIRITUAL HOMEWORK: Be aware of how you use "I AM." Do you declare that you are guilty and unworthy, or Lovable and Beloved?

CLOSING: Select a song you like. I suggest "Tender and In-nocent" on the audio tape, *Musical Companion to Sharing the Course or* "I Love Myself the Way I Am," on audio tape, *Loving Your Self: Songs & Meditations* by Louise L. Hay and Jai Josefs, Hay House, Inc.

SAMPLE LESSON SEVEN

This lesson is appropriate for Lent. It could easily be divided into enough classes to use as a Lenten series. See Section Three of Chapter 25 for additional Practice Exercises and Spiritual Homework.

TOPIC: *Individuation/Boundaries - Right Use of Refusal*

OPENING: Whom do you fear and what is it about them that is fearful to you?
Share about Spiritual Homework from your last class.

CONTENT: We all need to learn RIGHT USE OF REFUSAL. Consider for a moment: What is it you most want and don't have? --- Consider, also, that this is what you most fear having and without realizing it, you are refusing to fulfill your heart's desire. What we don't realize about fear is that we are sending out harmful vibration, alarm from our gut, calling for others to re-spond to us on that "channel." Note how *refusal* here works against ourselves and invites others to respond with alarm (harm) to us. In truth, we are *refusing* to be Loving. **We are ask-ing for our self-defeating ego results.**
We all need to learn to say "No" to harm whether it is coming from within ourselves or from others. This means **we need to**

recognize our own defensive stances and *refuse* to take them. It also includes learning to not put up with, tolerate, go along with, overlook, give consent to, or perpetuate harmfulness in any way. When we perpetuate harm, we prolong chaos in our lives by our own *refusal* to be Loving.

There is no difference between initiating harmfulness, and using harm done to us to justify more blame. Blame is invisible war. We bombard the other with weapons unseen by our eyes. They are felt by the other who justifies attack in return. Though we don't "see" that we are sending missiles, we need to learn that this is true of such feelings as resentment and blame. We all know how we feel when we receive such projections from others. We can *refuse* littleness. We can *refuse* to stay narrow in our options. We can *refuse* to see ourselves as helpless. We can *refuse* to blame.

Areas of pain indicate where we are unhealed. Pain is resistance against Spirit. If we have pain, we are *refusing* some gift of Spirit. We have a door closed. We have mostly learned to hate pain, fear it, be angry with it, and medicate it away. We can *refuse* to ignore it or make it wrong. It is our child speaking to us. True healing addresses the whole problem and always involves meeting our area of suffering with Loving-Kindness. We hurt where we are *refusing* to receive our own Good. The choice we once made to prevent pain of separation now separates us and brings us pain.

This Sample Lesson No. 7 is appropriate for Lent. One way to look at Lent is as a time to cleanse and purify negation from our minds. In Miracle Principle #7, T p. 1/3, we read that miracles are everyone's right and we must purify first. Reversing our refusal from refusing Love's way to refusing fear's way is one of those purifications. **We are always refusing Love's way or fear's way. We accept pain or Joy.** The forty days of Lent are adequate to *refuse* fear's way and transcend to Love. This is a time of crucifixion of our ego and resurrection of our Spirit.

Free will says "No" as well as "Yes" in ways that contain things without suppressing, like stones placed in a ring around a fire. They allow the fire to be safe and brilliant rather than a threat that smolders off, invading grasses that surround it. Wisdom is our own sense of what is totally appropriate for us at any moment.

Each appropriate "Yes" or "No" is like these stones, containing the flow of our Spirit and directing its creations. We need to be willing to follow inner knowing. This means *refusing* to give in to escalation's of our own defensive thinking as we let it go. This means *refusing* to give in to pressure from the masses who are following ingrained restrictions. This means *refusing* to go along with misnaming of things.

An example of misnaming is always saying that women get raped and never saying that men rape women. An example of misnaming a problem is focus on the abortion issue rather than sexual responsibility for both men and women. A third example of misnaming is calling those with free will "crazy." This is done by those who function from their ego (which in truth is insane). Functioning on free will does not mean violating laws. There is a difference between Universal Laws, laws of the land, and ingrained restrictions based on fear. Free will has released these restrictions. For example, when someone runs for public office, there is no law that says they must go all over the country to meet people. There is a law that says they must account for money spent in campaigning. Most "laws" of campaigning are from tradition or fear of not being elected.

Refuse to make yourself wrong for going up in awareness. Some people will be angry when you see what you see and say what you see. Waking up gets misnamed, also.

Refuse to believe that you will be all alone. Saying "No" to what isn't right for you opens a space for what is. Our hips symbolize individual independence, free will, self-support, and balance. They give us our major thrust in moving forward. Do you Love your hips??? We *refuse* to move forward if we do not see a favorable outcome. This tells us where we need to change our thinking in order to use RIGHT USE OF REFUSAL. We need to do early scene work. (See Healing Methods, Chapter 5.)

As you read these references from *A Course Miracles*, look for what you are being told you are to *refuse*.

MT p. 64/67, "Teacher of God, your one assignment could be stated thus: Accept no compromise in which death plays a part." (Read on.) **Inhibition is to be used to control your own destructive urges, not to inhibit your growth and that of others.**

T p. 124-6/133-5, "The Confusion of Pain and Joy." **Refuse to believe that anything that opposes health, happiness, or ease will bring you Joy.** We do not deny conditions, we deny beliefs that miscreate the conditions. We deny that there is no way to find Joy. We deny the belief that substitutes bring Joy. This applies to abuse of any substance. We can also look at any illness, injury, or state of deprivation in terms of what is "gained" from it. Secondary gains of such things include: time off work, release of responsibilities, getting attention from others, an opportunity to sleep in, time to read, time to focus inwardly, and any excuse to avoid whatever we want to avoid.

T p. 277/298, Refuse to teach yourselves from your ego. Refuse to blame. **Use any blame statement to identify your unmet need and then meet it.**

T p. 189/203, Breaking out of bondage from acquiescing in oppression releases energy. To acquiesce is to go along with without protest. It requires courage, conviction, and willingness to go with the impulse of the Self. Ego forces call us backward. God/Holy Spirit or the Voice of Love in us calls us forward. **Only denial of your feelings keeps you willing to submit to authoritative control which is power over you.**

T p. 555-557/598-600, "The Greater Joining." Refuse to be part of fearful dreams. **Refuse to be stuck in entertaining only catastrophic outcomes.** Think of best possible outcomes.

Additional readings on this topic include T p. 573-77/617-21 on idols (addictions) and T p. 586-93/630-38, looks beyond idols to free will and your only purpose.

No self-definition will stand unchallenged for long. The law of life is growth. As soon as you master one thought, transfer it from fear to Love, the next in line will come to your attention. Your life will get bigger and better as your self-definition gets bigger and better.

PRACTICE EXERCISES: Any in SECTION THREE, Saying "YES" and "NO," Chapter 25, especially:

a. No. 22, SAYING NO
b. No. 26, "STOP IT"
c. No. 27, "I REFUSE"

In order to feel safe to be different and give a new response you need to see some favorable outcomes.

d. No. 68, BEST OUTCOMES

HOMEWORK: Assign readings based on your next lesson.

SPIRITUAL HOMEWORK: Assign the homework that is listed with these four exercises or any Practice Exercise you choose from Chapter 25.

CLOSING: Circle and rock as you sing, "Spirit Am I" on the audio tape of the same name by Jay Minoru Inae, Kokoro Music Publishing Co., lyrics selected by Bob Rogosich from *A Course in Miracles*, and distributed by Hay House, Inc. Or you might choose to sing "Om Namaha Shivaya," (See Sample Lesson No. 3), or "I Say No" on the audio tape, *Musical Companion to Sharing the Course*.

SAMPLE LESSON EIGHT

To extend this lesson into a series of classes see Practice Exercises and Spiritual Homework in Sections No. 4 and 5 in Chapter 25.

TOPIC: *Asking/Seeing*

OPENING: I'm beginning to believe (see) _____.
Share about Spiritual Homework from your last class.

CONTENT: See T p. 14-19/17-22. **To *ask* is to remove fear of joining.** To *ask* is to lower defenses that separate you from others (and God, of course). **To *ask* is to remove your blocks to awareness of Love's presence in your life, which means to see.** The most proper thing to *ask* for is peace which comes from Atonement. This means you trust the presence of Love (which may be your inner parent, or may be an experience of a holy figure or God). In a state of peace you believe you are seen, heard, and will receive a Loving response to fulfill your needs. You know you are protected and safe.

To *ask* and to pray are the same thing. They both are a shift of consciousness which shifts your energy from fear to Love. See WB Lesson #183, "I call upon God's Name and on my own." The "Name of Jesus," the "Word of God," and the "Name of God" are all symbols referring to Love expressing. It is your true vibration. It is this Love for which you long. See MT p. 51/53, Words of a prayer are not the prayer. Moving to the energy of Love calls a new response to you.

See Miracle Principles #26, T p. 2/5, "Miracles represent freedom from fear. 'Atoning' means 'undoing.' The undoing of fear is an essential part of the Atonement value of miracles."; #29, T p. 3/5, "Miracles praise God through you. They praise Him by honoring His creations, affirming their perfection. They heal because they deny body-identification and affirm spirit-identification." (Body-identification means your view of yourself when you are in your ego survival mode.); and #49, T p. 4/6, "The miracle makes no distinction among degrees of misperception. It is a device for perception-correction, effective quite apart from either the degree or the direction of the error. This is its true indiscriminateness."

Every problem we have is from separating due to fear. The goal of *A Course in Miracles* is for us to identify as Sons of God, remembering who we are as innocent children of Loving holy parents. This can be taken to mean the masculine and feminine in us, or the poles of Spirit and Soul.

See T p. 40-41/45-46, "Beyond Perception"; T p. 152-55/163-66, "The Answer to Prayer"; and T p. 195-99/211-14, "The Problem and the Answer."

See MT p. 48/50, "Pray for God's justice ...." God's Justice means receiving what we deserve in response to extending Love. It means knowing we are innocent and accepting the miracle of Love. This is the opposite of the way the world defines justice where a person is viewed as guilty, deserving revenge and punishment.

See T p. 236/253, "Awakening unto Christ (Love) is following the laws of love of your free will, and out of quiet recognition of the truth in them. The attraction of light must draw you willingly, and willingness is signified by giving."

PRACTICE EXERCISE: See LOVE YOURSELF (Practice Exercise No. 76 in Chapter 25.)

HOMEWORK: Assign readings based on your next lesson.

SPIRITUAL HOMEWORK: Assign that which goes with Practice Exercise No. 76.

CLOSING: Rock in a circle silently to "Rocking Song - A Lullaby" on the audio tape, *Musical Companion to Sharing the Course.* Imagine light going out from your eyes, hands, heart, and smiles.

SAMPLE LESSON NINE

TOPIC: *Virtues*

OPENING: What do you see as your Holy gifts to our planet? Share about Spiritual Homework from your last class.

CONTENT: Virtues are qualities we express when we trust our own Being, know our Belovedness, and express without judging ourselves as wrong. **Knowing we are Loved, we unfold instead of withhold.** The Holy Instant is the moment of transition when we choose forgiveness instead of guilt. It is when we listen to the voice of the nurturer inside us instead of the voice of the ego. It is the moment of the miracle instead of the grievance. **The Holy Instant is the moment of our WILLINGNESS to receive the miracle.**

We either bless others by extending our virtues, or curse them by projecting our ego energy. Virtues support Life, and everything else is murder. See T p. 461/496, "What is not love is murder. What is not loving must be an attack." We do not need to be perfect to be virtuous. We need to keep our energy flowing. This means we must accept all of who we are. When we accept ourselves, the energy we have been using to *try* to make ourselves acceptable is released and graces us and everyone else. **We create that to which we give most of our attention. The virtuous focus on Goodness and accept the rest as part of learning and healing.**

JOY and PEACE are signs of balance. They are goals of *A Course in Miracles*. Their presence means we are neither stuck in contraction nor expansion. Human beings pulse and cycle naturally like everything in nature. Knowing our own natural rhythm is Joy and Peace.

As a group, name other virtues. Here are some examples: compassion, understanding, harmony, wisdom, beauty, vitality, health, courage, patience, trust, clarity, honesty, attitude of gratitude, discernment, endurance, acceptance, freedom, grace, love, zeal, true (inner) authority, curiosity, humor, light-heartedness, humility, meekness, devotion, confidence, generosity, and serenity.

Select from the following to read on other virtues:
MT p. 8-15/9-16, "WHAT ARE THE CHARACTERISTICS OF GOD'S TEACHERS?"

FAITH and GRACE, T p. 373/400 and WB Lesson #169, "By grace I live. By grace I am released."

We are in a state of grace when we are happy learners. This means that when problems arise, we simply see that there is something we need to know. Instead of making ourselves wrong, we open to see what we haven't seen yet. Grace allows us to look forward and have foresight because we aren't afraid to see what might lie ahead. Until then, we live with hindsight, learning from our mistakes. Open-mindedness is necessary for grace.

PATIENCE, T p. 70/76, "The Voice..." Patience means we remember our strength and have faith in miraculous outcomes from choosing extension over contraction even if we do not see immediate results. ("I am ready and willing to know what I need to know, to do what is mine to do.")

A virtuous person never tries to teach a pig how to sing. It wastes their time and annoys the pig. (Just kidding! Go ahead if you are called to do so.)

WILLINGNESS and HUMILITY, T p. 354-56/380-82.

NON-DEFENSIVENESS, T p. 345/370, "The Conditions of Peace."

PRACTICE EXERCISE: See Practice Exercise No. 10 in Chapter 25. Each of you write a pledge of allegiance to your Soul using the rhythm of The Pledge of Allegiance. Here are some examples from our group.

> *I pledge allegiance to my self and to all that nurtures me, and to the Universe, of which I am a part, indivisible, with love and compassion for all.* (Bill G.)

> *I pledge allegiance to be free of the old rules for being loving and to be true to my Inner Guide, one voice, of Good, with Peace and Joy as results.* (Nancy G.)

SHARE your pledges with each other. Take a stance with them. Pledge your allegiance to live your virtues. Live Peace rather than war.

HOMEWORK: Assign readings based on your next lesson.

SPIRITUAL HOMEWORK: Continue to appreciate your virtues and affirm them.

CLOSING: Dance virtues. Using music that touches the heart, select some virtues and call them out one at a time. Say to your group, "If you don't want anyone to see you, close your eyes!" It is always worth a laugh. Enjoy sculpting and illustrating virtues with your bodies. Hug.

SAMPLE LESSON TEN

TOPIC: *Kingdom of Heaven*

OPENING: What is your most demanding current problem? Share about spiritual homework from your last class.

CONTENT: Discuss what you can do with the key to something. **The key to the Kingdom is willingness to forgive** (release ego's way to go God's way). Forgiveness opens the gate to Heaven for you.

> Heaven is not a place. It is an awareness of perfect Oneness and knowledge of nothing else. Heaven is your state of Being fully alive and awake. It is a process. The cells of your body are constantly replacing themselves. Your Soul is constantly taking on more light, moving to higher and higher rates of vibration. Vibrating with the Name of God is Love. It is a conscious choice you make continuously. The result is happiness within you, so Heaven is within you. Being a quality of your Soul, it is independent of what we call death of the body. For the Soul there is only Life, and that Life is now, in the present, eternal "time."

This is what *A Course in Miracles* says about the Kingdom of Heaven:

T p. 44/49, Heaven is what I AM. "Instead of 'Seek ye first the Kingdom of Heaven' say, 'Will ye first the Kingdom of Heaven,' and you have said, 'I know what I am and I accept my own inheritance.' "

T p. 54/60, "The Kingdom of Heaven *is* you." "The Kingdom is perfectly united and perfectly protected, and the ego will not prevail against it. Amen." Discuss this prayer in terms of what your state is when you connect your own inner parent and child. Here, you are safe and Home where you belong.

WB p. 469/479, "What am I?"

WB Lesson #306 says Heaven is ancient memory from before the world I made (ego).

MT p. 36/37 says Heaven is sorrow turned to Joy and war turned to Peace.

T p. 358/384, "There is nothing outside you. This is what you must ultimately learn, for it is the realization that the Kingdom of Heaven is restored to you." The Kingdom is your natural dwelling place.

WB Lesson #138, "Heaven is the decision I must make."

WB Lesson #193, "All things are lessons God would have me learn." One way you know when you are in Heaven is its quality of Simplicity. Discuss this. When you "finally" figure out a problem, the answer seems almost too simple to be true. Then you know it is true!

T p. 80/87 says Heaven is the greatest threat to the ego because it is the ego that is undone to claim your holy inheritance. "'The wicked shall perish' becomes a statement of Atonement, if the word 'perish' is understood as 'be undone.' Every loveless thought must be undone, a word the ego cannot even understand. To the ego, to be undone means to be destroyed. The ego will not be destroyed because it is part of your thought, but because it is uncreative and therefore unsharing, it will be reinterpreted to release you from fear. The part of your mind that you have given to the ego will merely return to the Kingdom, where your whole mind belongs. You can delay the completion of the Kingdom, but you cannot introduce the concept of fear into it."

T p. 318/342, Read this page to see how the Kingdom of Heaven relates to "special relationships." Heaven is completion from extension of Love bringing union. In all "special relationships" we live the hell of separation.

T p. 380-84/407-12, "The First Obstacle: The Desire to Get Rid of It." Every ego thought is the desire to get rid of Heaven which is Peace. Heaven is beyond your veil of fear where you look with perfect gentleness on yourselves and others.

T p. 65/71, "God is praised whenever any mind learns to be wholly helpful. This is impossible without being wholly harmless, because the two beliefs must coexist. The truly helpful are invulnerable, because they are not protecting their egos and so nothing can hurt them."

T p. 69/76, "You *are* the Kingdom of Heaven, but you have let belief in darkness enter you mind and so you need a new light. The Holy Spirit is the radiance that you must let banish the idea of darkness."

T p. 74/80, "The ego made the world as it perceives it, but the Holy Spirit, the reinterpreter of what the ego made, sees the world as a teaching device for bringing you home."

T p. 91/99, "...your part is only to allow no darkness to abide in your own mind." Your part is to not hold dark thoughts in your mind. Dark thoughts separate you from Light/God. You are to correct/undo them. This *is* your spiritual journey.

WB Lesson #265 tells you to let no appearance (fear) obscure the light of Heaven shining on the world.

T p. 100/108 tells you to be vigilant only for God/Loving thoughts. In error, you are vigilant against these. When you reverse your vigilance and undo ego thoughts instead, you have consistency rather than chaos in your life.

You are hostage to the ego or host to God. You either serve yourselves guilt under direction of the ego, or Love under counsel of the Holy Spirit. The ego asks for the problem to continue and the Child of God receives the answer.

T p. 56/62, "Watch carefully and see what it is you are really asking for. Be very honest with yourself in this..."

T p. 318/341, "...Heaven is completion." **Completion is Peace and Joy.**

See Chapter 7 of *A Course in Miracles*, "THE GIFTS OF THE KINGDOM." (This chapter includes topics: holy relationships, free will, purity, clarity of vision, glory, grace, joy, eternity, peace, and remembering God.)

PRACTICE EXERCISE: Use Speaking Visualization No. 23, Chapter 26. Create a safe space and then speak and see what your life IS without your most demanding current problem situation. (See the opening for this sample lesson.)

HOMEWORK: Assign readings based on your next lesson.

SPIRITUAL HOMEWORK: Take some problem you have been struggling with for a long time and put it "on a shelf." "Remember the Sabbath" means to rest. This breaks your ego intention and allows things to reverse to Love. Honor the Sabbath to keep things Holy.

CLOSING: Sing "Peace Be to You" on the audio tape, *Voices of the Heart,* by Michael Stillwater, Heavensong Recordings.

28

HOW I LESSON PLAN
(AND LEARN MY LESSONS)

In this chapter I share the double meaning of lesson planning. **At one level we learn lessons about our own ego. This can be the most difficult part of teaching. This is our transformation from teaching what we learned with ego intent (fear), to being a Teacher of God (Love).** In this phase we go through blame, anger, scare, and physical symptoms of all kinds, to finally surrender to tender tears of acceptance. After learning these lessons, we demonstrate our power and radiance as we present our new self as Teacher. **The other level of lesson planning is technical.**

LEARNING MY LESSONS

Teachers teach what they need to learn. I pick a topic which is always something I need to learn, of course. I do this about six months before I plan to share with group. I need to be living it to truly Teach it. Here is an example of learning my lessons.

I began wearing glasses when I was sixteen. Every few years I got stronger lenses. In April of 1990 strange things were going on with my eyes like I had never heard of, or experienced. I thought I was going blind. Then two things happened. I received the inner message that I was to take off my glasses. And, in the mail, I received my copy of *EastWest, The Journal of Natural Health & Living*. In it I read an article on seeing better without glasses. I was about to go on a trip to visit my older children. I was about to go on another trip, too, and didn't realize it yet.

The *EastWest* article listed some references. I found *Total Vision* by Richard Kavner and Lorraine Dusky at the library to read on my trip. I ordered *Help Yourself to Better Sight* by Margaret Darst Corbett, *Seeing Beyond 20/20* by Robert-Michael

Kaplan, and *Natural Vision Improvement* by Janet Goodrich. Up until this time I had lightly read over the word, "vision," in *A Course in Miracles*. I really was not aware that the message of the Course is to wake up and SEE.

I learned about eyesight and experimented with various exercises in the books. Over a period of six months my vision cleared enough that I now only occasionally use a pair of glasses. They have a slight magnification. I bought them at a local drug store.

> My major learning was that when we defend as a child, we literally alter our visual memory so we do not see, and therefore do not feel, that which overwhelms us. Our eyes also adapt to help us not see what we decide to not see. Blinding ourselves is an idol. We think it saves us. Wearing corrective lenses is like all addictive processes. We cycle to stronger and stronger lenses. Glasses serve the blinding by binding us in the non-seeing state. Now, that is a new thought, isn't it! Coming off glasses is like coming out of any addiction.

Of course, I taught a whole series on vision related to *A Course in Miracles*. I needed to learn it. The word "see" now seemed to pop right out of the pages at me. My experience of life transformed from feeling like I was watching it, to one of truly feeling it. Until this transformation, I didn't realize I wasn't seeing.

Some of those who have studied with me are now leading their own groups. They asked for a chapter in *Sharing the Course* on handling problems that come up in group. While on the topic of seeing I will simply say that I have shared with you a model that works for me. Every problem you face is a place where there is more for you to SEE. These are your lessons to learn and your opportunities to become ever more radiant as a Teacher of God.

LESSON PLANNING

For the technical aspects of lesson planning, I have a box under my desk. Once I select a topic, I start throwing anything that comes to my awareness on that topic in the box. By Natural Law, energy follows thought, so as soon as I name the box, all kinds of things come to fill it. I start SEEING things all over the place. The next magazine that comes in the mail will have an article on it. I start talking about it and friends give me articles on it. I start seeing examples in my own life and in that of others. I make notes and throw those in the box, too.

After a while I have a full box. Then I go through all my scraps and start subdividing them into categories. I put these in folders. The process continues and now I slip new pieces of information into the folders. By the time I go to a folder to actually write out a lesson plan I am thrilled to see what is in there. It is like opening a precious gift.

Meanwhile, I have a "box" called EXERCISES. All ideas that come to my mind I place in that box. I have collected hundreds of ideas over the years. At first I used ideas from other people as I invite you to use any from *Sharing the Course.* Ideas from others inspired my own creativity. I have a similar "box" for OPENINGS, CLOSINGS, and HOMEWORK. With all these boxes I get crowded out of my dining room office at times. To actually plan my lessons I use the format suggested in this book and find appropriate material from these boxes.

THE NATURAL YEAR

I find that the year naturally divides into segments. I plan a series of about thirteen weeks between September and Christmas, another between January and Easter. I then plan a shorter topic for spring and one that allows us to feel free in summer.

In the **fall,** nature calls us to go inside ourselves and this is conducive to study of *A Course in Miracles.* Just like plants, what came to fruition in us has had its time of glory and becomes the mulch for new seeds that begin to germinate in our consciousness, not visible at first. **Christmas is when we acknowledge birth of a new spiritual aspect of ourselves.** Through the **winter** we embrace that aspect of self, nurture, and receive nurturing. **Easter represents when we are ready to let our restricted way die out and let Spirit's way reign.** Our Soul then takes on greater light. We also call this resurrection. After Easter we feel lighter. **Spring** is a good time for a lighter topic. In the **summer** we want to feel free.

My style has been to use *A Course in Miracles* heavily from September through Easter. Then I switch to a lighter topic. This year I did a four week series on ritual, symbols, ceremony, and initiation. You say, lighter?? Well, I told you I am always learning my lessons. What I learned about these four topics is that in four weeks we looked at one grain of sand on the ocean shore. One thing stands out that intrigues me. **Idols bridge to our ego and symbols bridge us to God. We need to learn about symbols, don't we!** See *A Dictionary of Symbols* by J. E. Cirlot if you are curious.

I have also found that using a book complementary to *A Course in Miracles* works well in the summer. I have selected *The Seat of the Soul* by Gary Zukav, *Spiritual Growth* by Sanaya Roman, and *The Sermon on the Mount* by Emmet Fox. These books all easily divide into lessons. This way, those who are on vacation read assigned chapters and feel a part of what is going on in group.

REFERENCES

To research a topic in *A Course in Miracles*, I use *A Course in Miracles Concordance* by Barbara Findisen. I also use *Glossary-Index for A Course in Miracles* by Kenneth Wapnick. His Scriptural Index found in the back of this book cross references *A Course In Miracles* and the King James Version of the Holy Bible. I am grateful to him for this. Both of these reference books refer to pages in the first edition of *A Course in Miracles*. I will welcome the new expanded concordance which is in process of publication. It will assist with the new second edition as well as facilitate using the workbook and manual.

Two other reference books that have helped me generally have been *Metaphysical Bible Dictionary* by Charles Fillmore, a Unity School of Christianity publication, and *Harper's Bible Dictionary*.

IN CLOSING

It may seem like I approach lesson planning all backwards. Often, the last thing I do is research *A Course in Miracles* on a topic. In Truth, because I consistently read and study *A Course in Miracles*, (I ask) my Soul knows I am ready and willing to grow spiritually. Therefore, my soul indicates my next lesson by bringing a problem to my awareness. And, through the principles of *A Course in Miracles* I have learned to recognize them for what they are, errors in my mind showing up in life events for me to see and correct. My struggle to awaken involves searching inside myself. *A Course in Miracles* is a guide to me. I Love *A Course in Miracles.* I wrote words to an old familiar tune, "I Love to Tell the Story." I share them with you. This song is recorded on *Musical Companion to Sharing the Course* by Michael Root.

I LOVE A COURSE IN MIRACLES

I love A Course in Miracles, a gift from God to me.
I'm learning how to open. I'm learning to be free.
I'm learning to be loving. I'm learning how to see.
I'm grateful for my growing, I'm truly being me.
I love A Course in Miracles. I love to learn and sing.
I love the joy and glory, that all my learnings bring.

BLESSED BE

I would like to hear how you use the information in *Sharing the Course* and the results you receive. If you choose to share with me, write me in care of Noelani Publishing Company, P.O. Box 24029, Cleveland, OH, 44124-0029. Enclose a self-addressed, stamped envelope for my reply.

Nancy

REFERENCES

A Course in Miracles. Tiburon, CA: Foundation for Inner Peace, 1976.

A Course in Miracles. 2d ed. Glen Ellen, CA: Foundation for Inner Peace, 1992.

Cirlot, J.E. *A Dictionary of Symbols.* New York: Dorset Press, 1991.

Corbett, Margaret Darst. *Help Yourself to Better Sight.* No. Hollywood, CA: Wilshire Book Company, 1949.

Diamond, John. *The Re-Mothering Experience: How to Totally Love.* Valley Cottage, NY: Archaeus Press, 1986.

East/West, The Journal of Natural Health & Living. Sections on Vision. Vol. 16, No. 12 (December 1986); Vol. 20, No. 4 (April 1990).

Metaphysical Bible Dictionary. Unity Village, MO: Unity School of Christianity, 1931.

Findisen, Barbara. *A Course in Miracles Concordance to Volume One: Text.* Farmingdale, NY: Coleman Graphics, 1983.

Fox, Emmet. *The Sermon On The Mount.* San Francisco: Harper & Row, Publishers, 1938.

Goodrich, Janet. *Natural Vision Improvement.* Berkeley, CA: Celestial Arts, 1986.

Gray, John. *What You Feel, You Can Heal.* Mill Valley, CA: Heart Publishing Company, 1984.

Harper's Bible Dictionary. San Francisco: Harper & Row, Publishers, 1985.

Hay, Louise. *Feeling Fine Affirmations.* Santa Monica, CA: Louise L. Hay, 1988.

Hay, Louise. *Love Yourself, Heal Your Life Workbook.* Santa Monica, CA: Hay House, 1990.

Holy Bible. Dallas, TX: The Melton Book Company, 1946/1952.

Jaeger, Mary M. and Juline, Kathleen. *You Are the One.* Los Angeles: Science of Mind Publications, 1988.

Jampolsky, Gerald. *Teach Only Love.* New York: Bantam Books, 1983.

Johnson, Ethel. *Draw Me a Tree.* New York: Andrews, McMeel & Parker, 1984.

Johnson, Sonia. *Going Out of Our Minds: The Metaphysics of Liberation.* Freedom, CA: The Crossing Press, 1987.

Kaplan, Robert-Michael. *Seeing Beyond 20/20.* Hillsboro, OR: Beyond Words Publishing, 1987.

Kavner, Richard and Dusky, Lorraine. *Total Vision.* New York: A & W Publishers, 1978.

Levin, Pam. *Becoming the Way We Are.* Berkeley, CA: Pamela Levin, 1974.

Levin, Pamela. *Cycles of Power.* Deerfield Beach, FL: Health Communications, 1988.

Levine, Stephen. *Healing into Life and Death.* New York: Anchor Books, 1987.

Master Mind Goal Achiever's Journal. Warren, MI: Master Mind Publishing, annually from 1983.

Miller, Alice. *Banished Knowledge.* New York: Anchor Books, 1990.

Ray, Sondra. *Drinking the Divine.* Berkeley, CA: Celestial Arts, 1984.

Roman, Sanaya. *Spiritual Growth.* Tiburon, CA: H.J. Kramer, 1989.

Skutch, Robert. *Journey Without Distance.* Berkeley, CA: Celestial Arts, 1984.

Wapnick, Kenneth. *Glossary-Index for A Course in Miracles,* third edition. Roscoe, NY: Foundation for "A Course in Miracles," 1989.

Wapnick, Kenneth. *Absence From Felicity.* Roscoe, NY: Foundation for "A Course in Miracles," 1991.

Williamson, Marianne. *A Return to Love.* New York: HarperCollins Publishers, 1992.

Zukav, Gary. *The Seat of the Soul.* New York: Simon & Schuster, 1989.

INDEX

Major definitions of terms are found on pages listed in **bold** print.

183, 205, 240, 351-2, 362, 366

asleep, **15**, 48, 112, 256

Atonement, **236-9, 52, 85-6, 317**, 67, 246-7, 267, 356, 361

attack, (see projecting, blaming, idols), **17-19**, 20-1, 23, 43, 52, 55, 60, 67, 69, 80, 89, 100, 107-8, 115, 177-8, 212, 241, 269, 341, 345, 358

attention, (see awareness, focus), **228**, 4, 51, 234, 278, 290

attract, (see magnetism, polarity), **261-2**, 147, 161, 240, 313

auditory, 186

author, (see authority), 173

authority, **173-81**, 9, 95, 143, 155, 233, 355

awakening, **106, 184, 317**, 17, 35, 68, 70-1, 78-9, 88, 103, 113, 115, 131-2 256, 303, 306

aware/awareness, **107, 228, 288-93**, 18, 22-3, 29, 31, 39-40, 55, 62, 67, 71, 73, 77, 86, 88, 93, 95, 105-6, 109, 111-12, 119, 130, 139, 160, 167, 174, 183, 207, 211, 215, 223, 226, 235, 237, 240-1, 255, 271, 273, 282, 286, 306, 337-8, 346, 351

B

balance, 294, 298, 358

balloon, **12**, 15, 17, 22, 86

basic skills, 231-242

Be Good, (see Good Girl), 41, 44, 51-2, 100, 175

Beatitude, 29, 203, 206

beauty/beautiful, 179, 233, 284-5, 288

Beholding, (see holding), 210

being, (see human being), **63, 79, 311**, 22-3, 30, 53, 55, 70-1, 78, 95, 135, 140, 183, 195, 205, 210-11, 216, 232-3, 252, 269, 276, 287, 291, 321, 358

belong/belonging, **136**, 143, 183, 272

Beloved Child, (see Child of God, Son of God), **15, 78, 347-52**, 22, 24, 69, 80, 114, 132, 177, 183, 186, 206, 229, 240, 347, 350-1, 358

birth, 132, 142

blaming, (see anger, projecting), **18-20, 55, 254, 353, 235, 239**, 14, 22, 24-5, 30, 35-7, 39, 43-5, 47, 52-6, 61, 71, 95, 97, 106, 112, 135-6, 147, 156, 166, 178, 198, 204-5, 212-13, 231, 234, 250, 257, 264, 273, 279, 285, 290, 292, 306-7, 314, 322, 328, 343, 345, 347, 350, 355, 363

bless/blessing, **69**, 195, 202, 205, 211, 234, 239, 304, 309, 318-19, 348, 358

blind/blinding, (see visual memory), **364**, 114-15

block/blocking, **16-17**, 19, 62, 68, 115, 149, 322

body, **69, 357**, 45, 47, 58, 62, 70, 98, 101, 130-2, 135, 139, 190, 214, 216, 245, 269, 272-3, 289, 300, 311, 329, 332, 340, 345

H

honest, **308**, 183, 286
hope/hopeful, **34**, 115, 131,
143, 280, 299
hopeless/hopelessness, **34**,
44, 115, 164
horizontal axis, **132**, 115
hugs, **188**, **192**, 156, 201
human being, **78**, 51, 93,
358
human doing, **78**, 51,
humiliating, 319
humility, 69
humor, 165
hurts/hurtful, **238**, **227**,
229-30, 243, 245, 271,
273, 276-7, 279, 290,
306, 309, 320, 325, 351

I

"I accept," **39**, **237**
"I Am," **117**, **121**, 132, 173,
179, 181, 242, 244-5,
247, 261, 298, 350, 352,
360
"I can't," **253**, **34**, 52
"I don't know," 246
"I guess," 246
"I haven't yet," 34
"I pass," **183**, 190
"I'll show you," 307
identify/identity, (see Christ
identity, Face of Christ),
347, 22, 24, 55, 69, 75,
77-8, 83, 132, 197, 242,
244, 247, 273, 282, 348,
351, 357
idols, **137-42**, 40, 48-9, 63,
115, 118, 130-2, 197,
256, 286, 333, 348, 355,
364, 366
"if only," **72**, 49, 52,
ill/illness, (see sickness,
symptoms), 9, 355

illusion, (see errors,
perception, ego), **79**, **105**,
114, **236**, **317**, 109, 115,
119, 132, 168-9, 228,
239, 283
image/imagery, 47, 94, 102,
294
imagine/imagination, 37,
43, 58, 212
impressed/impression, **85**,
131-2, 203
in the Name of (God), (see
name), 81, 175
incest, 327
include, 76, 80-1, 137, 185,
206, 252
incomplete, 235
information, **277**, **276**, 43,
44, 94, 158, 273, 319,
343
inner Authority, 143
inner child, **12**, 21-2, 24, 26,
28-30, 48, 51, 55-6, 95,
138-9, 147, 213-14, 217,
272, 276, 279, 294, 302,
316, 343, 351
inner guide/guidance, **78**,
174, 22, 24, 77, 97, 107,
173, 180, 243
inner parent, 1, 12, 21-2,
39
innocent/innocence, **15**,
204, **347-9**, 24, 28, 37-8,
67, 78, 82, 95, 101, 119,
132, 135, 181, 206, 226,
239, 241, 279, 303, 311,
340, 357
insane, **35**, 78, 107, 132
inspire/inspiration, **8**, 176,
184, 259, 294
integrate/integrity, (see
joining), **233**, **297**, 174-5,
177, 241,

vitalization stance, 268
voice, **13**, **69**, **73**, **342-3**,
    190, 21-2, 28, 32, 34, 41,
    45, 51, 57-8, 68, 78, 88,
    93-4, 100, 108, 111, 120,
    128-30, 132, 154, 160,
    174, 183-4, 187, 214,
    226, 240, 244, 247, 251,
    259, 264, 272, 280-1,
    288, 311, 328, 358
voiceless, 63

W

wait/waiting, **22**, **37**, **254**,
    311, **314**, 39, 245, 250,
    274, 292, 343
waking, (see joining), 325,
    354
walls, (see defense), **15-16**,
    34, **339-41**, 20, 24, 29,
    135-7, 317
want/wanting, (see asking,
    prayer), **251-2**, **270**, **307**,
    261, 267
want list, 120, 196, 256
weak, 72-3, 204, 247, 338
welcome/welcoming, **73**, 81,
    143, 145, 185, 268, 280
wellness, (see wholeness), 97
"what if," 277
whole/wholeness, (see
    holiness), **12**, **225**, 69,
    72, 76, 128, 164, 174,
    190, 241, 294, 302, 307,
    338, 351
will/willing/willingness, (see
    intent, free, freedom), **7-9**,
    223, **253**, **283**, **20**, **22**,
    24, **74**, **95**, **107**, **217**,
    239, **244-5**, **260**, **269**,

291, **297**, 23, 43, 68, 73,
    81, 93, 101, 103, 108,
    112, 114-5, 118, 122,
    135, 138, 141, 159, 178-
    9, 184, 189, 194-5, 211,
    228-9, 241, 247, 252,
    255, 257, 261, 264, 267,
    298, 306-7, 313, 354-5,
    358, 360
Will of God, 28, 68, 71, 93,
    136, 175, 210, 243, 302,
    317
willful/willfulness, (see
    resistance), 28, 122, 184,
    257, 317
winter, 140, 365
wisdom, 280
wish/wishes, 254, 257
withholding, 234
Word of God, 238, 250, 264,
    267
worry, **105**, **118**, 140, 147-8,
    233-4
worth/worthy/worthiness,
    7-9, **12**, **14**, **19**, **25**, **37**,
    77, **306**, 30, 78, 143,
    148, 155, 160, 163, 180,
    195, 204, 234, 238-9, 307
wounded child, **12-13**, 19,
    34, 45, 55, 77, 83, 321

Y

"yes," **243-52**, **353**, 159,
    207-8, 228
"yes, but," **28**, **87-9**, **227-8**,
    235, **261**, 280
"yet," 34

SHARING THE COURSE by Nancy H. Glende
may be obtained through:
Noelani Publishing Company, Inc.
P.O. Box 24029
Cleveland, OH, 44124-0029

Make check payable in US funds to Noelani Publishing Co.

QTY _____ at $25 each ...._____
Ohio residents add 7% tax ($1.75 per book) ...._____
Shipping first book, $3 ...._____
Shipping each additional book, $1 ...._____
                              Total enclosed _____

     Send to:
     Name _____
     Street _____
     City _____State _____ Zip_____

Thank you for your order.

❋   ❋   ❋   ❋   ❋

A MUSICAL COMPANION TO SHARING THE COURSE
by Michael Root
A set of two, 40-minute audio cassette tapes with lyrics
may be obtained through:
Music of Miracles
P.O. Box 1071
Shaker Heights, OH, 44120-1071

Make check payable in US funds to Music of Miracles

QTY Tape sets _____ at $20 each ...._____
Ohio residents add 7% tax ($1.40 per set) ...._____
Shipping first set, $2 ...._____
Shipping each additional set, $1 ...._____
                              Total enclosed _____

     Send to:
     Name _____
     Street _____
     City _____State _____ Zip_____

Thank you for your order.